DATE DUE

MY 14 '98		
MY 27 '99		
DE 18 '99		
MY 30 '01		
JE 11 '01		
NO 20 '01		
AG 8 '02		

DEMCO 38-296

STEE-RIKE FOUR!

STEE-RIKE FOUR!

What's Wrong with the Business of Baseball?

Edited by

Daniel R. Marburger

PRAEGER

Westport, Connecticut
London

Library of Congress Cataloging-in-Publication Data

Stee-rike four! : what's wrong with the business of baseball? / edited
   by Daniel R. Marburger.
        p.   cm.
   Includes bibliographical references and index.
   ISBN 0–275–95706–3 (alk. paper)
      1. Baseball—United States—Finance.   2. Collective bargaining—
   Baseball—United States.   3. Baseball players—Salaries, etc.—
   United States.   4. Antitrust law—United States.   I. Marburger,
   Daniel R.
   GV880.S84   1997
   338.4′7796357′640973—dc20   96–44685

British Library Cataloguing in Publication Data is available.

Library of Congress Catalog Card Number: 96–44685
ISBN: 0–275–95706–3

First published in 1997

Praeger Publishers, 88 Post Road West, Westport, CT 06881
An imprint of Greenwood Publishing Group, Inc.

Printed in the United States of America

The paper used in this book complies with the
Permanent Paper Standard issued by the National
Information Standards Organization (Z39.48–1984).

10 9 8 7 6 5 4 3 2 1

Contents

Tables and Figures

Preface

Seeking to make productive use of my outrage following the cancellation of the 1994 baseball season, I immediately set forth to edit a book on the economics of baseball (a.k.a. the state of the game). In short order I accumulated a list of willing contributors whose insightful essays were to breathe life into *Stee-rike Four!* Recognizing that most baseball fans do not have a formal background in economics, our goal was to make the economics of the game understandable to individuals across all disciplines. I believe we have succeeded.

Interestingly my urge to write a book like *Stee-rike Four!* came several years earlier. In 1991, economists from across the United States converged on Middlebury College in Vermont for a three-day conference on the economics of baseball. Middlebury students ran shuttles from the Burlington airport to the college, and I was accompanied by economists Bruce Johnson, Larry Kahn, and George Daly in my van. Although the four of us were more or less strangers to each other, our shuttle had not even left the airport parking lot when the conversation turned to baseball. Not the conference, mind you, nor the economics of baseball. Just... baseball. At that point I realized that our common bond was not that we were economists but that we were baseball fans, and that the state of the game merely allowed us to marry our professions to our first love.

This experience sowed the seeds for *Stee-rike Four!* The economics of baseball is relevant to fans across all academic and nonacademic persuasions and, therefore, deserves to be stripped of the language that limits its discussion to small circles of economists. References to monopsonies, marginal revenue products, and other freshman-level economics terminology have, accordingly, been surgically removed from *Stee-rike Four!*

If readers will pardon the shameless metaphor, I like to think of *Stee-rike Four!* as sporting an All-Star lineup. In addition to Bruce Johnson,

I also met contributors Rod Fort, Bill Kaempfer, and Andy Zimbalist at the Middlebury conference. Collectively with the other participants, the research we presented at the conference was compiled in the book *Diamonds Are Forever: The Business of Baseball.*

Fort was later to hook up with Jim Quirk in *Pay Dirt*, an outstanding book, which a publisher once described to me as "the Bible of the economics of sports." Zimbalist became wellknown for penning *Baseball and Billions*, the most comprehensive and detailed description of the business of baseball to date. And each of these books appeared after Jim Dworkin's *Owners versus Players: Baseball and Collective Bargaining*, which was published in 1981 (the year that the players first walked out in midseason).

In the summer of 1995 I renewed acquaintances with my fellow baseball fan/colleagues in San Diego, where a number of economists, including Larry Hadley, Elizabeth Gustafson, Bruce Johnson, Bill Kaempfer, Rod Fort, and John Fizel, were presenting their latest research on the economics of baseball. The research was subsequently captured in the book *Baseball Economics: Current Research.*

Serving as the editor for a book that includes contributions from a dozen essayists has given me a unique appreciation for the quality control manager at the end of an assembly line. Because *Stee-rike Four!* was my own inspiration, I suppose I have no one but myself to blame.

The truth is that piecing together this book was a pleasure from start to finish. Nonetheless, *Stee-rike Four!* would not be complete without the acknowledgment of those whose combined efforts made for a finished product. First and foremost I thank the 12 contributors who exercised extreme patience while responding promptly to my many demands. As a self-acknowledged klutz when it comes to word-processing skills, my wife Carleen was a lifesaver in making the tables and text presentable. Additionally, my secretary, Jen Vincent, was instrumental in taking *Stee-rike Four!* from early draft to final copy. Thanks also to Nina Pearlstein, who gave this project encouragement in its earlier stages and to David Palmer, my production editor, who walked me through the fine art of book publishing.

Several of the references deserve special mention. John Helyar's *Lords of the Realm,* Marvin Miller's *A Whole Different Ball Game,* and Bowie Kuhn's *Hardball: The Education of a Baseball Commissioner* proved to be invaluable in establishing the chronology of events that are detailed in the first chapter. Additionally I know that I am speaking for all of the contributors in acknowledging the trailblazing contributions of Henry Demmert, Rodney Fort, Roger Noll, James Quirk, Simon Rottenberg, Gerald Scully, and Andrew Zimbalist; their influence and perspectives on the economics of major league baseball are felt throughout this book.

Introduction

Daniel R. Marburger

Shortly after the 1994 major league baseball season was unceremoniously canceled, channel surfing replaced The Game as my favorite pastime. With my trusty remote in full operation, I stumbled onto the hypocrisy that inspired *Stee-rike Four*! PBS began its 18-hour broadcast of Ken Burns's "Baseball," with its memorable history whimsically narrated by John Chancellor. I managed to catch every episode of the marathon, and went to bed each night reminiscing about the days when my father took my brother and me to watch the Pittsburgh Pirates at Forbes Field. Forbes, I recalled, was so expansive that the batting cage sat in deep center field during games, under the safe assumption that batted balls would never travel that far. I sat in the box seats near first base during a July 4th doubleheader and watched Willie Stargell launch a Tom Seaver fastball over the right field stands. (Babe Ruth was the first of a small handful to accomplish this rare feat. It was here that the Bambino hit the final three home runs of his fabled career.)

I held tickets to the first game at Three Rivers Stadium in 1970. The Pirates lost to the Cincinnati Reds on that day. Pete Rose had created a piece of baseball folklore only two days prior, having barreled into catcher Ray Fosse for the game-winning run in the All-Star game.

The following year I paid an outrageous eight dollars to watch Bob Robertson hit a game-winning three-run homer in game three of the 1971 World Series. I was also in attendance on the day that Roberto Clemente got his "real" 3,000th hit. The Great Roberto tapped a swinging bunt to the right side of the infield in the first inning. Second baseman Ken Boswell unsuccessfully tried to bare-hand the ball to make the play. The official scorer, wishing to make for a more memorable historic event, scored the play as an error. The starting pitcher, Tom Seaver, went on to pitch a two-hit shutout (neither of which belonged to Clemente)—and

I was left to only listen to Clemente's 3,000th hit on the radio the next day.

I cheered Bill Mazeroski and Matty Alou, and I booed Orlando Cepeda and Pete Rose (whom I never forgave for beating out Alou and Clemente for the batting title in consecutive seasons). I watched Bob Gibson strike out 17 Detroit Tigers in the first game of the 1968 World Series, and I patiently sat through all 15 innings of the 1967 All-Star game. No doubt about it: Baseball, just like rock and roll music, was better in those days.

In the midst of these fond remembrances, my channel surfing landed me on C-SPAN, where I found Bud Selig, Don Fehr, and some of baseball's best donning suits and ties rather than caps and uniforms. Orel Hershiser was making a pitch to Congress rather than to the Giants. This was the baseball of today, and the contradiction between the fanciful days of yore and the impersonality of the present game irritated me to no end. Baseball had become an endangered species, and it had only itself to blame.

Shortly thereafter, I began compiling the essays that make up *Stee-rike Four*! Despite the resistance of many a baseball fan, the business of baseball is no longer relegated to the smoke-filled boardrooms of wealthy investors. The sports pages, previously laden with box scores and player statistics, are now as likely to present the details of the latest revenue-sharing proposal as they are to recount the highlights of the previous night's games.

But why should baseball fans care about revenue-sharing and luxury taxes? Don't they only care about the *game* of baseball? Alas, despite their relative indifference to balance sheets and cash flow statements, baseball fans have come to recognize that the *business* of baseball and the *game* of baseball are indelibly intertwined. What happens at the bargaining table determines the names and faces of those who suit up in the home team's uniforms. For that reason alone, the fans have a vested interest in the final outcome.

My belief in stripping the economics of baseball of "economese" was reinforced in the spring of 1995, when I presented the paper "What Would Babe Ruth Earn Today?" at the Baseball and the Sultan of Swat conference at Hofstra University. Expecting the conference to be swarming with a collection of academics, I found myself surrounded by major media and baseball-lovers who had traveled the length of the globe to attend.

My address was preceded by University of Missouri-St. Louis history professor Charles Korr, who likened Marvin Miller to Babe Ruth in his presentation. Our speeches were subsequently followed up by a question-and-answer session, which quickly ventured away from a discussion of Babe Ruth and into the economics of baseball. These were not economists who wanted answers but baseball fans who understood that the economics of baseball affected the game they know and love.

Given the inevitable link between the game of baseball and the ongoing discussions at the bargaining table, this book provides fans with a few insights and predictions regarding the future of the game. *Stee-rike Four!* is divided into five parts. I authored Part I which provides an historical background on collective bargaining in major league baseball. Chapter 1 reviews the evolution of the bad blood that eventually led to the 1994 canceled season. Chapter 2 provides insight into collective bargaining strategy, including a discussion of strikes, lockouts, and basic strategies of negotiation as they pertain to baseball.

Part II deals with free agency, salary arbitration, and salary issues in general. James Richard Hill explains in Chapter 3 why millionaire salaries are not necessarily a cause for alarm; that rising salaries are merely indicative of an industry that generates tremendous wealth. In Chapter 4 John Fizel reprises "the invariance hypothesis": the landmark theory originally developed by economist Simon Rottenberg in 1956. The hypothesis asserts that the only impact free agency has on major league baseball is to transfer wealth from the owners to the players, and that competitive balance is unaffected. James Dworkin and William Kaempfer offer unique perspectives on salary arbitration in Chapters 5 and 6. Dworkin labels arbitration as a "win-win" situation for players, and he blames it for escalating salaries. Although arbitration is apparently on the collective bargaining chopping block, Kaempfer predicts little change in player salaries should salary arbitration be replaced with free agency.

With revenue-sharing, salary caps, and luxury taxes dominating the discussions at the bargaining table, Part III examines each of these issues individually. In Chapter 7 James Quirk explains why salary caps don't work very well, and why luxury taxes *won't* work very well. Lawrence Hadley and Elizabeth Gustafson illuminate readers in Chapter 8 with the surprising revelation that increased revenue-sharing between teams may not improve competitive balance. James Whitney, in Chapter 9, ties these issues together, criticizing salary caps and luxury taxes and advocating increased revenue-sharing as the desired alternative.

Part IV provides readers with opposite perspectives on baseball's antitrust exemption. In Chapter 10, Bruce Johnson claims that the exemption is the source of many of baseball's problems, and he advocates lifting the exemption as a means of improving league balance, team finances, and easing tensions at the bargaining table. In Chapter 11, William Shughart, on the other hand, argues not only for preserving the exemption, but for extending it to other professional sports leagues.

Part V looks toward baseball's future. Rodney Fort examines the issue of third party financing of stadiums in Chapter 12. Andrew Zimbalist, in Chapter 13, provides his perspective on antitrust, revenue-sharing, stadium financing, and expansion. Finally, in Chapter 14 I seek out the common thread that binds together the previous 13 chapters.

Readers will undoubtedly detect that many of the essays were written prior to the eventual labor agreement. This makes our analysis all the more interesting, as fans will be able to see if our predictions hold. The collection of essays that follows contains a great many insights and more than a few surprises. Just as economists don't always agree on other issues, neither is there an absolute consensus among contributors to *Stee-rike Four*! No matter. Readers, just like economists, are free to make up their own minds.

I

COLLECTIVE BARGAINING AND BASEBALL

1

Whatever Happened to the "Good Ol' Days"?

Daniel R. Marburger

From its poetic beginning firmly rooted in the myth of Abner Doubleday, professional baseball positioned itself as a staple of American life. As unfailing as the American Stars and Stripes flying over Fort McHenry, baseball showed its resiliency in weathering two World Wars, the Great Depression, and even a San Francisco earthquake. Baseball had even proven impervious to the Black Sox scandal in 1919. And despite the many predictions of impending doom by amateur soothsayers over the years, interest in baseball never faltered. Record attendance at games had been the rule rather than the exception. Burgeoning interest in cable television allowed fans in the remotest regions of the country to track their favorite team. For all practical purposes, baseball was invincible.

Perhaps it is all too fitting that the Titanic and the Hindenburg were also once considered models of perfection—for in 1994 the national pastime came to a grinding halt. Of course, it was not an economic recession that had caused the season to end, for baseball had withstood many of those. And it was not the perils of war that interrupted the game, for baseball can claim veterans from all but the earliest American conflicts. The single disaster that baseball was ill-prepared to endure, that ended its season prematurely and endangered its future was, of all things, a collective bargaining impasse.

A collective bargaining impasse! How could a sport that suited up players three months after the bombing of Pearl Harbor jeopardize its long-standing love affair with the American public over a collective bargaining disagreement? Work stoppages had become as commonplace as bubblegum cards in recent decades, but few aficionados of the game would have ever predicted the cancellation of a season. With the average baseball salary well over $1 million and franchise values skyrocketing at a mind-boggling pace, fans wonder if baseball is nearing the straw that will break the camel's back.

Of course, the more-seasoned fans of the game are quick to point out that baseball was not always this way. There was a time when baseball was not threatened with strikes and lockouts and when the business of baseball was behind-the-scenes activity not easily evidenced by its spectators. In reflecting upon baseball's "good ol' days," however, one should note that the peaceful coexistence of labor and management was hardly synonymous with harmony.

Throughout most of its history, major league baseball was dominated by the reserve clause. In the game's early days, bidding wars among competing teams for stars drove up player salaries at the expense of the clubs' profits. To counter these bidding wars, the reserve clause was established. Under the reserve system, no player was permitted to shop his wares to competing clubs. In effect, the reserve clause made the players the property of their clubs for life. Further, if the player's contract was traded or sold to another team, the individual became the property of the new team, subject to the same rigid rules of enforcement. Unlike most American workers, who take for granted the right to seek out alternative job opportunities, baseball players had to play for their current teams indefinitely or retire from the game.

For years, the clubs successfully defended the reserve clause as necessary to preserve competitive balance in the game. Perhaps the best summation of the necessity of the reserve clause came from Justice Smyth in the U.S. Supreme Court case of *Federal Baseball Club of Baltimore v. National League, et al.* Presenting the majority opinion, Smyth wrote:

If the reserve clause did not exist, the highly skillful players would be absorbed by the more wealthy clubs, and thus some clubs in the league would so far outstrip others in playing ability that the contests between the superior and the inferior clubs would be uninteresting and the public would refuse to patronize them. (Scully 1989, 5)

Chief Justice Smyth's opinion did more than rationalize the need for the reserve clause. The Supreme Court decision effectively exempted baseball from federal antitrust legislation, an exemption that has only recently come under serious fire.

Thus, with the deck heavily stacked in favor of the clubs' owners, it is no wonder that baseball continued to be played year after year without interruption. Individually, players could protest the state of affairs by threatening to withhold their services, but because baseball salaries tended to exceed compensation outside of baseball, it was only a matter of time before the holdouts came scurrying back to sign their contracts.

Among the more legendary battles between players and management was the alleged exchange between Pittsburgh Pirates slugger Ralph Kiner and Branch Rickey, the team's general manager. In refusing Kiner a raise, Rickey remarked "We finished last with you; we could have finished last without you" (Zimbalist 1992, 13). Of course, the comment was a vast oversimplification of the situation, because as one of the game's premier home run hitters, Kiner was the only drawing card on a losing team. Last place or not, Kiner's presence in the lineup was essential to attract crowds on game days. In reflection, the celebrated quote is more an indication of the power of the reserve clause than it is about the value of Ralph Kiner. The Kiner affair, and the many more that preceded and followed, made the case clear that absent a union and with the reserve clause intact, there was no incentive for any player to expect to receive meaningful concessions from management.

Despite the fact that the reserve clause deprived baseball players of leverage in contract negotiations, players acceded to the reserve system as an unfortunate but necessary component of the game. Throughout most of baseball's history the system went unchallenged. In 1946 outfielder Danny Gardella challenged the reserve clause, when after a stint with the Mexican League, he returned to the States only to find himself blacklisted by major league baseball's elite. The clubs avoided a federal ruling on the legality of the reserve clause, however, by settling out of court. A second challenge came a few years later when farmhand George Toolson sued after being reassigned to the minors by the Yankees. The reserve clause escaped doom when the Supreme Court ruled that a reversal of baseball's antitrust exemption was a legislative matter not a judicial one.

The reserve system's most recent threat came when St. Louis Cardinal outfielder Curt Flood filed suit against Major League Baseball in response to his trade to the Philadelphia Phillies. The case eventually went before the Supreme Court in *Flood v. Kuhn* in 1972. In his suit, Flood challenged the constitutionality of the reserve clause, which he likened to slavery. However, when the Supreme Court handed down the decision in favor of the clubs, the legality of the reserve clause, as well as its apparent acceptability, was reaffirmed.

Although the reserve clause dictated labor relations in baseball's first 100 years, the winds of change began to blow when Marvin Miller was selected by the players as the Major League Baseball Players' Association's (MLBPA) executive director in 1966. Interestingly the MLBPA was initially conceived with the blessing of the club owners, who even offered to finance the Association with proceeds from the All-Star game. Miller, however, was a product of the United States Steelworkers of America, one of the nation's largest and most powerful labor unions, and the thought of a union professional butting heads with baseball management was unpalatable to the owners at best. Even some of the players were wary of their new executive director, fearing that Miller might bring racketeering into the industry.

In the end Marvin Miller was the best thing that ever happened to major league baseball players. And for his ample achievements he was also the owners' worst nightmare.

Prior to Miller's arrival, baseball's minimum salary was $6,000, and the average baseball salary was $19,000 (Zimbalist 1992, 85). Multiyear contracts were virtually unheard of, and the reserve clause bound players to their clubs for life. There was no salary arbitration, no free agency, and no grievance arbitration. Topps, the baseball card company, complemented the players' salaries with a meager $125 payment to each player (Miller 1991, 144). In sharp contrast, by the end of 1982, Miller's last year in the official capacity of executive director, the minimum salary in baseball was $33,500, and the average salary exceeded $240,000 (Zimbalist 1992, 85). The reserve clause now applied to only a percentage of players, with the rest having the ability to choose their own employers or have their salary determined by an independent arbitrator. Grievance arbitration allowed for the enforcement of the collective bargaining agreement by permitting an independent third party to interpret the terms of the contract. Further, the Players' Association now negotiates licensing agreements with Topps, Fleer, and other baseball card manufacturers to the tune of tens of millions of dollars annually (Zimbalist 1992, 80).

Because most of these gains entailed a direct transfer of revenues from the pockets of the owners to those of the players, Miller's legacy continued well beyond his retirement. Many of the issues at stake today are remnants of the former executive director's accomplishments.

Whether Marvin Miller was a true genius in his repeated triumphs over baseball management or just the right person in the right place at the right time is subject to analysis and debate. What may be less controversial is the simple notion that his entanglements with baseball brass were a gross mismatch. Miller had been schooled in labor negotiations by the Steelworkers' Union, which had 1.25 million members and 3,000 locals in nearly every state (Helyar 1994, 19). Advancing through the ranks, Miller knew that the secret to any union's success was to simultaneously increase the size of the pie and then to take the largest slice.

Banging heads with the Steelworkers' Union protégé were baseball's owners, none of whom had any real experience in jawing with a labor professional over a collective bargaining agreement. Many of the owners had been around the game for years, and many firmly believed that baseball was an industry unlike any other. They resented the fact that Miller was driving a wedge between them and the cozy, cooperative relationship they'd had with their players. Some truly believed that the paychecks and perks they gave their players were acts of benevolence.

In a perverse way, the owners were right on all counts. Baseball was a different industry—different inasmuch as the reserve clause, coupled with the exemption from antitrust legislation, made each team immune from competition. The antitrust exemption granted baseball the right to protect its teams' territorial rights against encroachment. In stark contrast, the lack of similar protection in the National Football League (NFL) permitted Oakland Raiders owner Al Davis to pack his team's helmets and jerseys and invade turf that was supposed to belong to the

Los Angeles Rams.   The same lack of an antitrust exemption left Los Angeles without *any* NFL team 10 years later.

If the antitrust exemption turned the lock, the reserve clause threw away the key.   Not only did the clubs not have to fear a fellow competitor setting up shop next door, the reserve system ensured that other teams could not pick their pockets for their most precious resource, the players.   In this regard, paying and rewarding the players for their services was, in fact, an act of generosity.   Most of the players had been snatched from the womb as teenagers and relatively few had college degrees.   Further, disciplined instruction on the fine art of sliding or hitting the cutoff man had little marketability outside of baseball.   For this reason it would have been perfectly feasible for the Branch Rickeys of the baseball kingdom to promote a player to the major leagues and refuse him a raise for the entirety of his career with minimal fear of losing him to another occupation.

In squaring off against the owners in his earliest years, Miller sought to win the easiest victories: raising baseball's minimum salary (which had been raised only once—by $1,000—in 20 years), increasing the pension fund, and establishing a formal grievance procedure.   Quite possibly the most important achievement in Miller's early years was that of obtaining impartial grievance arbitration in the interpretation of the collective bargaining agreement in 1970. Ironically, as monumental as the attainment of grievance arbitration was, it is quite possibly the most understated accomplishment of the Players' Association.   Ultimately it was grievance arbitration that ended the reserve clause, and it was grievance arbitration that resulted in baseball's collusion rulings and damages in the mid-1980s.

In 1973 the Players' Association bargained for salary arbitration. Actually, "bargained for" is a misrepresentation of fact. "Handed on a silver platter" is a more fitting description.   Miller made no secret that the number one item on his wish list was an upheaval of the reserve clause.   For this reason, the owners offered the players salary arbitration in much the same way that one might offer table scraps to a pack of hungry wolves. Salary arbitration was by no means a substitute for the free market. It might, however, present the illusion that the owners sympathized with the inequities inherent in reserve clause restrictions and, in so doing, soothe the savage beast.

Prior to baseball, interest arbitration (where an independent arbitrator determines the terms of a new contract) existed primarily in public sector occupations such as law enforcement and firefighting.   In those industries, arbitration served as the substitute for a strike. In baseball, however, salary arbitration was offered as a means of living within the restrictions of the reserve clause; that arbitration would eliminate the inequities in salaries across (or within) clubs.   Under salary arbitration, each side would submit an offer to an independent arbitrator. The arbitrator would then determine which of the two offers would be binding.

Miller also bargained for the "10-and-5" rule in the 1973 negotiations. This allowed players with at least 10 years of major league service (the last five years with the same club) the right to veto any trade.

The most significant event during Marvin Miller's tenure did not come during collective bargaining negotiations, however. Miller was convinced that Paragraph 10a of the Uniform Player's Contract limited the powers of the reserve clause. This section read:

On or before January 15 . . . the Club may tender to the Player a contract for the term of that year by mailing the same to the Player. If prior to the March 1 next succeeding said January 15, the Player and the Club have not agreed upon the terms of such contract, then on or before 10 days after said March 1, the Club shall have the right . . . to renew this contract for the period of one year. (Helyar 1994, 35)

According to Miller, the reserve clause did not give the club the right to the player indefinitely; it only gave the club a one-year option on a player's services after the expiration of his contract. Thus, if the parties were unable to agree upon a contract, the club could renew the old contract for one additional year only. After that, the player would be free to negotiate with any club.

Although he eyeballed dissolving the reserve system not unlike a dog surveys a steak hanging from a butcher's window, Miller stashed Paragraph 10a in his back pocket, to be wielded at the proper time. Prior to 1970, any disagreement over the interpretation of the clause would likely have been resolved by the commissioner of baseball. Miller viewed the commissioner as a puppet whose strings were pulled by the owners; he was hired by the owners, paid by the owners, and therefore was bound to represent the best interests of the owners.

After the 1970 negotiations had been completed, however, the scenario had changed. Now, an impartial arbitrator would resolve any disputes regarding the language of the Basic Agreement. Miller was convinced that a nonpartisan observer would agree that the reserve clause was only valid for one season beyond the expiration of the current contract. In professional basketball in 1967, Rick Barry left the National Basketball Association (NBA) to join the American Basketball Association. When Barry's NBA team, the San Francisco Warriors, sued to keep their star from jumping leagues, a federal judge ruled that Barry was bound to the Warriors for one year subsequent to the expiration of the contract. The relevant section of Barry's NBA contract from which the judge's decision was based was practically verbatim the same as baseball's (Miller 1991, 246).

While awaiting the ideal test case for which to place the interpretation of Paragraph 10a to the scrutiny of an arbitrator, Miller made repeated attempts to relax the reserve clause via negotiations. John Gaherin, who headed the owners' Player Relations Committee, secretly believed that Miller's interpretation of the contract was correct, and he implored the owners to retain some control over their own fate by negotiating modifications to the reserve clause, rather than to risk losing it all at the hands of an arbitrator (Helyar 1994, 36).   No such modifications were made.

At the end of 1974 Jim "Catfish" Hunter was to demonstrate the almighty power inherent in free agency.   Hunter was one of the premier starting pitchers in the game and an eventual Hall of Famer.   Having signed a two-year contract in 1974 with the Oakland A's, the team was obliged to pay half of his salary into a fund for the eventual purchase of an annuity.   In fact, however, no such annuity had been purchased. The Players' Association filed a grievance on behalf of Hunter, claiming that Charlie Finley, the owner of the A's, had breached Hunter's contract, and that the pitcher should, therefore, be declared a free agent.   On December 13, 1974, arbitrator Peter Seitz ruled in favor of Hunter.   In the weeks that followed, a parade of suitors trekked to Hunter's North Carolina home to pitch their offers.   Interestingly, whereas the terminated contract called for a total payment to Hunter of $100,000 for the 1974 season, the competitive bidding war that ensued resulted in a five-year $3.5 million contract with the New York Yankees (Helyar 1994, 148).

With the power of free agency to increase player salaries in full evidence, Marvin Miller anxiously awaited his test case.   In recent years the number of players entering into a season without a contract had been increasing.   By and by, the players eventually signed contracts, however, putting the test of Paragraph 10a to rest. The test case finally came through in 1975, when pitcher Andy Messersmith played the entire season without a contract.   At dispute was Messersmith's insistence upon a no-trade clause in his contract—a notion staunchly refused by Messersmith's Dodger management. Although Miller was chomping at the bit to use Messersmith as the test case, he recognized that Messersmith was less interested in filing a grievance than he was in getting the no-trade provision.   Sifting through his files, Miller came upon pitcher Dave McNally as a backup in the event Messersmith were to sign.   McNally was once an outstanding pitcher for the Baltimore Orioles.   After many years of service, he was traded to the Montreal Expos. Feeling he had been misled by Expo management and frustrated by his own performance, McNally retired from baseball in midseason and returned to his home in Montana. Because he was an unsigned player at the time of his retirement, Miller requested that he file a grievance at the season's end.

The two grievances were filed in October of 1975.   The arbitration panel was to consist of one management representative, John Gaherin; one player representative, Marvin Miller; and a neutral chair, Peter Seitz, the same arbitrator who had declared Catfish Hunter a free agent only a year earlier.   Of course, the opinions of Gaherin and Miller were known to all even before the opening arguments had begun. Seitz was to determine the fate of the reserve clause.

Unfortunately for Seitz, presiding over this particular grievance hearing was akin to attending one's own funeral. The stakes were high, and Seitz's career as an arbitrator would likely be over regardless of his decision.   He desperately wanted to avoid casting the deciding vote. He begged the two sides to wash his hands of the affair and come to their own settlement. When the owners refused to negotiate, the decision went to Seitz. Seitz ruled in favor of the players: Messersmith and McNally were free agents. Before the ink on the decision had even dried, Gaherin handed Seitz his walking papers.

The Seitz decision registered 8.0 on baseball's Richter scale. As of that moment, all players need do is suit up without a contract for one season and they would be fair game for competitive bidding. The owners feared anarchy and bankruptcy, not necessarily in that order. In an act of defiance, the owners locked the players out of spring training, demanding that less drastic reforms to the reserve clause be implemented.

Ironically, no one was more anxious to moderate Seitz's decision than Marvin Miller. Miller had seen the result of the Catfish Hunter ruling: one player available for hire, and 24 teams knocking at his door. The executive director viewed this type of setting as the most favorable for escalating salaries. He wanted the clubs to compete for players, and not the reverse.

Eventually, baseball commissioner Bowie Kuhn ended the lockout, and negotiations over how to implement free agency continued. The owners wanted to limit free agency. Secretly so did Marvin Miller. The "compromise" the two sides eventually agreed upon was roughly the equivalent of handing the Players' Association a blank copy of the Basic Agreement and asking them to fill in their desired free agency eligibility standard. Eligibility for free agency was granted after the player had attained six years of major league service, just at the time the players perceived the stars of the game would be at the peaks of their careers.

The competitive bidding wars that soon took place were beyond the wildest dreams of any of the players involved. Players who had hoped free agency would double their money were aghast to find themselves being offered multiyear guaranteed contracts in the multimillion dollar range. Wayne Garland signed a 10-year contract with the Cleveland Indians for $1 million (Helyar 1994, 207). Ditto for outfielder Richie Zisk, whose 10-year contract was to earn him pocket change totaling $3 million (Helyar 1994, 238). These were not just baseball's thoroughbreds that were cashing in their chips; along with the stars of the game were the hasbeens and Hall of Fame wannabes. Move over Babe Ruth: The Padres just signed Oscar Gamble for $2.85 million over six years (Helyar 1994, 238). Thirty-five-year-old Bert Campaneris was signed for $950,000, guaranteeing that he could play for no other team but the Texas Rangers until he was 40 years young (Helyar 1994, 206). Claudell Washington, whose invitation to Cooperstown must be accompanied by the price of admission, was signed by Ted Turner's Atlanta Braves to a $3.5 million, five-year contract (Helyar 1994, 252-253).

In their zeal to get something for nothing, the owners repeatedly found themselves in the position of getting nothing for something. At the end of the 10 years, Wayne Garland was to log only a few more innings than the team batboy. Campaneris was paid to play baseball during the first two years of his contract, and then paid to watch it the final three. To avoid such distasteful scenarios, the owners resorted to buyout clauses. Here, if the player's ability deteriorated to the point where he was no longer a welcome member of the 25-man roster, the team could dodge the remainder of his contract by simply paying the player not to show up for spring training.

Prior to free agency the average salary was $51,501 (Zimbalist 1992, 85). One year later the average salary had risen to $76,066 (Zimbalist 1992, 85). By 1980 the average baseball player could expect to bring home $143,756 (Zimbalist 1992, 85).

One should not be surprised that the owners increasingly became frustrated by baseball's state of affairs. They cursed the free market, they cursed baseball's biggest spenders, and most of all, they cursed Marvin Miller. The Seitz decision was to be the apex of the executive director's career. The remainder was spent protecting his gains from the owners, who desperately sought to roll back the system to better days.

As the owners plotted to beat the horror they'd helped to create, another surprise crept into their pocketbooks. Prior to the establishment of free agency, the owners had offered salary arbitration as a means of placating the players. Although the players could use salary arbitration as a means of reducing inequities in salary scales, there was little reason to believe arbitration could play a significant role in escalating pay. Now, however, the game had changed. Players who were not eligible for free agency, who were still the personal property of their clubs, began submitting the salaries of the free agents as evidence of their value.

The landmark case came at the hands of pitcher Bruce Sutter in 1980. By the end of 1979 Sutter was arguably the game's best relief pitcher. In 1979 Sutter racked up 37 saves and was named the National League's Cy Young Award winner. Unable to come to terms with his Chicago Cubs, Sutter filed for arbitration. The Cubs submitted an offer of $350,000—the highest offer ever submitted in an arbitration hearing. Had he signed for that figure, Sutter would likely have been a hero to his relief pitcher brethren. But Sutter countered with an offer of $700,000. Among pitchers, only Nolan Ryan earned more money. Several other players, none of them pitchers, also earned salaries in the $700,000 range or better. However, the common thread among baseball's salaried elite was that they had earned their pay as free agents. Free agent salaries were a privilege, not a right. Arbitration-eligible players simply were not entitled to earn that kind of money.

The owners were convinced that the Cubs would win the arbitration case. Other top relievers were paid more in line with the Cubs' offer, not Sutter's. Further, the relevant salary comparison for Sutter was with other players with three years of major league service. Comparisons with 10-year veterans was apples and oranges. Sutter's representative at the hearing, attorney Jim Bronner, argued that Sutter had emerged as the one of the game's top pitchers and therefore was entitled to be paid as one. The arbitrator hearing the case was New York University law professor

Tom Christenson. Like Peter Seitz before him, Christenson knew that in filling the "appropriate" figure into Sutter's contract, he was preparing his own epitaph. Like the Seitz decision, Christenson's choice of Sutter's offer sent shock waves throughout baseball. When future arbitration decisions, most notably in the cases of Steve Kemp and Fernando Valenzuela, echoed that of Sutter, players increasingly seized upon the opportunity to use arbitration as a means of increasing their take-home pay. "Pay me what the free agents get paid," the message was clear, "or an arbitrator will force you to."

Until now the changes that Marvin Miller brought into baseball have been referred to in this chapter as "achievements," "accomplishments," and "gains." Clearly, such wording emanates from the perspective of the user. In this case the verbiage is intended to reflect Miller's role: As executive director of the Players' Association, his job was to bring home the bacon for the rank and file. From this angle, Marvin Miller's changes were an unmitigated success. From the viewpoint of the owners, however, "achievements" and "accomplishments" are the most inappropriate choice of words. To them, Miller was the devil incarnate. He pulled baseball's balance of power out from under the owner's feet. The changes he initiated were the equivalent of taking a blank check from the owners' pocketbook and marking it "payable to the players."

The incessant power struggles that existed between management and the Players' Association during these times, as well as today, were hardly confined to smoke-filled boardrooms. From the perspective of average baseball fans, who had come to view spring training, opening day, and the Fall Classic as guaranteed constants in their lives, the reality of collective bargaining brought with it the unwanted baggage of work stoppages. In baseball, such things became the rule rather than the exception.

For any union, its sole source of bargaining power is the threat of a strike. Absent a union, an individual is always free to protest his or her pay or working conditions by threatening to withhold services. Because individuals are relatively easy to replace, however, personalized strikes are unlikely to result in meaningful concessions by management. Plantwide or industrywide strikes orchestrated by a well-organized union, on the other hand, are quite another story. An entire fleet of employees is difficult for any employer to replace, and for this reason, it may be less costly for the firm to concede to some of the union's demands than it is to weather the losses incurred during a strike.

Baseball's first-ever strike occurred in 1972. At issue were the players' health care plan and retirement benefits. The Players' Association requested increases in the funding of both to reflect rising inflation over the course of the current agreement. To persuade the owners that the request was reasonable, Miller noted a surplus in the existing pension fund (Miller 1991, 204). The surplus, he suggested, could be applied to the increased pensions. The owners countered with a proposal for a smaller increase in health care benefits and no change in pensions.

In his more tenuous days as executive director, Marvin Miller worked overtime trying to instill the same sense of unity that was deeply ingrained within the psyche of the Steelworkers' Union's rank and file. To say that the players were green to the union mentality was a gross understatement. By 1972, however, the players were staunchly pro-union and anxious to exercise their right to strike. As the players' enthusiasm for striking grew, Miller's attitude toward orchestrating the walkout began to wane. The players had no experience in strikes, they had no strike fund built up, and they hadn't been paid since October. If the players went on strike and later scurried back to resume playing on management's terms, the damage to the Players' Association could be irreparable. Now, thought Miller, was not the time to strike.

In fact, the executive director seriously underestimated the sense of solidarity that he had cultivated among the players. They were eager to take the opportunity to stand up to the owners. The vote in favor of a strike was unanimous.

As the strike moved into its second week, the owners suddenly backed off their hard-line "Take it or leave it" stance and offered to add $500,000 to health care benefits plus a cost-of-living increase in pension benefits (Miller 1991, 220). Just as Miller and Gaherin thought they had come to a settlement, some of the owners threw a monkey wrench into the negotiations: The players would have to make up the lost games without pay. Not surprisingly, the proposal was patently unacceptable to Miller, and the strike continued several more days before management relented. The 86 games lost during the strike were never made up, nor were the players paid during the work stoppage. The players did, however, receive credit for major league service days during the walkout: the key component in determining player pensions.

The next work stoppage occurred in 1976. This time, however, it was the owners who initiated the action. The off-season had produced the dreaded Seitz decision, and the owners wanted to nip free agency in the bud. They had seen the Catfish Hunter affair as a precursor of things to come, and they wanted no part of it. Inevitably, dozens, maybe hundreds of players would play out their options and place themselves on the auction block. Management was quickly running out of options. They appealed the Seitz decision to the federal district court and then the federal circuit court of appeals. When the decision to uphold the Seitz ruling came down from the courts, the owners realized that their only hope of limiting free agency would be at the bargaining table. They promptly made the decision to lock the players out of spring training until a collective bargaining agreement had been reached.

An employer lockout has essentially the same impact as an employee strike. The adage "Everyone loses in a strike" was never a position taken by the AFL-CIO. Although both sides do lose money during a strike, a walkout is timed in such a way as to gain leverage. Hence, a more proper representation of the union credo is "He who stands to lose the most concedes the most."

Employers scheduling lockouts rely on the same philosophy. In this case, the owners believed that they could starve the players out. The players had no strike fund and hadn't been paid in several months. True, the exact same scenario had existed four years earlier, but in 1972 there was no real reason for the owners to prolong the strike. Relatively little was at stake. They were the ones who had given in. But this time was different. Now it was free agency, already upheld by the courts; status quo meant bidding wars and the specter of declining profits, rising losses, and even bankruptcy. This time the rallying cry belonged to them. The players were no longer *requesting* free agency, they *had* it—handed to them on a silver platter by a man who had never had to worry about making payroll. It was the owners' responsibility to hold it at bay.

The approach taken by the owners was to pretend that the Seitz decision was simply a pipe dream; that it was their own unilateral act of magnanimity in suggesting a relaxation of the reserve clause. In drafting their strategies to derail free agency, the owners assumed that Marvin Miller envisioned himself as a champion over slavery, that in affixing his name to the Seitz ruling he was a modern-day Abraham Lincoln signing the Emancipation Proclamation.

In fact, Miller was hardly the free-marketeer he was often thought to be. As executive director, his assignment was to bring home the most attractive package to those who paid him their union dues. If free agency could deliver the goods, so be it. If the owners were to offer the players 90 percent of their revenues and keys to the executive washroom in exchange for a return to the reserve clause and its involuntary servitude, Miller would likely have shipped the proposal off to the players for rapid-fire ratification. (In the next round of negotiations, of course, he would likely have bargained to have the reserve clause revoked.)

In short, both camps were brainstorming on how to limit free agency. On the player's side, there were chinks in the armor. In 1972 they knew from Miller's consultations how much money they ought to receive in health care and pension benefits and how much they were being offered by management. The difference was something they could measure. But free agency had never existed before, and its benefits were intangble. Much to the chagrin of Miller, hundreds of players flooded Florida and Arizona, organizing their own workouts and, in the mind of Miller, giving the owners ample reason to believe a lockout would eventually cause the players to crack. Then, on March 17, on a godsend from union heaven, Bowie Kuhn unbarred the gates of spring training. Let the games begin. Whether Kuhn was acting for the best interest of baseball or at the request of influential owners who stood to profit with or without free agency is subject to debate. What is relevant is that the players began receiving paychecks, and paychecks do not a successful lockout make.

In baseball, management labor negotiators come and go as frequently as baseball managers, and in 1978 Ray Grebey came and John Gaherin went. By 1980 free agency had helped to raise the average player salary to over $140,000 (Zimbalist 1992, 85). With legal challenges to free agency long a moot point and a change of heart by the players as to the merits of the reserve clause about as likely as snowfall in Barbados, the owners now argued for free agency compensation.

Free agent compensation meant that a team losing a free agent would be compensated for the loss by selecting a player from the signing team's roster. In effect, compensation schemes turned free agent signings into trades. From a management point of view, free agent compensation had worked quite well in the National Football League. In a nutshell, the NFL system was the equivalent to a rule that states if Team A decides to take $10 from Team B, then Team A must compensate Team B by giving it $15. Not surprisingly, football teams had little interest in signing free agents.

Baseball's version of free agent compensation was a softer sell than football's hard-line approach. In comparison, baseball's compensation formula was set up in such a way that if Team A takes $10 from Team B, it must compensate Team B by giving Team B $5. Thus, contrary to football's compensation scheme, baseball's version was less likely to impede the movement of free agents between teams. Nonetheless, Marvin Miller understood the full ramifications of the plan. If A had to give B $5 in exchange for the $10 it received, then A's $10 was actually worth only $5, the net value after the exchange was complete. Compensation may not hinder the movement of free agents, but it could hold down their salaries.

Persuading the players to turn their noses up at compensation schemes was easy. By now, the philosophy Miller had conveyed to the players since the Seitz ruling was simply this: Everything management has done, is doing, and will do has, as its sole intent, the dismantling of free agency.

Early in the 1980 negotiations, free agent compensation was clearly going to hold up progress toward reaching an agreement. Eventually, the negotiators decided to table the compensation issue until 1981 and salvage the 1980 season without a strike by settling other issues. The two sides would assign a joint committee to study the compensation issue.

Before continuing, readers need to understand just how joint committees in collective bargaining operate. In the typical scenario, management assigns members to the committee to demonstrate why their perspective should be adopted in the collective bargaining agreement. The union handpicks persons whose sworn duty is to substantiate the reverse. In other words—joint committees represent an agreement to waste each other's time. In the case of baseball's compensation issue, the committee fulfilled its purpose with flying colors.

In early 1981 the owners made a stunning announcement: They had agreed to institute free agent compensation. Perhaps something needs to be clarified here. The announcement was that the owners had agreed to institute compensation. The Players' Association was still vehemently opposed to the idea. The feeling of déjà vu prevailed when the players set a strike date in late May.

The compensation scheme "enacted" by the owners was as follows: Players would be ranked according to position, and the top 50 percent were subject to some form of compensation. If a team signed a player who ranked in the top third of his position, the team could protect 15 members of the major league roster. The team that had lost the player could select one of the remaining 10 players as compensation. Thus, the system implied a trade whereby the signing team acquires a player in the top third of his profession and in doing so must forego the services of a player in the bottom 40 percent. For a player in the top 50 percent at his position (but not the top third), the signing team could protect 18 players on its roster (Helyar 1994, 223). Again, although it is true that the signing team would always emerge as the winner in the transaction, compensation reduced the value of the free agent, which would almost certainly slow the free agent bidding wars.

Although the owners insisted that the compensation proposal was aimed at promoting competitive balance within baseball, Miller was convinced that its real purpose was to stunt salary growth. His response to the issue had not been altered by the passage of time. Either compensation goes or the players go.

That Miller had not embraced free agent compensation over the off-season did not surprise the owners. In anticipation of a showdown, the owners purchased strike insurance from Lloyd's of London.

The walkout began on June 12. Unlike the strike of 1972, which merely delayed the start of the season, this was the first time that a season had been interrupted in midstream by a work stoppage. Over the next several weeks, enormous strides had been made to bridge the gap in negotiations. The owners, through Ray Grebey, made it painfully clear that compensation must exist in baseball, and the players, through Marvin Miller, announced to the world that free agent compensation was unacceptable. Some progress!

Suddenly, after weeks of impasse, Marvin Miller received an unexpected phone call from Lee MacPhail, now pinch-hitting for Ray Grebey. The owners clearly were anxious to settle. Undoubtedly, their collective resolve to resume the season was attributable to their love of the game and their desire to resurrect baseball as an American institution. It bore no relationship to the fact that the strike-insurance pack with Lloyd's of London was about to expire. MacPhail soon scheduled a meeting with Miller at which he resolutely announced the owners' intent to settle immediately. Miller, with a long career as a labor negotiator behind him, correctly inferred the owners' stance as "You tell us what you want and we will agree." Miller's settlement outlined a pooled compensation scheme he had devised. Clubs that signed free agents could protect 24 players from their 40-player roster (nonsigning teams could protect 26 players). Unprotected players became part of a compensation pool. If a team lost a free agent who ranked in the top 20 percent of his position, that team could select from any of the players in the compensation pool (Helyar 1994, 286). In this manner, the signing club was not assured of losing a player. Oh, and another thing. Although the players did not play any games over the past six weeks, they were to receive credit for major league service days as if they had. (To this day, the owners have failed to grasp the leverage inherent in this bargaining chip.)

In the aftermath of the settlement came the damage assessment. The players lost nearly $34 million in salaries, or about $52,000 a player (Zimbalist 1992, 23). The owners' losses totaled $72 million, although they recovered $44 million courtesy of Lloyd's of London (Zimbalist 1992, 23). Baseball lost 50 days of the season and a total of 713 games. And Ray Grebey lost his job.

Labor relations in baseball were fairly peaceful over the next couple of years. That is to say, relations between labor and management were peaceful; labor-labor relations were in an uproar. Marvin Miller announced his retirement as executive director of the Players' Association. His replacement was Ken Moffett. Moffett had served as federal mediator during the 1981 strike and had become quite friendly with some of the player reps. Unlike Miller, Moffett was not a career union man. Moffett's pronouncements of his labor philosophy reeked of status quo, preaching labor peace and advocating a more cooperative relationship with management. To Miller, this was treason. Retired or not, the Players' Association was his baby. He had nurtured it to maturity from its earliest days; he had staged the revolution against the robber baron industrialists; he had given the Association leadership, solidarity, and a who-o-ole lot of money; and he was not about to let it slip away. To him, handing the union baton over to Moffett was like George Bailey giving Mr. Potter the keys to the Bailey Saving's & Loan, only to watch helplessly as Bedford Falls was leveled and replaced with the amoral corporate Pottersville.

Moffett had barely begun settling into his new office before Miller initiated a coup d'etat. He wrote a memo to the players warning them about Moffett. The memo was dictated to Miller's former secretary (who was now Moffett's secretary) and was to be mailed on Players' Association letterhead. Needless to say, using the union office to issue warnings about its current director did not win the former director brownie points with Moffett. The locks on the office were changed (an employer lockout with a new twist), and Moffett issued a strong memo effectively banning Miller from active participation in the Players' Association unless it came at his (Moffett's) request. Several months later, Moffett and his appointees were fired. Miller served as interim director until Don Fehr, who had sat alongside Miller as legal counsel for several years, took over as executive director.

As the 1981 collective bargaining agreement approached expiration, the Players' Association began to eyeball baseball's skyrocketing television revenues. Historically, management funded the players' pension, life insurance, and health care plan with one-third of the money from national broadcast revenues. In the early 1970s, when the players struck for the first time, national media revenues averaged roughly $20 million (Quirk and Fort 1992, 505). By the mid-1980s, annual broadcasting revenues were nearly 10 times higher. It didn't take a financial wizard to know that this was serious money, and the Players' Association let it be known that they were entitled to their share.

Not surprisingly, the owners backed off the customary one-third formula. If the players wanted more money, they would have to bargain for it. The owners also countered the players' demands with a claim that the industry was in dire financial straits. This claim had been made before, and the owners' cries of hysteria were usually met with yawns by the Players' Association. This time, however, the owners supported their assertions by opening their financial statements. The Association turned the books over to economist Roger Noll, who accused the owners of concocting the losses through creative bookkeeping.

In any case, the scenario was ripe for another work stoppage. Turnover among Players' Association executive directors was not the only factor that could influence negotiations. Baseball player careers are finite in length, and usually very short. Few of the players who had been around in the union struggles of the 1970s were still active. Most duespayers to the Association in 1985 had been handed free agency, salary arbitration, and ample compensation without a struggle. The veteran players believed that they had already paid their dues, and they were more willing to sacrifice the earnings of their less-experienced underlings than they were to forego their own money during a strike. In short, Don Fehr found little of the solidarity that had united the players to weather its first two strikes.

As the strike deadline neared, the promise of another midseason interruption appeared imminent. In addition to holding the line on handing the players one-third of their broadcasting revenues, the owners wanted caps on salary arbitration awards and demanded that the requirement for arbitration eligibility be raised from two years to three years (Helyar 1994, 327).

In the course of the negotiations, the owners unilaterally conceded the compensation pool that had interrupted the 1981 season for 50 days. The compensation pool had seemed like a reasonable compromise in 1981. The owners believed it to have some potential for slowing salary growth, and the losers of key free agents could receive bona fide players as compensation. What the owners did not consider was the fact that their own contributions to the player pool might be selected as compensation. Dissatisfaction with the system mushroomed quickly, and the owners were anxious to dispose of it.

The players easily saw through management's "concession" but were happy to oust the procedure nonetheless. This did not bring the two sides any closer to an agreement. The players walked out on August 6.

Just as the Players' Association had a new executive director leading the walkout, baseball had a new commissioner, Peter Ueberroth. Ueberroth was not about to erode fan support for the game by allowing for another strike. He called the negotiators and gave them an ultimatum. Either they come to an agreement or he would put the issues to binding arbitration. Naturally, the thought of an independent third party imposing a collective bargaining agreement sent chills up the spines of the negotiators. In rapid fashion, they designed a mutually acceptable agreement, halting the work stoppage after only two days. There would be no cap on arbitration salaries, an increase in the arbitration eligibility service standard to three years, and the two sides compromised on pension funding. Under the new contract, the players would receive less than their customary third of broadcasting revenues. Nevertheless, their take of $32.7 million was nearly double their share from the previous contract (Lidz 1985, 15).

This chapter began with a statement that the lack of a work stoppage in baseball's first century was not to be inferred as an indication of labor harmony. Nothing could be more true of the three years that followed the 1985 negotiations; this was a period that would forever be remembered as "The Collusion Years."

Bowie Kuhn was never well suited for collective bargaining. He was hired to be the commissioner of baseball, a figurehead to preside over the integrity of the game in the shadow of Kenesaw Mountain Landis. His role was never intended to extend into intense negotiations between a pair of labor pros.

In contrast, Peter Ueberroth had been tapped as the successor to baseball's throne owing to his much-publicized stint as director of the 1984 Olympic Games in Los Angeles. The Games were long considered a death blow to the finances of the hosting city. Ueberroth, however, turned the 1984 Olympics into a tribute to Adam Smith: the first capitalistic Olympics. The most basic tenet of the laws of supply and demand were applied: Charge each patron and each sponsor the highest price the market can bear. As a result, the Ueberroth Olympic Games turned a $222 million profit (Helyar 1994, 312).

Such a track record was of obvious significance to baseball owners, who selected Ueberroth to lead them out of their financial abyss. Ueberroth's approach was to centralize the process. He increased the authority of the commissioner to fine individual owner who were not in sync with the New Order. At meetings, he assumed totalitarian control; the owners could not speak unless they were spoken to (Helyar 1994, 321). The owners were unaccustomed to such condescension; after all, Ueberroth worked for them, not the reverse. Nonetheless, with the Players' Association having put a permanent dent in the clubs' collective finances, the dictatorial approach of Ueberroth was tolerated.

Ueberroth made it painfully clear to the owners whom he thought the enemy to be: It was not Marvin Miller, it was not Don Fehr, and it was not Peter Seitz. The real enemies were seated at the meetings, and they bore the name "owners." Free agent mania did not bring world championships, he asserted, it only pushed players into higher tax brackets. To support his contention, he circulated some startling statistics on the fiscal irresponsibility of clubs: Nearly $50 million in salaries were owed to players who were no longer in baseball (Helyar 1994, 332). Players with long-term contracts spent considerably more time on the disabled list than those on single-year contracts. Players with multiyear contracts exhibited deteriorating performances throughout the duration of their agreements.

In the end, Ueberroth's admonitions against fiscal waste worked only too well. Since the Seitz decision, the owners complained loudly about free agency but then rushed to the winter meetings with deep pocketbooks, anxious to deliver a Messiah to the home-town crowd at any price. When the free agent didn't pan out, or the team didn't win, or the club lost money, another Messiah was called upon to do the job. This was standard operating procedure until the arrival of Ueberroth. Ueberroth whipped the owners into submission, browbeating them into accepting his point of view. In lieu of the speeches, the statistics, the public humiliation, only a fool would have subjected himself to the wrath of the groupthink by signing a free agent.

The first player to experience the free agent drought was Detroit Tiger outfielder Kirk Gibson. Gibson, a former football star at the collegiate level, played baseball with the same reckless abandon that he did on the gridiron. To the highest bidder, he promised power, speed, and a fiercely competitive spirit. In an abrupt and unexpected change in environs, he meandered through baseball's free agent signing period as a man without a team. Defeated in his attempts to solicit bids from other teams, Gibson returned to Detroit. The other premium free agents fared no better. In fact, of the 33 players who declared free agency that year, 29 re-signed with their old teams, having received no offers from competing clubs (Zimbalist 1992, 24-25).

Going into the 1986 free agency period, the new commissioner had created a monster operating on automatic pilot. For the first time since free agency began, the increase in the average salary showed signs of slowing to single digits. The owners discovered that the key to fiscal sanity was to turn their backs on free agency. Had an individual owner or two opted to turn their nose up at free agency, few eyebrows would have been raised. The marketplace ultimately would have determined whether such behavior was laudable or foolish. Now, however, there *was* no marketplace; by refusing to bid on free agents and not having to fear one's own stars being bid away, the teams' profits had nowhere to go but up.

The curious disinterest in the game's free agents did not get past the watchful eye of the Players' Association. Its office had been inundated with complaints from players and their agents. The Association filed grievances for each of the 1985–1986, 1986–1987, and 1987–1988 periods. The Basic Agreement plainly forbade clubs from acting in concert in the bidding for free agents, and it was just as plain that the clubs were doing exactly that. In the first two hearings, the arbitrators, Tom Roberts and George Nicolau, sided with the Players' Association and ruled that the clubs were guilty of collusion. In addition to damages, which would be settled at a later date, free agents during this period would be granted the opportunity to shop the market again if they chose to do so. Ironically, Kirk Gibson took the opportunity to jump to the Los Angeles Dodgers, leading them to the World Series and winning the National League's Most Valuable Player award. It is also somewhat poetic that his dramatic ninth-inning limp-hit home run trot remains indelibly laced into baseball folklore. The third collusion ruling, also by Nicolau, came about after the owners concocted a scheme to skirt the charges of collusion. Free agent bidding was fine, but each bidder must submit his or her bid to an information bank. Unlike the free agent bidding of the 1970s or early 1980s, when player agents would play clubs off each other to set off a bidding war, each club would now know exactly what its competitors had bid. Theoretically, then, a club could win a free agent's services by bidding the highest existing bid plus one dollar. The Players' Association filed a grievance against the information bank, and once again, the arbitrator sided against the owners. Eventually, the opposing sides settled on collusion damages totaling $280 million (Quirk and Fort 1992, 197). As the expiration of the 1985 Basic Agreement drew near, there were murmurs of another work stoppage. Of course, by now, contract expirations and work stoppages had become synonymous; one simply couldn't exist without the other. The only relevant issue was over which side would initiate the attack.

Baseball's collusion years, hardly relegated to nasty rumors, were now a matter of public record. The owners had earned a pretty penny over the temporary throwback to the "good ol' days", and now it was about to enter payback time. Don Fehr was not about to enter the negotiations on congenial terms. Unlike his predecessor, he'd been burned by the owners. Fehr had also been publicly scorched by Marvin Miller for giving up a year of eligibility for salary arbitration, and the executive director was certain to place it at the top of his agenda. To head off the possibility of a midseason strike, the owners decided to launch the first missile. Absent an agreement, the gates at spring training would be locked. Chuck O'Connor (who succeeded Barry Rona, who had succeeded Lee MacPhail, who had succeeded Ray Grebey, who had succeeded John Gaherin) was now management's chief negotiator and the messenger of the owners' hard-line.

With big money gleefully being tossed around to free agents once again, the owners decided to take the offensive. They presented Fehr with a request for a salary cap, accompanied by a pay-for-performance formula to replace arbitration. Baseball's new commissioner was Fay Vincent. Like his predecessors, work stoppages fell well within the scope of the "interests of baseball" of which the commissioner was to be the guardian. Convinced that Fehr would never buy the package, Vincent unilaterally pulled it from the bargaining table and replaced it with his own proposal. Shortly thereafter, O'Connor received word that Vincent had seized the chief negotiator hat for himself and was privately negotiating with Fehr at the request of no one (Helyar 1994, 420). In the events that were to haunt Vincent over the coming year, his unsolicited involvement in labor negotiations could be referred to as "strike one."

Almost as if scripted, Fehr entered the negotiations determined to win back the year of arbitration eligibility he had given away four years earlier. Much to his chagrin, however, there was much division within the ranks. The most vocal dissenter among the rank and file was veteran catcher Bob Boone, who surprisingly had been a key player in the 1981 strike. Boone was unwilling to sacrifice salary to enhance the financial welfare of a handful of younger players, and he'd uncovered quite a few other veterans who felt the same. Fehr lured Marvin Miller out of retirement to cut off the tongue of the union's loose cannon. Boone became angered by the union brass and accused them of directing a top-down rather than grass-roots operation. Fehr and Miller worked feverishly to patch up the dissent and restore unity in the players.

Fehr's latest proposal included a flat-out compromise on the arbitration issue: Half of the players with between two and three years of service would become eligible. Fay Vincent's hands-on dealings during the negotiations had hardly endeared him to his employers, and their silent contempt for the commissioner ran high when he beckoned them to accept Fehr's offer. Before the weekend came to an end, an agreement had been reached. Baseball's minimum salary would jump to $100,000, and the salary arbitration eligibility issue, which had stalemated the negotiations, had achieved a compromise (if one were to define "compromise" as getting less than initially desired). In fact, the new terms of the agreement consisted entirely of management concessions to the players. Baseball negotiations were back to normal.

The Players' Association had already gone through its internal squabbles in the early 1980s. Now it was management's turn. The new chief negotiator for the owners, Dick Ravitch (who had succeeded Chuck O'Connor, who had succeeded . . . well, you know) was wary over Commissioner Vincent's involvement in labor negotiations during the lockout. He pushed to have Vincent's duties as commissioner redefined so as to keep his nose away from the bargaining table. Vincent steadfastly refused. The Major League Agreement had a rule that forbade the clubs from diminishing the powers of the commissioner while he was in office, and Vincent waved it like a flag. He agreed verbally to adhere to some of the owner's requests, but an amendment to the Major League Agreement was out of the question.

"Strike two" came about over the National League's decision to add two expansion clubs. Historically, the fees charged to newcomers were somewhat nominal ($7 million per team in 1977), and the revenues were split among the clubs in the new teams' league. The 1993 expansion was different. The price for membership in the Club had now risen to $95 million (Helyar 1994, 466). The notion that a windfall this large should be distributed among National League teams only was unconscionable to the American League clubs, who demanded their fair share. After a tug-of-war between the leagues failed to achieve a resolution, the issue fell on the lap of Fay Vincent. The case had all the trimmings of the Messersmith decision: No matter what the split, one of the leagues would walk away miffed.   Vincent decided to award 22 percent of the fees to the American League (Helyar 1994, 467). The result: *Both* leagues got miffed.

"Strike three" was a spitball tossed by the Tribune Company, owners of the Chicago Cubs. The National League was preparing for realignment. Chicago and St. Louis had been in the Eastern Division since 1969, despite the fact that they were geographically west of Western Division teams Cincinnati and Atlanta. The logical move was for the four teams to swap divisions. Chicago balked.   Chicago Cub baseball was a cash cow for the Tribune Company, which beamed its games nationwide on superstation, WGN. A move to the Western Division would mean more games with San Francisco, Los Angeles, and San Diego, and the late starting times would certainly cut into the TV station's advertising revenue. Vincent came down from the mountaintop and ordered the move as "in the best interests of baseball."   Though the rest of the clubs agreed that the Tribune Company had been rather pigheaded in this matter, they did not regard it as one to be resolved by "executive order." Fay Vincent's fate had been sealed.

Unable to fire the commissioner, the clubs gathered together to draft a statement of no confidence. Vincent dug in his heels and vowed a legal battle. The events had constituted a holy war to Vincent, and he saw himself as the sole protector of a religious shrine. He would not be removed from office without a fight.   When the no-confidence vote passed by a two thirds majority, the owners prepared for Vincent to make his first move toward litigation. To their surprise, the commissioner resigned.

One by-product of the 1990 lockout was the creation of a joint committee to report on the economic status of baseball. Like most committees of this sort, the owners and players each selected their own appointees, which included former Chairman of the Federal Reserve System Paul Volcker.

In 1992 the committee completed its report. The group pointed to the growing disparities in the revenues of the large- and small-market clubs as a cause for concern. Because national broadcasting revenue, which had become the lifeblood of smaller markets, was likely to decline, the committee urged the owners to adopt a more aggressive means of sharing revenues between teams. This, they argued, would preserve not only the financial stability of smaller-market clubs but also competitive balance within the league.

Regarding the proposal of salary caps, which would tie player salaries to a fixed percentage of league revenues, the committee did not commit itself to a position.   Reflecting perhaps the partisanship of the owners and players who had appointed them, the committee limited its comments to a discussion of the pros and cons of having caps.

Unfortunately, like most joint committee work, the time spent developing the analysis was largely for naught. The two sides scoured the report for conclusions that supported its contentions and casually ignored the rest. The next showdown was to be resolved by owner and player reps at the bargaining table, not by a group of preeminent economists.

With major league baseball commissionerless following the ousting of Fay Vincent, the owners prepared for their next confrontation with labor. The collective bargaining agreement negotiated in 1990 had a reopener clause, which allowed either side to reopen the agreement after 1992. At the urging of Ravitch, the owners did so. By reopening the agreement prior to its expiration, the owners freed either side to enact yet another work stoppage.

The negotiations that ensued were probably the most intense confrontations witnessed in 20 years. Each side took extreme positions and stubbornly refused to budge. Never before had such obstinacy threatened to derail any hope of productive bargaining. Only something was missing from the negotiations: the Player's Association. This round of bargaining had nothing to do with negotiations between labor and management. This time it was management against management.

Baseball had always been characterized by large- and small-market teams. The New York, Chicago, and Los Angeles clubs had a greater drawing base than clubs like Kansas City or Seattle. In recent years, however, the gap had become substantially larger, due primarily to growing disparities in local broadcasting revenues.

As recently as 1985, the difference in broadcast dollars between the high-revenue club (the Yankees) and the low-revenue club (the Mariners) was barely $12 million (Zimbalist 1992, 49). By 1990, on the other hand, the Yankees were drawing $55.6 million in local broadcast revenues, compared with the paltry $3 million pulled in by Seattle (Zimbalist 1992, 49).

The wide disparity between the financial resources of the large- and small-market clubs had begun to infiltrate the field in a way not quite witnessed previously. The small-market Pittsburgh Pirates, through astute trades for major league prospects and player development within its own farm system, suffered through several years of growing pains awaiting harvest time. Eventually its crop of youngsters developed into stars and led the team to three consecutive division titles. Then, as if torn apart by a hurricane, the dynasty was instantly dismantled, as its core of stars were bid away by large-market dollars.

Even more pathetic was the plight of the San Diego Padres. The Padres, also bearing the scarlet letter "S," had finished the 1992 season in second place. Presumed by its fans to be a contender in 1993, the club promptly shed itself of anyone whose salary totaled seven digits. Fred McGriff, who had pieced together more consecutive 30-plus home run seasons than any player in the game, was dealt to the Atlanta Braves in exchange for a host of no-names for whom baseball cards had to be hastily manufactured. Likewise for Gary Sheffield, who flirted with baseball's Triple Crown only a year before. The flood of players exiting San Diego could have stocked an All-Star team. The incoming players, on the other hand, could only be identified with the aid of a high school yearbook.

The small-market clubs were not about to let this trend continue. Decreased national broadcasting revenues were on the horizon, which would only increase the imbalance. They demanded more-aggressive revenue-sharing from the larger-market teams. Suddenly, Dick Ravitch, who had been hired to lock horns with Don Fehr, found himself refereeing a battle between the owners.

With no hope of a revenue-sharing agreement in sight, Ravitch had to come to grips with the double-edged sword inherent in reopener clauses. The players could organize a strike in midseason. Hoping to stave off such a possibility, Ravitch promised a no-lockout pledge from the owners in exchange for a reciprocal no-strike guarantee from the players. Fehr agreed, and baseball was spared a midseason impasse.

For the better part of the year, the owners ferociously debated revenue-sharing. The reluctance of large-market clubs to share their revenues with small-market teams was only natural. Owners are in business to make money, and agreeing to increased revenue-sharing is like the Sheriff of Nottingham handing Robin Hood his wallet.

There was more to it than just the money. The owners also like to field winning teams. Given their druthers, they would prefer to see their own team in the World Series over someone else's. Revenue imbalances improved the odds for large-market teams. Market-related revenue differentials, for example, allowed the New York Mets to bid Bobby Bonilla away from small-market rival Pittsburgh. The Mets knew they could outbid the Pirates and stay in the black, and they liked having it that way. (The fact that the Mets' bevy of high-priced free agents wound up being big-time losers is another story.) Thus, not only did revenue-sharing cut into the larger teams' profits, it also meant handing over money to competitors, who could then use it to try to bid away the large-market teams' players. Why would any sane large-market owner be agreeable to this?

Eventually, the two sides agreed to a system of revenue-sharing. It came, however, with a catch. The large-market teams would agree to revenue-sharing only if it were tied to a salary cap. In other words, the large clubs would only give up money if the players made up the difference. To no one's surprise, the players were not amiable to such a deal. They walked out on August 12, 1994.

The 1994 season had been a dandy. Both Matt Williams and Ken Griffey Jr. were chasing after Roger Maris's non-asterisked home run record. Tony Gwynn's batting average was hovering around .400. Cal Ripken, Jr.'s consecutive game streak was now within sight of Lou

Gehrig's. Perpetual loser Cleveland was one game behind the division leader. Yet all would be for naught if the season were not to resume.

The Players' Association had been preparing for this showdown for some time. It had stockpiled $175 million of licensing revenue to be used as a strike fund (Verducci 1994a, 26). The average player would lose nearly $7,000 per day during a strike (Verducci 1994, 26). If the Association were to disburse the fund to the players at the same daily rate, it would not be depleted for a month. If the players had been prudent enough to stash away some of their own pay, they could easily last through the remainder of the season.

Salary caps had existed in professional basketball and football, the owners argued, so why not baseball? (Of course, the fact that both basketball and football players bemoaned their respective caps was beside the point.) The deal the owners laid out on the bargaining table called for all revenues in baseball to be split 50/50 between the clubs and the players (Grover, Bernstein, and Schiller 1994, 26). In fact, the players already earned 58 percent of the revenues. If the 50 percent was not acceptable, said Ravitch, give us your figure.

Don Fehr stated unequivocally that no salary cap would ever be acceptable and that the strike would continue as long as a cap was on the table. Fehr believed that baseball's woes could be traced solely to revenue imbalances and that the industry's problems could be resolved simply by sharing revenues on a more equitable basis. In other words—it was unacceptable for the clubs to expect the players to give up some of their money to help out Pittsburgh and San Diego; it was perfectly OK, however, for the New York Mets and Los Angeles Dodgers to give up some of theirs.

And so the gridlock continued. In between press conferences, the two sides managed to squeeze in some time at the bargaining table. No negotiations actually took place, nor were any compromises discussed. Rather, the opposing sides would get together to reiterate their stances on the issues, apparently in the event the other side had forgotten.

The Players' Association was certain that the owners would blink first. Unlike the small-market teams, for whom the status quo was patently unacceptable, there were plenty of teams that would be profitable with or without the current proposal. To them, a show of solidarity came at an enormous cost. Prior to the strike, however, the owners had adopted a new rule: No settlement could be approved without a three-fourths majority (Verducci, September 1994b, 20). This placed the larger-market teams in the minority and put the small- and medium-market teams in charge. The impasse continued.

On September 14, 1994, the remainder of the season was officially canceled. The announcement came without fanfare. Bud Selig, the un-commissioner, disseminated the edict in a four-paragraph fax (Verducci 1994b, 20).

The cancellation did not bring the two sides any closer together. Congress toyed with the notion of lifting baseball's antitrust exemption as a means of ending the strike. The owners offered to drop the salary cap and replace it with a luxury tax, which would punish teams with excessive payrolls. To the Players' Association, however, a luxury tax was simply a salary cap in subtitles.

On December 22 the owners finally declared an impasse and unilaterally imposed the same salary cap that had begun the negotiations. Along with the establishment of payrolls and benefits equal to 50 percent of the previous year's revenues, each team's payroll would be constrained to being within 84 percent and 110 percent of the average payroll (Bernstein and Greising 1994, 38).

The new system also implemented changes in free agency and salary arbitration. Arbitration, long regarded as a thorn in the owners' side, was discarded. In its stead, players with between four and six years of major league service would be restricted free agents, meaning that they would be bound to their current clubs only if the team matched an outside offer for the player's services. Unrestricted free agency for players with at least six years of experience would continue (Bernstein and Greising 1994, 38).

The response of the Players' Association was to move away from the bargaining table and into the legal arena. The Association filed a charge with the National Labor Relations Board (NLRB), alleging that the owners failed to bargain in good faith when they unilaterally implemented the salary cap. If the NLRB were to file a complaint against the owners, it could move for an injunction, which would prevent the owners from implementing their plan.

In early February of 1995 the Board hinted that it would, in fact, file a complaint against management. In rapid fashion, the owners dropped the salary cap and replaced it with a proposal calling for a luxury tax, which would impose a series of penalties for payrolls existing a predetermined threshold.

After the salary cap was removed, the Players' Association dropped its self-imposed ban on player signings. Ironically, however, management moved just as quickly to impose its own ban, arguing that issues such as free agency- and salary arbitration-eligibility were unresolved and made meaningful salary negotiations impossible. In response, the Players' Association filed another charge of unfair labor practices against management.

The Players' Association was also busy politicking for the lifting of baseball's antitrust exemption. Removing the exemption would allow the union to sue major league baseball for antitrust violations, giving it additional leverage in bargaining. Earlier in the fall, the players pledged that the strike would end if the exemption were repealed. Members of Congress, seeing a chance to take credit for ending the dreaded baseball strike, looked favorably toward removing the exemption, but then agreed to table the discussion until the start of the new year.

Although Congress's interest in lifting the exemption appeared to wane since the September hearings, President Clinton initiated his own involvement. Having already assigned William Usery as mediator to the disputes several months earlier, the President beckoned the two sides to come to an agreement before the scheduled start of spring training. In fact, he proposed a deadline of February 6, Babe Ruth's 100th birthday, for a settlement. Although the executive office has no legal power to intervene in the negotiations, he hinted that a failure of the two sides to come to an agreement by the deadline could lead to legislation calling for binding arbitration. He also suggested that Usery propose his own nonbinding solution if the parties were still at impasse at the deadline.

The players and owners doggedly tried to come to an agreement in the days that followed. Nonetheless, it was no secret that the President's threat lacked teeth. Baseball's impact on the gross domestic product is so small that it can only be detected with a magnifying glass. The industry generates little income, few jobs, and does not impact national security. Direct government intervention in an industry that generates little more than civic pride and entertainment would have been unprecedented.

In the meantime, the owners began their own offensive. They publicly discussed the possible use of replacement players should the strike continue into spring training. The National Football League had made effective use of scab players several years earlier when the players struck to obtain free agency. The crowds were smaller, but the game went on, and in time the players crossed the picket lines in droves.

As the prospect of an opening day with replacement players drew nearer, the momentum favored the owners. Productive bargaining had come to a grinding halt. If the clubs could draw enough fans to cover their game costs, it would just be a matter of time before the players cracked; hence, there was no reason for the owners to negotiate.

Then, suddenly, the bargaining leverage shifted gears as abruptly as the swirling wind changes directions at Candlestick Park (or 3Com Park to nonpurists). In late March the National Labor Relations Board ruled that the owners had not bargained in good faith when they banned player signings in early February. In seeking an injunction, the Board ruled that the two sides must continue to bargain under the rules of the previous agreement. For the players, whose only demand was to preserve the status quo, the Board's action ventured well beyond establishing a level playing field for negotiations: It essentially awarded the players an unconditional victory for the 1995 season.

Management had little time to react to the decision. U.S. Circuit Court Judge Sonia Sotomayor was to rule on the injunction the following Friday, and the season was officially scheduled to begin before the weekend was through. The owners promptly announced their "willingness" to play the 1995 season under the old set of rules (a generous act of magnamity, given the court's power to enforce the NRLB injunction) and offered the players essentially the same luxury tax deal that had been on the table previously for the 1996 season and beyond. The players countered with their own illusion of compromise. No deal was reached, and the two sides remained miles apart.

When Judge Sotomayor sided with the NLRB's decision on March 31, the owners ran out of options. A lockout of the players was potentially illegal, and the damages resulting from a suit could add up to $5.5 million per day in back pay (Bernstein 1995, 58). They had no choice but to allow the games to begin (albeit three weeks behind schedule).

As baseball prepared to enter into the 1995 season without a collective bargaining agreement, the only view shared by the two sides throughout the strike was that baseball was impervious to permanent and irreparable damage. They had learned through all of the threats, all of the lockouts, and all of the strikes that a baseball fan's love and devotion to the game were unshakable; and that the psyche of the baseball's loyal following could be summarized by a reconstructed line from the movie *Field of Dreams*: "If you play it, they will come."

Unfortunately, both sides faced a rude reality once the season got under way. Having spent the entire winter arguing over how to split the pie, they returned to the game only to discover that the pie had shrunk. Despite slashing ticket prices, despite offering giveaways, and despite taking great pains to restore the image of the game (there were even unconfirmed reports of players tipping their caps to the fans at some ballparks), the fans they had so dutifully alienated over the past several months stayed home. Attendance declined by 20 percent despite the reductions in ticket prices, national broadcasting revenues dropped by 20 percent, and local broadcasting revenues and cable advertising were down 30 percent (Greising and Baker 1995, 50). Baseball was damaged goods.

The diminished interest in baseball had ill effects on the players as well. The average player salary fell from $1.26 million to $1.07 million (Greising and Baker 1995, 50). The decline was the first decrease in player salaries since the collusion period. If the collusion period is ignored, the 1995 decline marked the first drop in player salaries since baseball became unionized (Zimbalist 1992, 85).

One might have thought that the 1994–1995 strike, which cost both sides dearly, and whose aftershocks carried into the 1995 season would have caused everyone to rethink their priorities, but alas not. The bargaining table gathered dust as the owners once again appealed the NLRB decision. Don Fehr hinted at the possibility of a midseason strike unless the owners pledged not to lock out the players in 1996. Both sides spoke eloquently about the need for a new labor agreement to restore America's faith in the game, but no meaningful negotiations took place over the course of the season. Was the new agreement expected to come about through osmosis? Or were the two sides jockeying for position, trying to develop a strategy that would gain the advantage at the bargaining table? Then, in August 1996, in the midst of the second year of the automatic-pilot-labor-agreement, came news of a divine intervention. Randy Levine (management's labor-negotiator-of-the-week) was close to an agreement with Don Fehr. The proposed deal included provisions for a luxury tax in the first three years of the agreement. It also returned the service days lost during the 1994–1995 strike to the players in exchange for a promise to drop litigation charges against the owners for their unfair labor practices. Acceptance of the deal would pave the way for a new-and-improved revenue-sharing scheme, the beginning of interleague play, and most importantly, a five-year period of relief for the fans.

The optimistic reports brought a glow to the faces of baseball fans who were too young to know better. Twenty-three owners had to vote in favor of the proposal to complete the agreement. Sports reporters took straw votes as to how many owners would support the deal. Preliminary reports suggested that as many as eight owners opposed the agreement. Periodic updates fluctuated between eight and 12 "No" votes. Interim Commissioner Bud Selig refused to tip his hand on which direction he was leaning.

On Wednesday, November 6, the owners delivered the bad news. Eighteen of the 30 owners voted against the deal (Bodley 1996, 1C). Baseball appeared to be back to square one.

But then, three weeks later, on November 26, common sense accomplished what the gods could not. The owners reversed their previous stance and overwhelmingly voted to accept the deal by a lop-sided 26–4 margin.

What was responsible for the change of heart? Why would an agreement that was patently unacceptable to 60 percent of baseball's brass suddenly be fine and dandy only three weeks later? Could it be that the owners recognized the importance of preserving the integrity of the national pastime? Doubtful, unless one believes that canceling a World Series and preparing to suit up replacement players had similar appeal to the fans of Mudville.

To the contrary, the evidence suggests that a series of events that transpired shortly after the initial vote may have caused the tides to turn. Two weeks after the "No" vote promised yet another year of a court-ordered status quo, the Chicago White Sox signed Albert Belle to a reported $55 million five-year contract. The signing turned more heads than Madonna's announcement that she was pregnant. Belle, whose explosive bat was matched only by his explosive temper, was to become baseball's first player to sport an eight-figure annual salary. The $11 million per year salary easily dwarfed the $9 million figure pulled in by Cecil Fielder in 1996.

The Belle signing was not an aberration. John Smoltz re-signed with the Braves and became the game's highest-paid pitcher. Bobby Bonilla, who was heavily criticized in New York for being baseball's least-worthy $6 million player, signed on with the Florida Marlins for a hefty raise. The owners, it appeared, were preparing for a spending binge—and without the benefit of extra revenues from interleague play or expansion fees.

Moreover, not all of the clubs were preparing to empty their pocketbooks. The Pittsburgh Pirates made a tactical decision to make a bad team worse, and were in the process of dumping any player whose salary totaled seven figures. The Pirates' total payroll in 1996 was already less than what Albert Belle and Frank Thomas stood to earn in combined salaries in 1997, and Pittsburgh seemed hellbent on lowering it by even more.

By voting to accept the deal, the owners might halt the trend. If the recent signings were any indication, the $51 million tax threshold specified in the proposed labor agreement for 1997 would affect more than just a small handful of clubs.   Only four clubs reported payrolls exceeding $51 million in 1996 (Dodd 1996, 3C). A luxury tax would not only discourage teams from paying Belle-like salaries to other free agents, it would also serve as a source of much-needed revenue for small-market teams such as Pittsburgh and Milwaukee. Further, approving the deal would also allow baseball to enact its revenue-sharing plan, begin interleague play, and expand the league to include the Arizona Diamondbacks and Tampa Bay Devil Rays—after all, if the owners are going to pay eight-figure salaries, they're going to need some money! In short, the owners believed that perhaps the deal was better than they had previously thought—in any case, it sure looked better than the status quo. Peace was at hand!

As the 1997 baseball season proceeds, guided by the terms of the new collective bargaining contract, the scars from the 1994–1996 skirmishes will gradually heal. As they do, it will become easy for us baseball fans to be lulled into complacency and to adopt the belief that perhaps baseball will finally begin to resemble the fond days of yesteryear—when "strike" referred to a pitch. Let us be reminded, however, that baseball has not had a collective bargaining agreement expire without a work stoppage in over twenty years. And let it not be forgotten that it was Hall of Fame catcher Yogi Berra, and not Thoreau or Emerson, that was credited with saying "It isn't over until it's over." Are baseball's labor problems finally over? Only time will tell.

REFERENCES

Bernstein, Aaron. 1995. Let's See the Owners Pitch Their Way Out of This One. *Business Week* (April 3): 58.

Bernstein, Aaron, and David Greising. 1994. Baseball's Strike Talk Turns Serious. *Business Week* (June 27): 38.

Bodley, Hal. 1996. Baseball Owners Vote Down Labor Deal. *USA Today* (November 7): 1C.

Dodd, Mike. 1996. Four-year Struggle Ends. *USA Today* (November 27): 3C.

Greising, David, and Stephen Baker. 1995. The Bozos of October. *Business Week* (October 16): 50.

Grover, Ronald, Aaron Bernstein, and Zachary Schiller. 1994. Ste-e-e-rike? *Business Week* (August 15): 26–28.

Helyar, John. 1994. *Lords of the Realm: The Real History of Baseball*. New York: Villard Books.

Lidz, Franz. 1985. The Strike of '85: Called on Account of Reasonableness. *Sports Illustrated* 63 (August 19): 15.

Miller, Marvin. 1991. *A Whole Different Ball Game: The Sport and Business of Baseball.* New York: Birch Lane Press.

Quirk, James, and Rodney D. Fort. 1992. *Pay Dirt: The Business of Professional Team Sports.* Princeton, N.J.: Princeton University Press.

Scully, Gerald W. 1989. *The Business of Major League Baseball.* Chicago: University of Chicago Press.

Verducci, Tom. 1994a. In the Strike Zone. *Sports Illustrated 81* (August 1): 26–28.

———. 1994b. Making Small Talk. *Sports Illustrated 81* (September 26): 20–24.

Zimbalist, Andrew. 1992. *Baseball and Billions: A Probing Look inside the Big Business of Our National Pastime.* New York: Basic Books.

2

Why Can't Baseball Resolve Its Differences in the Off-season?

Daniel R. Marburger

Ever since the Players' Association was established as the bargaining arm of the players, baseball and work stoppages have gone together like peanut butter and jelly; it's hard to imagine one without the other. In fact, since 1970, baseball has not settled a single collective bargaining agreement without the accompaniment of either a strike or lockout. To the average baseball fan, whose only request is that the season start and end on schedule, the persistence of early- and mid-season interruptions is annoying, to say the least.

A reasonable question to ask is why these disputes are not resolved during the off-season. If they were, no games would have to be canceled, no player would have to sacrifice a paycheck, and no owner would have to forego so much as a day's ticket receipts. An off-season settlement would also ensure that the goodwill of baseball's loyal following would not be jeopardized.

If the above statement gushes with logic to the extent of being downright obvious, the reader is long on common sense but may be short on an understanding of collective bargaining. To truly understand baseball's history of work stoppages, a primer on management-labor negotiations is needed.

UNION TACTICS AND STRATEGY

As with any group of organized labor, the players' only tool to force concessions from management is the strike. The alternative is to wait for management to unilaterally decide that it has more money than it needs and that the proper thing to do is to share the windfall with the players. In other words—the only tool is the strike. Major league baseball players have struck on four occasions: in 1972, 1981, 1985, and

1994-1995. The costs of a player strike to management are obvious: No players means no games, and no games means no money. Therefore, it may be less costly for the owners to accede to the union's demands than it is to suffer the losses from the canceled games.

Of course, the players are not paid during a walkout. This leads to the oft-quoted aphorism "Everybody loses in a strike." If so, then why strike? Wouldn't everyone be better off if an equitable settlement were reached without a strike?

This is the great paradox in collective bargaining. The standard union strategy is to force concessions not by striking but by *threatening* to strike. In the case of baseball, the players hope they can pressure the owners to meet their terms without actually having to stage a walkout. If management has not offered acceptable terms by the strike deadline, the players may find that it is better to strike until further concessions are made than to settle quickly to avoid losing paychecks.

By the same token, however, the players cannot expect to gain meaningful concessions from management if their threats are perceived as empty. Therefore, strikes can sometimes occur for no other reason than to convince management that the union rank and file is united in its cause.

Given the strategic necessity of the strike threat, the union must next decide upon the proper timing of a walkout. Because the purpose of a strike is to put management on the "hot seat", logic dictates that the greater the losses to be suffered by the employers, the more willing they will be to negotiate, and the more the terms of a new agreement will favor the players.

However, because the players also lose paychecks during a strike, it is possible that the strikers will become even more uneasy about losing money than the owners and will therefore collapse and concede ground to the opposition. For this reason, the key to orchestrating a successful strike is timing the threat such that the owners will buckle before the players.

In this regard, baseball fans should note that the last three player strikes have occurred in midseason. Such timing is not an accident. In 1994, for example, by timing the walkout toward the end of the season, the bargaining leverage was tilted heavily in favor of the players. By the start of the 1994 strike, the players had received over 80 percent of their paychecks. The Players' Association had also been stockpiling licensing revenues to be used as a strike fund in the event of a walkout. In this case, the union had accumulated enough to keep the players from anxiously staring at their pocketbooks through the remainder of the season. Moreover, the late-season strike was timed to cause undue pain to the owners. September pennant races tend to fill the stands and post-season money creates powerful incentives for management to settle. Thus, the Players' Association believed that by staging an August strike, the deck would be stacked heavily in its favor.

In contrast, continuing to play in 1994 and threatening to strike at the beginning of the 1995 season was an option never seriously considered by the players. An early 1995 strike would have had the opposite effect. Here, the players would be entering into a strike having not been paid since October. Although the owners would still lose revenue, it would be April's revenue and not October's post-season bonanza that would be in limbo. Further, the month of April is often characterized by a larger than average number of offdays, smaller crowds, and postponements due to inclement weather. An April strike would have tipped the scales in favor of management.

MANAGEMENT TACTICS AND STRATEGY

To counter the players' strike threats, baseball management has relied on lockouts to force union concessions. A lockout is much the same as a strike. No one works, no one gets paid, and no product is sold. However, lockouts are timed by management so that the bargaining leverage favors the employers. Baseball's lockouts are inevitably timed to coincide with the beginning of the season, when the players are anxious to resume drawing paychecks. Management has locked the players out twice: once in 1976 following the Seitz decision and once in 1990. In both cases, the lockout occurred during spring training.

Unfortunately for baseball fans, strikes and lockouts can be as much a defensive maneuver as a strategic offensive. Given that the owners prefer early-season lockouts and the players favor midseason strikes, management may opt to lock the players out of spring training simply to avoid a midseason strike. The reverse is true when the players take a strike vote.

When the owners reopened the collective bargaining agreement in 1993, for example, they gave themselves the right to lock the players out of spring training until a new agreement was reached. However, because revenue-sharing was at the top of the agenda, the owners could not achieve an internal consensus much less force the players to the bargaining table. By reopening the agreement, the owners gave the players license to strike in midseason. Only by promising not to lock the players out of spring training the following year were the owners able to obtain a no-strike pledge from the players.

Similarly, the players' decision to walk out in 1994 may have been something of a defensive maneuver. Don Fehr's stated position in orchestrating the strike was that if he had not, the owners could have unilaterally implemented a salary cap in the off-season. Of course, absent a collective bargaining agreement, the owners could not force the players to go to work in the spring. By implementing the cap, the players would have to choose between playing under management's terms or striking. Hence, in choosing between striking in August or striking in February, the players maximized their bargaining leverage by opting for the former.

(Alternatively, in the event management arbitrarily slapped a salary cap on the players between seasons, the union could charge the owners with an unfair labor practice. This, of course, is the sequence of events that eventually transpired).

While a strike is underway, management can rely on a variety of options to lessen the impact of the strike. In 1981, for example, the owners took out strike insurance from Lloyd's of London. The insurance gave the owners back over half of the money that was lost to the canceled games, improving their ability to weather the strike. The settlement came immediately after the insurance deal had expired.

In response to the 1994–1995 strike, the owners made preparations to begin the 1995 season with replacement players. The replacement teams would have been similar to the "scab" teams employed by the National Football League (NFL) in 1987. The intent is to give the owners leverage in labor negotiations. If major league baseball could be profitable with the replacement teams, there would be little incentive to concede ground to the players. In time, the players would have no choice but to accept the demands of management.

Is there any reason to believe that baseball could have succeeded with replacement teams? If the NFL experience is any indication, the answer is "Yes." Although the NFL replacement teams were condemned by the media and attendance at the games was poor, the salaries paid to the replacement players were sufficiently low to allow most teams to sustain a profit (Flanagan et al. 1989, 444). Ultimately, the teams comfortably sat back and waited for the players' collective resolve to collapse.

Baseball's situation is similar. Stocking replacement teams could potentially work to the advantage of the clubs because it represents a brief return to the days of the reserve clause. Unlike the major league labor market following the Messersmith decision, the clubs would be free to set an industrywide payscale not unlike that which existed during the reserve clause era. The clubs could determine a salary level that allows for a profit even with diminished crowds. The proposed replacement salaries for 1995 were less than one-tenth the average 1994 salary level. Theoretically, management could have kept its head above water by attracting roughly one-tenth the normal gate revenue. Unless the replacement games were an unmitigated disaster (in some cities, they undoubtedly would have been), most clubs would have been able to cover their costs.

There is, however, one major difference between baseball's replacement games and football's. Revenue-sharing is so extensive in football that it was of no consequence if a small handful of teams could not draw minimally acceptable crowds at the replacement games. As long as the industry as a whole could cover its game costs, there was no reason for any particular team to squabble. In contrast, baseball clubs that would not draw well for replacement games would not stand to be bailed out by the more successful teams. Unless the owners had agreed to help out the least successful teams, some clubs may have chosen to break ranks shortly after the replacement season had begun.

This explains management's reluctance to bargain as spring training approached in 1995. Replacement games were a definite threat to the players' bargaining strength, and the owners knew it. If the games were successful financially, the strike would have ended quickly with many of management's demands being met. Even if the games were a bust, all would not be lost for the owners. The clubs could substitute a lockout for the replacement games, which also favored management (although significantly less so).

Unfortunately for baseball fans, the players had as much incentive to see the results of the replacement games as the owners did. Management would not concede an inch as long as it believed that the replacement teams could be successful. (Fans should recall the curious lack of negotiations as the replacement season drew nearer.) Only if the games failed would management accept anything less. Thus, had it not been for the National Labor Relation Board's (NLRB) decision to move for an injunction against the owners in late March of 1995, the players' only choice would have been to adopt a wait-and-see attitude.

WHY NO OFF-SEASON SETTLEMENT?

Whereas the use of strikes and lockouts as offensive and defensive strategies tends to explain baseball's propensity for work stoppages, it also casts light on why the two sides never settle during the off-season. Between the end of the World Series and the beginning of spring training, there are no games scheduled. Clearly, an off-season "strike" has no clout, because management is confronted with no impending losses in revenue. True, the strike threat does have some impact on management, which uses the off-season to promote season-ticket sales, but the threat pales to that which exists after the season is underway.

Similarly, the players are not accustomed to being paid during the off-season anyway. For this reason, it costs them nothing to resist the demands of management. Because neither side has a decided edge over the other in terms of bargaining power during the off-season, no one has even a shred of a reason to concede. Not surprisingly, the parties tend to hold their ground between seasons, thereby increasing the likelihood that the upcoming season will be interrupted.

NEGOTIATION STRATEGY

Although it should now be clear why settlements never occur during the off-season, the question as to why strikes and lockouts are not avoided by eleventh-hour settlements is as yet unanswered. After all, it is the *threat* of a strike or lockout that is designed to bring the two sides to the bargaining table. To understand why the two sides invariably fail to find common ground prior to the work stoppage, one needs to understand the dynamics of collective bargaining negotiations.

Collective bargaining, in a nutshell, is a nasty game, not intended for the faint of heart. For those who dare to play, its success is predicated upon a willingness to lie through one's teeth, to dutifully make enemies and strive to keep them at arm's length, and to stare eyeball-to-eyeball at an opponent who loathes one's very existence. Reasonableness and congeniality are viewed as signs of weakness and are typically cast to the four winds. The old saying that "All's fair in love and war" can very well be amended to state "All's fair in love, war, and collective bargaining," except that the mention of "war" and "collective bargaining" in the same phrase smacks of redundancy.

Perhaps the preceding is too strong a statement to describe all collective bargaining scenario—some management groups boast amicable relationships with their labor unions. Nonetheless, the confrontational games of chicken often associated with labor relations come about not so much out of stubbornness but as a necessary strategy to avoid unconditional surrender at the hands of the opponent.

To fully comprehend why this is so, consider the negotiations involved in the purchase of a car. In selling the car, the salesperson knows the cost of the car to the dealership, and hence, the minimum acceptable sales price. The salesperson's goal, of course, is not to sell the car at the minimum price but rather to bleed the buyer dry (at least, the salespersons I've dealt with aspire to this). Similarly, the buyer knows what he or she can afford but hopes to spend considerably less.

As long as the dealer's minimum price is below the buyer's maximum price, a deal should be consummated. The problem in negotiating a price comes about because each party recognizes the wisdom in keeping its minimum/maximum acceptable figure secret. If the buyer, for example, were foolish enough to reveal his or her maximum price to the dealer, the individual would probably wind up paying this price. In other words, the best deal will go to the bargainer who does the best job of concealing that magic number.

The secret to negotiating a good deal on a car also applies to collective bargaining. Both the players and owners know which settlements they would accept to avoid a strike or lockout. Each side also knows that its minimum acceptable position must not be revealed to the opponent. Successful bargaining is based on the bargainers' ability to convince the opponent that the offer placed on the bargaining table is their true position. Further, whereas each side strives to keep its true position secret, it is well aware that the other side is playing the same game. Because stated positions are potential bluffs, each side must distinguish the true positions from the bluffs.

As each side concedes during the negotiations, the true and stated demands begin to converge. As a result, however, the bluffs become much more difficult to discern. Strikes and lockouts invariably occur when at least one side improperly gauges the distance between the true and stated positions.

Because of the importance in concealing true positions, the designated bargainers insist upon being the official spokespersons for the "party line." For bargainers to be effective, the other side must be convinced that the opponents are united in their resolve. If dissenters are perceived to exist within the ranks, the incentive is to sit back and wait for the other side to crack. In fact, dissenters on both sides invariably do exist, but their representatives "take them to the woodshed" if they make their protests public.

For example, the cancellation of the 1994 season quite possibly may have been avoided absent the public statements of dissent offered by some of the large-market owners. These individuals stood to profit with or without a salary cap, and toting the party line came at a sizable cost. Would the perception of dissension among the owners have anything to do with the fact that the players' first counterproposal came over a month after the owners' proposal was handed to the players?   And what of the timing of the counterproposal? By waiting until mid-September to offer a counterproposal, the owners were handed an ultimatum of "Withdraw your demands for salary caps and the season will be salvaged; stick with the demands and the season will have to be canceled." Clearly, the Players' Association hoped that the large-market owners would pressure the others for a quick settlement (at the players' terms). In addition, the player reps were undoubtedly convinced that certain peculiarities of the 1994 season weighed in their favor. Small-market clubs Montreal, Texas, and Cleveland were in a position to win their first division titles in years. Normally, these teams might comprise the hardest of the hard-liners. Silenced by their obligation to the party line, the players bet that these clubs would join the ranks of the dissenters after the season was truly in jeopardy. Instead, the players miscalculated, and the season was lost.

Likewise, one would be naive to think that strikebreaking statements made by Greg Swindell and Lenny Dykstra were not followed up by swift attempts to cut off their tongues. Not only do signs of cracks in the armor inhibit the attractiveness of the eventual bargaining agreement, they might even increase the likelihood of a prolonged stalemate, because the other side has reason to believe that its demands will be met without further concessions.

Ultimately, because the stated positions at the bargaining table may or may not be bluffs, the bottom line in negotiating is that each side must assume that his or her opponent is inherently greedy, with no interest whatsoever in fairness or justice. If one enters into negotiations without such preconceived prejudices, the bargainer stands to be taken to the cleaners. In fact, labor negotiations represent the classic syndrome referred to as the "prisoner's dilemma." If both sides enter into negotiations with an eye on fairness, then each will come away with an equitable settlement without the threat of a strike or lockout. If one bargainer seeks a fair deal, whereas the opponent aspires to highway robbery, then the less congenial of the two will walk away with the lion's share of the riches, and without a strike.   On the other hand, if both sides play the hard-line, each seeking to pick the other side's pocket then the final settlement will tend to approximate the congenial setting, albeit accompanied by the serious possibility of a work stoppage.

THE ROLE OF GOVERNMENT

Baseball's Antitrust Exemption

Although the pros and cons of major league baseball's exemption from antitrust legislation will be discussed in greater detail later in this book, some elements of the exemption are relevant in terms of their impact at the bargaining table. In short, the antitrust exemption protects major league baseball from lawsuits that allege practices restricting interstate commerce. Because baseball players travel from state to state to play their games, baseball would be subject to such litigation in the absence of the exemption.

In contrast to management's position that baseball needs the exemption, the Players' Association has lobbied to have it removed. Although the owners' rationale for shielding themselves from antitrust suits is inherently obvious, the union's support for lifting the exemption is less evident. Perhaps the best way to understand the players' position is to look back at football's experience.

In 1987 the NFL players struck to obtain free agency.   Absent a strike fund, the walkout was poorly organized, and in time, the players crossed the picket line without any concessions from the owners. However, because football was not exempt from antitrust legislation, the players shifted their demands from the bargaining table to the courts. The union pretended to decertify (in all fairness, it disbanded in the legal sense, but its magical reappearance following its court case suggests that the decertification was little more than paperwork) and promptly sued the NFL, using antitrust legislation as its primary weapon. In time, the jury's ruling effectively handed the players much of what they had failed to gain at the bargaining table.

In 1995 several professional basketball players, led by Michael Jordan and Patrick Ewing, tried to pull off a similar stunt. Anxious to shed themselves of the salary caps and luxury taxes that the union had agreed to, they sought to replicate the strategy of their NFL brethren by decertifying the union and taking the National Basketball Association (NBA) to court. Implicitly, this would suggest that a collection of jurors who may not know a free throw from a full court press are in a better position to gauge an equitable settlement than those who must live by its terms.   At its worst, the court would become a surrogate for collective bargaining.

Along these lines,   another feature of antitrust legislation that makes lifting the exemption attractive to the Players' Association is found in Section 6 of the Clayton Act passed in 1914. Regarding the application of the antitrust legislation to union activity, Section 6 reads:

Nothing contained in the antitrust laws shall be construed to forbid . . . labor organizations from lawfully carrying out the legitimate objects thereof; nor shall such organizations . . . be held or construed to be illegal combinations or conspiracies in restraint of trade, under the antitrust laws. (Flanagan et al. 1989, 385)

Section 6 falls short of outright exempting labor unions from antitrust legislation, but the language comes pretty close. In point of fact, the very notion that a single labor organization collectively negotiates on behalf of the industry's employees is, by definition, an exercise of monopoly power. Nonetheless, the courts have repeatedly ruled that most collective bargaining activity by labor unions is antitrust exempt.

This apparent exemption provides a great deal of insight into the Players' Association's support for the lifting of baseball's protection from antitrust suits. In effect, removing the exemption gives the union a one-way access to the courts. The players can sue the owners without fear of a countersuit. In extreme cases, litigating collective bargaining demands may cost less than enduring a lengthy strike or lockout, thereby making it a preferred alternative to bargaining. At the very least, the mere threat of an antitrust suit is plenty of ammunition for the union to bring to the bargaining table every few years.

The oft-cited argument that lifting the exemption will eliminate unpopular strikes and lockouts belies the evidence from the nonexempt sports leagues. The 1994-1995 National Hockey League (NHL) season was interrupted by a costly and lengthy lockout of the players. Similarly, the lack of antitrust protection did not keep the NFL players from striking in 1982 and 1987. Finally, lockout threats loomed over professional basketball in 1994 and 1995. Although Professor Johnson will argue in his essay that eliminating the exemption will reduce the stress that leads to strikes and lockouts, he does not promise that removing the exemption will preclude work stoppages altogether.

Binding Arbitration

In February of 1995 President Clinton established a "deadline" for a collective bargaining agreement in an effort to keep the baseball strike from extending into the 1995 season. Although much attention was paid to the President's announcement, the federal government had no power to intervene in an industry that is not vital to the national security. After the President's bluff was called, the beginning of the 1995 season became imperiled. Federal mediator William Usery presented each side with his own proposal. His version allowed for 50 percent luxury taxes on payrolls exceeding $40 million (Impoco and Popkin 1995, 48). The proposed tax was only moderately less than that demanded by the owners. Not surprisingly, the owners hailed the proposal as a breakthrough, whereas the players condemned it as unacceptable.

Unable to reach an agreement, the President proposed that the issue be resolved by binding arbitration. Under binding arbitration, each side would be permitted to present its arguments to an independent arbitrator. The arbitrator would then be empowered to determine the binding terms of the collective bargaining agreement.

The purpose of binding arbitration is not to have an independent third party settle the disagreement. As with using the courts as a substitute for the bargaining table, heaven forbid that an arbitrator whose knowledge of baseball does not extend beyond scanning box scores determine the terms of an agreement that other persons must live by. Rather, the intent is for binding arbitration to threaten action if the parties cannot come to their own settlement by a set deadline.

Although the uncertainty surrounding the third-party decision should provide the impetus to settle, arbitrators often compromise the issues to maintain an image of fairness. In this regard, reaction to the President's suggestion for binding arbitration revealed which side had the most bargaining leverage. The owners, who had embraced Usery's proposal, staunchly opposed binding arbitration and advocated that the two sides continue to bargain. Clearly, this suggests a belief that they would fare better at the bargaining table than they would at an arbitrator's compromise. In contrast, the players welcomed binding arbitration, preferring a compromised agreement hastily put together to beat the arbitrator's deadline to continued negotiations without the arbitration threat.

How might the reaction to binding arbitration have differed if the proposal had been made in September of 1994? Clearly, with the leverage on the side of the players, management would have greeted the proposal with open arms, and the players would have screamed bloody murder.

Guidelines for Fair Play: The National Labor Relations Act

Collective bargaining negotiations must adhere to the guidelines of the National Labor Relations Act (NLRA). In the early days of organized labor, unionism was considered to be akin to Communism and was treated accordingly. Only through government legislation did unions gain legal recognition to organize and collectively bargain.

The National Labor Relations Act was passed in 1935 and was later amended in the Taft-Hartley Act in 1947 and the Landrum-Griffin Act of 1959. The National Labor Relations Board is the gatekeeper of the key tenets of the NLRA, which include a list of unfair labor practices for employers and unions.

Perhaps the thorniest issue on the list is each side's duty to "bargain in good faith." Unfortunately, bargaining "in good faith" is as nebulous as it sounds. Section 8(d) of the NLRA defines "good faith bargaining" as: "[the] mutual obligation to meet at reasonable times and confer in good faith with respect to wages, hours, and other terms and conditions of employment, or the negotiation of an agreement . . . but such obligation does not compel either party to agree to a proposal or require the making of a concession." (Flanagan et al. 1989, 365) In contrast, Boulwarism, where a party makes a hard-line "Take it or leave it" offer, is barred by the provisions of the NLRA as an unfair labor practice.

Clearly, discerning Boulwarism from bargaining in good faith can sometimes become quite sticky because section 8(d) does not require either side to make concessions. To avoid NLRB sanctions, a negotiator need only convince the Board that it was bargaining in good faith.

Throughout baseball's 1994-1995 impasse, both the owners and players accused each other of unfair labor practices. The Players' Association resolutely refused to accept a salary cap or any reasonable facsimile. Does that constitute a failure to bargain in good faith? The owners stated that cost control was an essential feature of any collective bargaining agreement to which they would be signatory. Does the owners' stance constitute an unwillingness to bargain in good faith? Because neither side is compelled to concede ground to the opposition, the merits of the charges are clearly subject to the Board's interpretation of their overt actions.

Even if a party is guilty of committing an unfair labor practice, the NLRB sanctions can be a slap on the wrist. Although the NLRB can issue a "cease and desist" order to halt the action that created the charge, the Board has no legal power to enforce it. The enforcement of the order must come from the U.S. Court of Appeals, which is not duty bound to adhere to the Board's request. Should the Appeals Court concur with the Board's decision, failure to comply with the order constitutes contempt of court.

In the 1994-1995 impasse, the Players' Association won a major victory when the Board declared its intent to file an unfair labor practice complaint against the owners in response to the salary cap imposed in December of 1994. The NLRB also hinted that it might speed up the process that would lead to an injunction. In response, the owners quickly disposed of the cap. However, as soon as the cap was eliminated, management imposed a ban on player signings. The signing ban was immediately accompanied by another unfair labor practice charge by the players. Unfortunately for the side that initially files a charge, the decision to issue a "cease and desist" order may come months after the initial charge and can sometimes be followed up by several years of appeal. By the time the matter is eventually resolved, the power of the victory is seriously diluted, if not entirely undermined. To make matters worse, the Board has no authority to impose punitive damages on the perpetrator of the illegal labor practice. For these reasons, refusing to bargain in good faith can be sound tactical strategy if compliance is potentially more costly than noncompliance.

Ironically, the reverse occurred in baseball's dispute. In late March of 1995, the NLRB ruled in favor of the players and deemed the owners' ban on player signings a refusal to bargain in good faith. In seeking the injunction, the Board's action required the owners to resume bargaining under the rules of the previous collective bargaining agreement. In effect, the Board mandated an unconditional surrender by the owners, because it required the two sides to play the 1995 season under the *precise terms demanded by the players*! Ultimately, the 1995 season was destined to be played under a set of rules determined not by negotiations at the bargaining table but by the federal government.

Although the injunction guaranteed that the 1995 season would not begin with replacement games or a lockout, by no means did it eliminate the likelihood of a midseason strike. Had the season begun with replacement players, the likelihood of a settlement would have increased dramatically, because a continued strike would have been a no-win situation for the players. Assuming that the owners could recover their game costs, the strike would have ended quickly, albeit at terms favoring management.

Instead, after the players began receiving 1995 paychecks and gate receipts began to roll in for the owners, however, the incentive to reach a collective bargaining agreement vanished. Courtesy of the ruling, the owners were powerless to force a settlement. Likewise, because the court order effectively forced the game to be played under the players' initial demands, the union had little reason to concede ground. In short, with no one on the hot seat, little progress was made on a new agreement.

The experience in 1994-1995 also lends some insight into the sticking point in subsequent negotiations as to whether a luxury tax would be included in the final year of the new collective bargaining agreement. The owners wanted the tax, the players did not.

Why should the tax status in the final year of the contract be of such importance? Clearly, should history repeat itself at the bargaining table in the year 2000, the players would like the court to force baseball to be played under the terms of the existing terms of the contract (i.e., one with no luxury tax). If this were to occur, the intervention would have the effect of completely undoing the tax altogether (another unconditional victory for the players), thereby forcing management to have to bargain to get it back.

In any event, governmental intervention during a work stoppage is not a neutral position despite its intention to be exactly that. The crucial importance of bargaining leverage is such that any attempt by the government to put a quick end to the deadlock automatically shifts the momentum away from the side that enjoys the advantage.

AVOIDING FUTURE WORK STOPPAGES

As the 1995 and 1996 seasons unceremoniously began with the dark cloud of yet another strike or lockout looming each day the game was played without a collective bargaining agreement, the real losers in baseball's work stoppages were not the fans, who lost only a source of entertainment, but the players and owners, who sacrificed a portion of their livelihoods during the stalemates. Both sides lost enormous sums of money in an effort to increase their take. Baseball also learned a valuable lesson during the 1994-1995 strike: that work stoppages alienate the very people who subsidize their life-styles, the fans. If strikes and lockouts breed fan disinterest, both sides will suffer financially. To preserve the long-term health and wealth of the game, baseball must look toward means of avoiding its costly work stoppages.

In this regard, baseball is unique inasmuch as it has an off-season where no product is sold and no player gets paid. Unfortunately, because neither side has an incentive to concede its demands during the off-season, the prime time for reaching an agreement inevitably passes without resolution.

History suggests that productive negotiations occur when at least one side faces imminent financial penalty for a continued impasse. As conditions exist now, each side attempts to gain leverage by timing its threat so as to place the opponent in a position of weakness. Too often, the result is a strike or lockout. If both sides were to face equal penalty, productive bargaining could exist with counterbalancing incentives to negotiate.

With this in mind, the secret to avoiding future strikes and lockouts is to shift the financial burden to the off-season. To achieve this end, future collective bargaining agreements should not expire until the end of a given season (making midseason strikes or lockouts illegal). Throughout the duration of the agreement, the two sides could agree to place some percentage of national broadcasting revenues into an escrow account each year. The revenues should constitute monies that would normally be shared equally between the two sides. After the agreement expires, an off-season deadline for a new agreement (i.e., November 1) could be set. For each day an agreement has not been reached beyond the deadline, 1/30th of the revenue in escrow would be donated to charity (how's that for public relations?). The account would be completely drained by the end of the month, never to return.

To be effective, the amount of money stashed into the account should be significant enough that both sides have strong (and importantly, equal) incentives to stop the flow of money to outside parties. If the percentage set aside is too small, one side may have more to gain by sacrificing the escrow funds and initiating a strike/lockout than by settling while the November clock is ticking.

Interestingly, this plan is not altogether different from one advanced by commissioner Peter Ueberroth in 1985. Unfortunately, Ueberroth's proposal came in mid-negotiations, and was therefore ill-timed.

Is the proposal workable? In fact, both sides have had no difficulty in accumulating their own private war chests to prepare for past confrontations. The players' 1994 strike fund was made up of baseball card money, which had been diligently set aside over the course of the 1990 collective bargaining agreement. Similarly, the owners are not strangers to establishing their own reservoir of cash, having earmarked two percent of revenues in 1979 and 1980 to purchase strike insurance in 1981 (Helyar 1994, 261).

Further, one lesson that should have been learned from the 1994-1995 impasse is that bargaining leverage can dramatically change hands overnight. The pendulum swung from the players to the owners after the 1994 season was canceled, and gradually picked up momentum as the prospect of a replacement season became more imminent. Then, just as suddenly, the leverage swung in favor of the players when the NLRB ruled that the 1995 season had to be played under the conditions of the 1994 contract. And, of course, there was always Congress, posturing to take credit for returning the national pastime to the fans at any cost. In any case, the standard collective bargaining strategies can be risky business. The alternative suggested here removes any possibility that one's own course of action could backfire.

Although the setting aside of a "joint penalty fund" is patently unattractive to either side, the implementation of such a proposal can pay huge dividends in the long run. A painful side-effect of the 1994-1995 impasse was the fans' reluctance to return to the game when baseball resumed in 1995. One is hard-pressed to imagine American consumers boycotting domestic cars because of a strike organized by the United Auto Workers. As an entertainment industry, however, baseball is different. To generate wealth for the players and owners, the game depends upon maintaining the trust and goodwill of its constituency. When the trust is broken, the losses affect the pocketbooks on both sides of the bargaining table. By transferring negotiations to the off-season, baseball is spared the losses in goodwill that cost both sides dearly in 1995 and 1996.

Having made the sales pitch, is such a proposal likely to come about? Don't bet on it. The history of collective bargaining negotiations in baseball suggests that each side views fan demand for the game as a constant—that the bargaining process itself is completely independent of the game's revenues (all evidence to the contrary.) For this reason, even if the two sides were to recognize the benefits from preserving the long-term integrity of major league baseball, hammering out an agreement to shift the financial burden to the off-season would become a bargaining exercise in itself. Each side would likely propose a means of setting aside revenues in such a way that it perceives itself as having an advantage during negotiations. Even if an agreement were to be reached, the percentage of revenues set aside would likely be so minimal so as to provide little or no incentive to negotiate. Baseball has a long history of shortsightedness. My suspicion is that strikes and lockouts are here to stay.

REFERENCES

Bernstein, Aaron. 1995. Let's See the Owners Pitch Their Way Out of This One. *Business Week* (April 3): 58.

Bernstein, Aaron, and David Greising. 1995. Owners: 1 Players: 0. *Business Week* (April 17): 32-33.

Bernstein, Aaron, and Kevin Kelly. 1995. A Three-Way Jump Ball in the NBA. *Business Week* (September 4): 58-60.

Bodley, Hal. 1996. End of Labor Pains Gives Birth to Hope. *USA Today* (August 12): 7C.

Flanagan, Robert J., Lawrence M. Kahn, Robert S. Smith, and Ronald G. Ehrenberg. 1989. *Economics of the Employment Relationship*. Glenview, Ill.: Scott, Foresman and Company.

Helyar, John. 1994. *Lords of the Realm: The Real History of Baseball*. New York: Villard Books.

Impoco, Jim, and James Popkin. 1995. Throwing a Sharp Curve. *U.S. News and World Report 118* (February 20): 48.

Impoco, Jim, Sara Collins, and James Popkin. 1995. Down to the Last Out. *U.S. News and World Report* 118 (February 13): 66-68.

Kurkjian, Tim, and Tom Verducci. 1995. Time is Running Out. *Sports Illustrated* 82 (March 20): 38-40.

Wulf, Steve. 1995. An Unwhole New Ball Game. *Time* 145 (April 17): 48.

II

FREE AGENCY, SALARY ARBITRATION, AND PLAYER SALARIES

3

Will Rising Salaries Destroy Baseball?

James Richard Hill

In the contentious negotiations for a collective bargaining agreement between professional baseball owners and the players' union that began in 1994, the owners insisted on some measure or measures to stem the rising tide of players' salaries. Owners maintained that unless something was done to stop or slow the rise in player salaries, major league baseball could collapse. The crux of their arguments revolves around the economic viability of small-market clubs, like Milwaukee and Kansas City. According to this line of reasoning, in order to compete for the best players in a free agent market, clubs in these smaller markets must offer salaries competitive with those of the big market areas like New York or Los Angeles. Unfortunately, these small-market clubs are not able to generate the revenue necessary for such salaries. So small-market clubs can either pay the big salaries and operate at huge losses, or they can operate a fiscally responsible club that is not able to compete well on the field.

The plight of the small-market owners gains enormous sympathy from baseball fans today because players' salaries are often published in the media. The reported average salary for a player for the 1996 season is $1,172,736, a far cry above the estimated average salary figure of around $52,300 in 1976, the last season before free agency (Bodley 1996, 1C and 14C). The picture is even bleaker when one considers that a large portion of a club's revenue is generated from local broadcast rights. Unlike the national broadcast rights, which are split evenly between all clubs, local broadcast rights are not. The disparity in these figures is astounding. For instance, in 1994 local rights for the New York Yankees totaled $47 million, but the Minnesota Twins earned only $4.5 million (McClellan 1994, 30–33).

If small-market areas do go under or decide to be fiscally responsible and field noncompetitive teams, major league baseball would be in terrible trouble. Leagues composed of only a few teams or leagues continually dominated by a few teams would not stir fan interest to the extent that larger, balanced league competition can offer. Given these arguments, it would be all too easy to join the chorus of voices calling for limits to the growth of players' salaries. However, looking back on the arguments just proposed in support of the owners' position, one cannot help but realize that two separate issues have become linked together: rising salaries and vastly unequal club revenues. To better understand the issues involved, it is instructive to first discuss each issue separately before linking them together.

Will rising salaries in and of themselves destroy baseball? There are many interesting facets to this simple question. Average fans, when confronted with the unbelievable high player salaries and the escalation in such salaries in recent years, are dumbfounded. It is difficult to believe that any business could profit under the burden of such heavy labor costs. Average fans consider their own salary and the meager increases doled out in the last few years in our competitive economic environment and often feel disgust for millionaire players protesting owners' attempts to constrict future pay raises.

Both blue-collar and white-collar workers in the U.S. auto industry, for example, have felt the sting of foreign competition. Car companies must contain costs to remain competitive in pricing with products produced abroad where wages may be lower. The clothing industry in America, a very labor-intensive enterprise, has seen hundreds of thousands of jobs lost as production facilities have been moved out of the country to low-wage areas.   The debates spawned by the North American Free Trade Agreement (NAFTA) agreement have made everyone more aware of the global economic environment.

Yet many industries do not face constraints such as these. Service and retail trade oriented businesses do not need to worry about low foreign wages. Nevertheless, these industries still face the same overall market constraints as do all industries: declining demand due to rising prices. If prices rise too greatly for fast-food meals or movies, for instance, there is always the threat that consumers may choose not to buy these items and/or may purchase lower-priced substitutes instead.

Baseball is in the entertainment business and thus can be broadly classed with other services-producing industries. Like other such endeavors, baseball must take care not to make its product so costly that consumers turn to alternatives. Unlike most other businesses, however, major league baseball enjoys a monopoly over the provision of its product.   Whereas other professional sports seasons overlap the baseball season somewhat, major league baseball is the only game around for a good deal of the time in the summer in many cities. Such economic clout may allow owners to sell their products at higher prices than they would be able to in a more competitive setting—the same as a restaurant or bar in an airport or convention hotel gouges trapped clientele.

Even though ticket prices for baseball games have been rising, evidence suggests that after adjusting for inflation, ticket prices today are no higher and are even lower for most major league teams compared to 20 years ago in the era before free agency (Quirk and Fort 1992, 219–222). The real explosion in baseball revenue has come from broadcast rights, both national and local. In 1976 national broadcast rights totaled $23–$24 million, while local broadcast rights totaled around $37 million (*Broadcasting*, A Big Lift, 1976, 50–60). In 1993 national broadcast rights, CBS-TV, CBS-radio, and ESPN combined, equaled $378 million, and local broadcast rights combined for all teams reached approximately $353 million (Jessell 1993, 39–42).

From the skyrocketing figures on broadcast revenues it is easy to see why and how baseball salaries have risen so greatly. The rise in baseball revenue from broadcasting due to its popularity with fans allowed owners to pay players big bucks. It is important to stress this cause-and-effect relationship very clearly. The rise in revenue was the cause, and the rise in player salaries was the effect. As in all markets in a capitalist system, the consumer is king. If the consumer is not willing to buy the product at the price offered, it will not be sold.

This point brings us to the current dilemma in professional baseball. CBS reported a loss of around $169 million in the third quarter of 1991, mostly due to its national professional baseball broadcast contract (McClellan 1994, 30–33). A drop in advertiser interest caused revenue from the sale of ads during baseball games to plummet while CBS was still contractually obligated to pay Major League Baseball (MLB) around $260 million a year through 1993. Fear of huge decreases in bids for the national television broadcast rights caused MLB to try a bold new joint venture in 1994 with ABC and NBC. In this new scheme, MLB attempted to produce its own coverage of games and to market these to advertisers on its own. The purpose of such a plan was to better promote and package the telecasts in order to revive lacking ad prices. By taking total control of production and marketing through its own company, The Baseball Network (TBN), major league baseball hoped to provide games of regional interest to the appropriate market segments as well as offer important games for divisional races to the overall market. Owners hoped this technique, combined with the additional division races created due to league expansion and the quest for wild-card spots for the playoffs, would improve the national broadcast revenue for professional baseball in the future.

Unfortunately, the baseball strike that began in August 1994, which prevented World Series play and delayed the beginning of the next season, proved devastating to baseball advertising revenues for this new venture. TBN generated only about $5.5 million per team in revenue each of the two years it operated, compared to the sum of $14.7 million per team from CBS in 1993 (McClellan 1995, 38). The drop in revenue created by the strike caused baseball salaries to decrease by approximately $140,000 on average in 1995, supporting the hypothesis that changes in revenue determine changes in salaries (Klapisch and Marantz 1995, 37).

Upset by the huge decline in revenue and the uncertainty of revenue from the TBN experiment, baseball owners abruptly ended this venture in favor of a fixed fee contract. Beginning with the 1996 season, major league baseball has a combined broadcast contract with Fox, NBC, ESPN, and Fox Sports/Liberty Media for $1.7 billion over a five-year period (McClellan 1996, 24–28). This generous broadcast package has allowed player salaries to rise from their 1995 levels and has given owners more certainty in revenue so that they can better adjust player salaries in advance of the season to minimize losses or maximize profits.

Although some might argue that perhaps the enormous salaries of players have upset fans and caused the downturn in TV audiences, the argument does not appear justified. Basketball is enjoying a tremendous upsurge in popularity among fans, and National Basketball Association (NBA) basketball players have average salaries that surpass those of MLB players. The strike appears to be solely responsible for the dismal attendance and revenue figures for the 1995 season, and time will undoubtedly heal this wound if players will only continue to play ball.

Turning attention to the other separate issue for discussion, one could ask: Will vastly unequal club revenues in and of themselves destroy baseball? A simple answer to this question would be no, the same reply that our first question would elicit if our answer were constrained to a one word response. As always, however, some qualifications must accompany this answer.

If baseball clubs can cover their costs of operation despite the varying levels of revenue, then no problem exists. This scenario merely suggests that average salary levels for the teams may vary greatly, just as production costs do for different firms in many various industries across the land. In 1996, average salaries per team in MLB ranged from $52,189,370 for the New York Yankees to $15,410,500 for the Montreal Expos (Bodley 1996, 1C). However, if some clubs cannot cover their operating expenses, then problems can arise. Unlike other industries where firms making losses can simply shut down and leave the business, professional baseball, like other team·sports, requires a certain number of teams for intraleague competition and division races. Franchises cannot be allowed to close without a replacement.

Several solutions exist for professional baseball to address the problem of clubs that cannot earn a profit. Franchises can be sold to other owners who may be better able to market the teams' games and generate added revenue and/or cut costs until profits are earned. Such sales could involve movement of the franchise to an area with improved financial viability, perhaps, although not necessarily, a bigger market area. The recent competition for expansion franchises in the major leagues suggests several different cities and owner groups that are anxious to "play ball."

As a group, however, owners have dismissed these obvious market solutions, claiming that such measures would create too much instability and would not be in the "best interest of the game." Another suggested solution would have profitable clubs share their larger revenue sources, particularly local broadcast revenue, with franchises unable to generate sufficient revenue to cover costs. Much discussion has taken place on this issue, but owners who are making profits from their teams are reluctant to subsidize money-losing franchises. Even though owners of profitable organizations realize that it is in their own best interest to see that their competitors' teams remain financially sound, they will not sacrifice too much of their own profits to achieve this result.

Now it is time to link our two issues together again. Owners of profitable franchises may be willing to share some of the burden necessary to restore profits to other clubs if players also help in the endeavor. Therefore, what has been characterized by some media writers as essentially a small-market area versus big-market area dilemma has become a unified struggle by owners to slow the growth in player salaries.

Obviously for clubs losing money every year, some measure to contain salary costs, be it a cap or luxury tax plan, would help their financial position. For clubs that are not in financial difficulties, however, such plans may represent a desire to reap higher profits at the expense of players' decreased earnings. Depending on the nature of the plan chosen, profitable clubs may or may not have to help offset the losses of their fellow owners with sacrificed profits of their own. All of the plans suggested however undoubtedly reduce future player salaries from those levels that would prevail under the current collective bargaining arrangement. Because natural market forces already dampen management's salary offers to players, just as declining car sales dampened United Auto Worker wage increases in the late 1970s and through the 1980s, players are obviously reluctant to compound this situation with a cap or tax plan measure.

Overshadowing all of the current owner-player negotiations is the suspicion that the owners have really exaggerated the financial situation of professional baseball. Owners claim that only a few teams turn a profit each year. At one point, league representatives stated that 19 of the 28 clubs in existence at that time were losing money (Sanderson 1995, 20). The players' union and some prominent economists suggest that though creative accounting may make it appear that most clubs lose money, in reality only a handful of teams really do. Given the rapid escalation of franchise prices, seen through sales of clubs that have changed hands in recent times, and the willingness of potential owner groups to pay enormous fees for new franchises, both common sense and business sense would suggest that if the financial outlook was as bad as owners claim, more clubs would be for sale and a majority of owners would be willing to change existing league rules to make franchise moves easier (Sanderson 1995, 20).

Regardless of the true financial picture of baseball, it appears likely that some form of drag will be placed on player salaries when a negotiated settlement is reached. If the experience of the NBA with its own salary cap measures is any indicator, however, such measures may do little to slow salary growth or help financially strapped franchises. Ultimately, as always, it is the consumers, through the marketplace, who will determine the path of the player salaries and franchise successes or failures.

In conclusion, it is not rising player salaries that endanger baseball. The marketplace will automatically adjust salaries as necessary. The biggest threat to major league baseball is the loss of fan appeal that occurs from the lack of games. Perhaps it is time to relax baseball's antiquated, anti-free market league rules so that financially viable franchises can be introduced that can compete under current collective bargaining arrangements. Several locations exist that offer promise of large revenue potential, including some cites outside the United States and Canada. Imagine franchises in Japan and Mexico, for example. It will happen sooner or later. Such franchises will give new meaning to the term World Series.

REFERENCES

A Big Lift for the Old Game. 1976. *Broadcasting* (March 8): 50–60.

Bodley, Hal. 1996. Baseball Payrolls Increase Only 1.8%. *USA Today* (April 5): 1C and 14C.

Jessell, Harry A. 1993. MLB's Local TV/Radio Take Tops $350 Million. *Broadcasting and Cable* (March 15): 39–42.

Klapisch, Bob, and Steve Marantz. 1995. Back to Basic. *The Sporting News* (November 13): 37–38.

McClellan, Steve. 1994. MLB Gets Its First Start. *Broadcasting and Cable* (March 14): 30–33.

———. 1995. The Baseball Network Stays in the Game. *Broadcasting and Cable* (March 27): 38.

———. 1996. The Foxification of Baseball. *Broadcasting and Cable* (March 25): 24–28.

Quirk, James, and Rodney D. Fort. 1992. *Pay Dirt: The Business of Professional Team Sports*. Princeton, N.J.: Princeton University Press.

Sanderson, Allen R. 1995. Bottom-line Drive. *The University of Chicago Magazine* (June): 18–23.

4

Free Agency and Competitive Balance

John L. Fizel

Competitive balance is a key ingredient to maintaining fan interest in baseball. Although fans enjoy watching their team win, fan interest is also sparked by one-run games, tight pennant races, and Cinderella stories. Each of these suggests relative balance in the playing strength of league members. If the league became sufficiently unbalanced with playing talent concentrated in one or two teams, perennial cellar dwellers would be unable to attract fans and even the fans of dominant teams will lose interest in the sport. As the Yankees won the pennant each year from 1950 to 1958, the attendance of the American League declined. Fans in New York and in every other American League city dozed, knowing that they would miss little because the season outcome was a foregone conclusion. Clearly, the financial viability of the league and each of its teams requires that Major League Baseball (MLB) preserve competitive balance.

A practical question is whether free agency has undermined this objective. Through 1976, player movement from one team to another in professional baseball was regulated by the reserve clause. Under the reserve clause, players could negotiate only with their current team, leaving decisions concerning player movement through trades or cash sales solely to the discretion of the owners. At the end of the 1976 season, players with less than six years' experience continued to operate according to the dictates of the reserve clause, but players with six or more years experience could opt for free agency. Free agents can negotiate with any team and at their discretion, not the team owner's, sign a contract with a different team.

Owners argue that with this freedom players will flock to the teams with the most financial resources, usually large-market teams. The large-market teams will then dominate league play, winning significantly more games than small-market teams that lost talented free agents. Thus, the owners conclude, restrictions on player mobility like those imposed by the reserve clause are necessary for competitive balance to exist.

Economists, however, argue that if teams can exchange players (via trades or cash sales), owner profit incentives prompt migration of talented players to large-market teams just as they do under free agency. Under the reserve clause, owners reap the financial rewards from player movement; under free agency, the players reap the rewards. Therefore, economists see owner insistence on use of the reserve clause as a ploy to transfer wealth from players to owners but not to preserve competitive balance. Ronald Coase (1960) recently won the Nobel Prize in economics for this theorem, which succinctly states that a change in property rights (like free agency) affects only the distribution of wealth (owner versus player) but has no impact on the allocation of resources (competitive balance).

This chapter provides an explanation of economic theory concerning the market for baseball players under free agency and under the reserve clause. The effect of free agency on competitive balance is then analyzed using 24 years of team performance data. Finally, the impact of free agency on player salaries and owner profits is discussed.

THE MARKET FOR BASEBALL PLAYERS UNDER FREE AGENCY

Owners are correct in suggesting that free agency, in conjunction with the financial disparities between large- and small-market clubs, creates imbalances in talent distribution. Free agents are able to negotiate with all teams and sign with the highest bidder for their services. It follows then that the teams with the greatest financial resources will be able to offer higher salaries, attract more free agents, and have stronger teams. In professional baseball, network television and licensing revenues are divided equally among the teams, but individual teams keep the lion's share of gate receipts and all local television revenue. When Toronto's gate receipts total $44 million and San Diego's only $12 million, and when the Yankees are blessed by a $47 million local television deal that dwarfs the $4+ million received by Minnesota for local broadcasts, large-market teams have the economic clout to outbid small-market teams for star players (*USA Today*, Baseball Bucks 1994, 8C).

Economic theory also suggests that large-market teams will be able to acquire more talent than small-market teams. Owners will typically follow the principles of introductory microeconomics by offering the free agent no more than the player's value to that team: the extra revenue the team would earn as a result of signing the free agent. If an owner signed the free agent by paying more than this value, profits of the team would decrease. However, a player's value will differ from team to team and so will economically sound bids. Consider the case of Barry Bonds and his move from Pittsburgh to San Francisco through the free agent market.

Although Pittsburgh ownership stated that Bonds was worth approximately $5 million dollars per year as a Pirate, San Francisco ownership was willing to pay Bonds over $7 million per year to become a Giant. Bond's extra value in San Francisco may be due in part to the fact that his father once played for the Giants and is currently a coach.   More important, his value is due to the fact that San Francisco is the center of a large metropolitan area with a well developed media. Bonds can sell more tickets and local media time in San Francisco than in Pittsburgh. Therefore, the Giants can offer Bonds $2 million more than the Pirates and still make a profit.

Was Bonds worth $7 million?   Emphatically, yes!   In Bonds' first season with the Giants, the team improved from second-to-last to second in their division. In response, one million additional fans attended the home games of the Giants. The increase in attendance alone translated into a revenue gain of approximately $20 million and a $13 million profit for the signing of Bonds. Bonds also generated increased media attention and income (Zimbalist 1994, 5A). Of course, Bonds is not singularly responsible for all this extra revenue but he did play the leading role. Thus, large-revenue market teams can offer players higher salaries than small-revenue market teams and still make significant profits.

Given that teams operate in markets with different actual and potential revenue, free agency appears to lead to league domination by large-market teams. However, four other economic considerations limit the acquisition of free agents by large-market teams.

First, some players will stay or sign with smaller-market teams because of locational or other nonmonetary incentives. Kirby Puckett (Minnesota), Tony Gwynn (San Diego), Mark Gubicza (Kansas City), and Cal Ripken (Baltimore) could have earned more with other teams but opted to remain as members of small-market clubs. Countless other players have refrained from signing in the New York market, sacrificing dollars in order to avoid intense media pressures, the life-style of the City, and, historically at least, the erratic behavior of George Steinbrenner.

Second, large-market teams will not stockpile free agent talent. After a team has attracted one or two free agents, it has a greatly reduced desire to engage in a competitive bidding war for another. The opportunity for a third free agent to add even more to team revenues is limited, so the value of that player is limited. Value can be severely limited if the team already has a good player playing the position of this free agent. Although Steinbrenner signed free agent closers Goose Gossage and Rawley Eastwick in 1978 when he already had Sparky Lyle (the Cy Young winner in 1977), he traded Eastwick and Lyle within a year. Teams with deficient talent would find these free agents much more valuable and be willing to bid more to sign one of the players. Thus, small-market teams can win free agent bidding wars when large-market teams face diminishing returns to the signing of additional free agents.

Third, free agent signings by any team is limited by the collective bargaining agreement (Article XX, Section B, 5A). If there are 14 or fewer free agents, no team can sign more than one player; if there are 15–38 players declaring free agency, each team is limited to two signings; if there are between 39 and 62 declared free agents, teams can sign up to three players; and so on.

Finally, because owners desire to earn profits as well as win games, they recognize the importance of competitive balance. Domination may be fun, but if fans lose interest, the pocketbook suffers. As a result, competitive balance is partially self-regulating due to the profit orientation of owners.

Nevertheless, the degree of competitive imbalance that occurs under free agency remains a concern. Former baseball commissioner Bowie Kuhn's anxiety was expressed this way: "If [free agent] transactions now and in the future were permitted, the door would be opened wide to the buying success of the more affluent clubs . . . our efforts to preserve the competitive balance would be gravely impaired" (Helyar 1994, 194). Former Dodger owner Walter O'Malley declared, "Pennants are not to be bought" (Helyar 1994, 193). Restraining player mobility was the owners' proposed solution. Then small-market teams would be able to keep good players rather than have the players seek higher salaries and move to large-market teams. The most restrictive of player restraint mechanisms is the "reserve clause."

MARKET FOR BASEBALL PLAYERS UNDER THE RESERVE CLAUSE

When a player signed his first baseball contract under the reserve clause system, he could negotiate only with his team. Even if the player had not signed a contract in subsequent seasons, the reserve clause continued to prohibit him from offering his services to other teams. The player's only options were to play with his team or retire from major league baseball. Should he retire and then want to return to baseball in the future, he would still remain the property of his original team.

The reserve clause effectively eliminated free agents, but player movement from one team to another was not completely blocked. Owners still had the option to trade or sell players to other teams. Economists argue that if teams exchanged players via trades or sales, market incentives induced the transfer of talented players to large-market teams—just as they do under free agency.

Let's reexamine the case of Barry Bonds. The value of Bonds to the Pirates was approximately $5 million. The value of Bonds to the Giants was at least $7 million and, perhaps, more near $20 million as described earlier. The difference is attributable to the extra ticket, concession, and media sales Bonds could generate in the San Francisco market that were not available in the Pittsburgh market. Hence, San Francisco could profitably offer Bonds a contract worth $2 million more than his Pittsburgh contract. Under free agency Bonds has a monetary incentive to become a Giant. Under the reserve clause Bonds cannot make such a move, yet Bonds remains an asset worth $5 million in Pittsburgh and $7 million in San Francisco. The Pirate owners now have the monetary incentive to initiate the talent transfer. If the Pirates sell Bonds to the Giants they pocket $2 million. The incentives are the same for trades between large- and small-market teams. Opportunities for exchange of talent yield salaries that allocate player talent to its highest-valued use.

The implication is that good players are worth more to large-market teams whatever the compensation system. In a free agent market, large-market teams *pay more to the player* to outbid small-market teams for his services. In a reserve clause market, large-market teams will *pay more to the small-market team* to purchase the contract of the player. In the former case the player receives the extra $2 million; in the latter case the small-market team collects the $2 million windfall. Because the revenue-generating ability of star players in large and small cities is similar under free agency and the reserve clause, economists claim that the distribution of these stars among the teams should be similar in free agent and reserve clause markets. The only impact of free agency is to redistribute revenues from owners to players.

The impetus for player movement through cash sales or trades in a reserve clause market is not simply theoretical speculation. Helyar (1994, 73) reports that from 1955 to 1960 alone, the New York Yankees, a large-market powerhouse, and the Kansas City Athletics, a small-market team always jockeying for last place in attendance and in the standings, exchanged 29 players. Through these transactions, the Yankees acquired blossoming stars such as Roger Maris, Hector Lopez, Art Ditmar, and Ralph Terry, and the Athletics received an improved "bottom line." Although data on player sales is limited, Quirk and Fort (1992, 281) point out that "player sales were an important element in business operations for most teams" when facing the restrictions of the reserve clause. They continue by stating that "the flow of players was from weak-drawing, low-profit, small-city teams to strong-drawing, big-profit, big-city teams, as the theory suggests. The teams with large purchases of players were the Giants, the Cubs, the Yankees, and, of course, Tom Yawkey's Red Sox" and "it was the weak teams—the Browns, the Braves, the Phillies, the Athletics—who were the big sellers."

COMPETITIVE BALANCE EVIDENCE

The conflict is clear. On one side the owners assert that the reserve clause is needed to prevent a decline in competitive balance that will occur with free agency. On the other side the economists insist that there are no inherent reasons why competitive balance will be any different under free agency than it was under the reserve clause. This conflict must be settled with data, not theory.

Three dimensions of competitive balance will be analyzed. First, data on team winning percentages and market size (population of city in which team plays) will be used to determine if large-market teams win more than small-market teams, and if the linkage between market size and winning is more pronounced under free agency. Second, competitive balance within a season is evaluated by calculating the number of teams contending for division championships.   More contenders means more competitive league play.   Third, competitive balance across seasons is assessed by identifying the number of different teams that win division and pennant championships—the greater the number, the more balanced is the league.

The analysis will include outcomes of previous research supplemented with a current evaluation of competitive balance. Beginning with the 1969 season, each season is included in the current evaluations except for the strike-shortened seasons of 1981 and 1994. The seasons are divided into the pre-free agency years, 1969–1976, and the free agency years, 1977–1993.   Each is long enough to reduce the effects of any unusual season. The strike-shortened seasons of 1994 and 1995 are not included. Also, the Florida Marlins and Colorado Rockies were omitted from the analysis because they had only played one complete season through 1993. If free agency does imperil competitive balance as alleged by owners, large-market teams should win more, and the competition within and across seasons should be less in the post-1976 era.

Market Size

Once again, economic theory asserts that player talent moves to where the talent is most highly valued, usually large markets.   Because large-market teams acquire talented players, they should win more games than small-market teams do. In other words—there should be a strong relationship between market size and winning percentage. This is true under the reserve clause and free agency. What we want to know is whether or not this effect is more pronounced with free agency.

The correlation between the rankings of team winning percentage and the rankings of market size is one measure of the dominance of large-market teams. If large-market teams acquire more talent so that they are able to win more games than do small-market teams, winning percentage rankings will increase as population rankings increase. If large-market teams totally dominate league play, the team in the largest city will have a population ranking of 1 and a winning percentage ranking of 1, the team in the second largest market will have a population ranking of 2 and a winning percentage ranking of 2, and so on. If small-market teams totally dominate play, winning percentage rankings will be low when population rankings are high. The team in the largest market will have a population ranking of 1 but a winning percentage ranking of 12.   The team in the second largest market will have a population ranking of 2 and a winning percentage ranking of 11, and so on.   If there is no linkage between market size and team strength there will be no relationship between the rankings.

Using such a ranking procedure, Christopher Drahozal (1986) examined the relationships between city size and team winning percentage for the pre-free agency years 1972–1976 and free agency years 1977–1982. He found no consistent relationship between market size and wins in either period, nor was there a significant increase in the winning percentages of large-market teams in the free agency period.

Feeling that Drahozal may not have allowed sufficient time for free agency to generate its anticompetitive effects, Gerald Scully (1989) extended Drahozal's study by adding five more years of free agency experience. The free agency period now included 1977–1987. The results were the same. Free agency still had not adversely affected competitive balance.

In Table 4.1, the analysis is complete one more time, using the latest available data. Casual observation shows little pattern in the relationship between the population and winning percentage rankings. Some large-market teams had high winning percentages, such as the New York Yankees with free agency and the Los Angeles Dodgers before and with free agency. Other large market teams did not, including Philadelphia before free agency, the Chicago Cubs with free agency, and Texas before and with free agency. The performance of small-market teams is equally mixed. Poor winning percentages were recorded by Milwaukee prior to free agency and San Diego before and with free agency. However, Kansas City performed well with free agency and Cincinnati had the best National League performance prior to free agency. Yet, in general, it is shown that large-market teams do not consistently win more than small-market teams nor do small-market teams consistently win more than large-market teams. Competitive balance appears to be alive and well, both with and without the reserve clause.

The small impact of market size on team performance is somewhat surprising and may be attributable, in part, to the difficulty of defining market size. Delineating market boundaries includes questions such as Should Anaheim be included as part of Los Angeles? Should Oakland and San Francisco or Washington and Baltimore be combined? Should the market size of Atlanta be increased due the national television coverage it receives through its "local" superstation WTBS? Should the population of two-team cities be divided in half?, and so on. Several alternative definitions of market size were used, but none altered the basic result. There is no apparent association between winning and large-market teams.

Pennant Contenders and Winners

Competitive balance can be interpreted as close pennant races within a given season. Fans become excited and involved when their team is in the chase for a championship. Increases in attendance and revenue are the result. Increase the number of contenders, and the number of teams benefiting from additional gate receipts increases. Spreading the wealth

Table 4.1
Winning Percentage and Population Rankings before and after Free Agency*

TEAM	Before Free Agency (1969–1976)			After Free Agency (1977–1993)		
	POP RANK	WIN RANK	WIN PCT	POP RANK	WIN RANK	WIN PCT
American League						
Detroit	1	7	.493	1	5	.520
NY Yankees	2	4	.532	2	1	.535
Chicago	3	9	.457	3	7	.502
Boston	4	3	.540	5	2	.531
Texas	5	11	.443	4	11	.485
Baltimore	6	1	.596	6	4	.521
Oakland	9	2	.575	10	9	.492
California	10	8	.468	8	8	.496
National League						
Milwaukee	11	12	.424	12	6	.508
Kansas City	12	6	.498	11	3	.528
L.A.	1	2	.561	1	1	.518
Philadelphia	2	10	.465	2	5	.510
NY Mets	3	4	.519	3	8	.489
Chicago	4	7	.494	4	10	.484
Montreal	5	11	.430	5	2	.515
Pittsburgh	7	3	.560	8	3	.514
Houston	8	8	.490	6	7	.495
Atlanta	9	9	.483	9	11	.481
San Francisco	10	5	.503	11	9	.485
Cincinnati	11	1	.599	12	6	.503
San Diego	12	12	.387	10	12	.470

*The population of two-team cities is split between the teams. Winning percentages were calculated from 1970 for Milwaukee (the year the Seattle Pilots became the Brewers) and from 1972 for Texas (the year the Washington Senators became the Rangers). The Toronto Blue Jays and Seattle Mariners were omitted from consideration because they were created in the 1977 expansion and played only after free agency.

among a number of contending teams should promote continued balance in talent acquisition and victories.

The "tightness" of pennant races can be measured in different ways. Lawrence Hadley and Elizabeth Gustafson (1994) and Quirk and Fort

(1992) used dispersion indices, which measure the difference in winning percentages of the top and bottom teams in the final standings. If "perfect" competitive balance existed all teams would win and lose half their games (a .500 record) and there would be no difference in winning percentages. The more teams deviate from .500, above and below, the greater the difference in winning percentages and the lower the level of competitive balance.

Hadley and Gustafson found no difference in the pre-free agency (1966–1976) and free agency (1982–1992) indices, again indicating that free agency has not undermined competitive balance. Quirk and Fort analyze dispersions in 10-year increments and find that from 1960 to 1990 competitive balance in baseball increased.

The measure of competitive balance used in our current analysis is the total number of teams that finished within 10 games of the division winner over each period. This number identifies teams that had realistic chances to win the division as the season came to an end. Three eight-year segments are examined: pre-free agency years 1969–1976; and two free agency segments 1977–1985 and 1986–1993. The results are reported separately for the American and National League and can be seen in Table 4.2.

Consistent with economists' predictions and previous studies, neither league had a worsening of competitive balance with the onset of free agency. In the American League competitive balance actually improved. Before free agency 17 teams over the eight-year period contended for the division crown. In the two periods with free agency the number of contending teams increased to 28, then to an incredible 39 in the most-recent years. In the National League, competitive balance increased in the first free agency period but has since reverted back to the level seen under the reserve clause. On net, pennant fever "afflicts" more fans with free agency than without.

Competitive balance can also be interpreted by which team won the division or pennant. An increase in the number of contending teams may give the appearance of improved competitive balance, but if the same team wins each year, competitive balance is actually compromised. Competitive balance requires turnover of champions, not dynasties.

Are there perpetual winners as the result of free agency? Returning to Table 4.2, the evidence suggests not. With free agency the American League had two to three more teams involved with division crowns and one more with league championships. The National League had two to three more teams involved with division and league championships. The total of 10 different division victors in the National League between 1986 and 1993 means that only two teams, excluding the 1993 expansion teams in Colorado and Florida, did not win a division title. That's competitive balance!

It is also indicative of why the 1991 World Series could be played by two teams, Atlanta and Minnesota, which had been last in their respective divisions the prior year.

Table 4.2
Contenders, Division Winners and Pennant Winners before and after
Free Agency

	Before Free Agency (1969–1976)	After Free Agency (1977–1985)*	After Free Agency (1986–1993)
Number of Teams within 10 Games			
American League	17	28	39
National League	21	25	21
Number of Division Winners			
American League	5	8	7
National League	7	9	10
Number of Pennant Winners			
American League	4	5	5
National League	4	6	7

*The strike-shortened 1981 season was not considered in these calculations.

FREE AGENCY AND COMPETITIVE BALANCE

The inescapable conclusion is that free agency does not destroy competitive balance. Since the introduction of free agency, competitive balance has actually improved. There is more equality among teams in any given year causing pennant races to be furious battles involving multiple contenders. The likelihood of building a dynasty is reduced because the number of teams that win division and pennant championships has increased under free agency. Finally, there is no evidence to indicate that large-market teams will win more than small-market teams.

Owners' protestations that free agency undermines competitive balance has no foundation. What free agency does do is direct more of the revenue that the player produces to the player than the team owner. Therefore, owner protestations are to induce policy that will move dollars from player accounts to owner accounts.

FREE AGENCY AND THE REDISTRIBUTION OF WEALTH

Although competitive balance has remained unaffected by free agency, the redistribution of wealth suggested by the Coase theorem has been dramatic. Prior to 1976, players were typically paid only 10–20 percent of their economic value (Scully 1974). This changed rapidly with the advent of free agency. In the first two years alone, player salaries increased by 47.7 percent and 31.3 percent, respectively (Scully 1989,

166).   Competitive bidding for players continues to up the ante for player services.   The extent of salary escalation is such that some analysts now argue that most players are paid their market value. The exception continues to be the players with less than three years experience who do not have the competitive option of arbitration or free agency and continue to be held captive by the reserve clause (MacDonald and Reynolds 1994). Some of the growth in salaries is the result of the growth in the baseball industry,   but the remainder represents monies transferred to players from owners. In the last 15 years, the cost of major league rosters has gone from approximately 35 percent of team revenues to nearly 60 percent (Baseball Bucks, *USA Today* 1994, 8C).

Redistribution, in and of itself, is not troubling given the favorable financial picture of the baseball industry and the number of investors clamoring to join the industry. For example, in the latest expansion movement in major league baseball, 18 investors from 11 different cities were willing to bid in excess of $100 million to develop their own major league team (Aaron et al. 1992, 14). What may be troubling is the disparity in incomes and payrolls between teams. Almost each year since the beginning of free agency the differences between high-income (payroll) teams and low-income (payroll) teams have grown. In 1996 the payrolls of the Yankees and Orioles were $52.2 million and $48.9 million, respectively, whereas the payrolls of the Expos and Royals were $15.4 million and $18.5 million, respectively (Bodley 1996: 14C).   Is this the powder keg that eventually explodes and destroys competitive balance? Perhaps, but concrete evidence that this problem stems from free agency is absent.

Still the problem remains, and a solution must be considered. Two options are generally discussed.   The first is to blame free agency and attempt to redistribute dollars from players to low-income teams.   This option includes expanding the years under which a player is controlled through the reserve clause, salary caps, and luxury taxes. The second option considers the income/payroll discrepancies to be an organizational weakness of the baseball industry. This option would redistribute income directly from the high-income teams to the low-income teams or allow movement of low-income franchises to more-lucrative markets. Because owners of small-market teams realize that the large-market teams are not likely to agree to share a larger portion of revenues and that baseball's antitrust exemption would come under scrutiny should "excessive" franchise movement occur, owners naturally try to attack free agency. Historically, owners have made direct attacks on free agency, with an independent third party finding that owners had colluded three times to reduce free agent bidding.   The newest salary proposals are thinly veiled attempts to again reduce free agent bidding. Neither direct nor indirect attacks on free agency are warranted because the Coase theorem has withstood the test of time. To reiterate: a change in property rights (like free agency) affects only the distribution of wealth (owner versus player) but has no impact on the allocation of resources (competitive balance).

REFERENCES

Aaron, Henry et al. 1992. *Report of Independent Members of the Economic Study Committee on Baseball* (December 3).

Baseball Bucks: Owners Should Open Books. 1994. *USA Today* (October 20): 8C-9C.

Bodley, Hal. 1996. Baseball Payrolls Increase Only 1.8%. *USA Today* (April 5): 14C.

Coase, Ronald. 1960. The Problem of Social Cost. *Journal of Law and Economics 3* (October): 1-44.

Drahozal, Christopher. 1986. The Impact of Free Agency on the Distribution of Playing Talents in Major League Baseball. *Journal of Economics and Business 38*: 113-121.

Hadley, Lawrence, and Elizabeth Gustafson. 1994. Free Agency and Competitive Balance. *By the Numbers (Newsletter of the Statistical Analysis Committee of the Society of American Baseball Research)* (March): 13-15.

Helyar, John. 1994. *Lords of the Realm: The Real History of Baseball.* New York: Villard Books.

MacDonald, Don, and Morgan Reynolds. 1994. Are Baseball Players Paid Their Marginal Product? *Managerial and Decision Economics 15* (September-October): 443-458.

Quirk, James, and Rodney Fort. 1992. *Pay Dirt: The Business of Professional Team Sports.* Princeton, N.J.: Princeton University Press.

Scully, Gerald. 1989. *The Business of Major League Baseball.* Chicago: The University of Chicago Press.

Zimbalist, Andrew. 1994. Baseball Owners, Not Players, Being Greedy. *Erie Daily Times* (August 2): 5A.

5

Final Offer Salary Arbitration (FOSA)– a.k.a. Franchise Owners' Self Annihilation

James B. Dworkin

HISTORY OF SALARY ARBITRATION IN BASEBALL

As most people are aware, baseball players for a long time suffered from a lack of bargaining power in salary negotiations with individual teams (Kuhn 1987, 74–90; J. Miller 1990, 213–228; M. Miller 1991, 170–202). Several labor market restrictions in baseball provided owners with a virtual monopoly, from which position they were able to keep player salaries remarkably low. These labor market features included the now famous reserve clause, under which a player was bound to the particular team into perpetuity unless traded or given an outright release. As the only buyer of player services, a particular team possessed enormous bargaining advantage over any player who wished to remain in professional baseball. This was not like employment in the normal private sector, where a person had the freedom to switch jobs from one foundry to another if he or she could find a higher wage and/or better working conditions. Baseball players had the choice of signing with the team to which they were reserved (at the terms specified by that team) or leaving baseball altogether. They did not possess the freedom to shop around from team to team looking for the best place to work.

Few were the options for the dissatisfied player prior to the implementation of arbitration. He could go into another profession. Some players might dare to stage a holdout (Sandy Koufax and Don Drysdale, for example) and some even ventured to play baseball in Japan. If a player did want to stay in professional baseball in the United States, his only choice was to deal with the one team that owned his contract and services. Of course, there was some bargaining over individual salaries, but team owners and players alike realized who held all of the cards.

A player who was not willing to sign on the terms offered by his club faced the unpleasant prospect of being "reserved" for the following season. This meant that his contract would be renewed at perhaps as much as a 20 percent cut in salary. Needless to say, most players simply signed on the terms offered by their clubs.

Resentment on the part of the players grew over time, as they realized some of the built-in inequities in the system under which they were forced to operate. But what could they possibly do? Antitrust prosecution was tried, but to little avail as baseball retained a historical exemption from our nation's antitrust laws. Turning to unionism was also a possibility and was attempted on several occasions throughout the history of baseball (Dworkin 1981, 1-20). Ultimately, it was to be the process of collective bargaining that led to the adoption of final offer salary arbitration in baseball. However, this was not to come until the year 1973. Players were very dissatisfied with their lack of salary bargaining power as far back as the late 1880s. How would they redress this lack of power? What could be done to allow players to have more of a say in setting their employment terms?

The notion of using salary arbitration to resolve the toughest player-club salary disputes first surfaced in a House Subcommittee hearing in the year 1952. The Commissioner of Baseball at that time was A. B. (Happy) Chandler. He told members of the Subcommittee that it was his belief that players should possess the right to demand salary arbitration. Others who testified in favor of arbitration at that time argued that it was a good way to enable players to redress the bargaining power imbalance they faced each spring when contract time rolled around. Obviously, owners were in no mood to change a system that had worked so fabulously for them in the past. Thus, the idea of salary arbitration lay dormant for about 20 years before rising to the surface once again.

The next big boost for salary arbitration came during the Curt Flood antitrust trial in 1972. Though Flood (1970, 228-236) was unsuccessful in challenging baseball's antitrust exemption, his trial did once again feature the notion of using salary arbitration in order to give players more bargaining power during salary talks. Salary arbitration was presented as one possible way of partially modifying the reservation system. An interesting thing to note is how many of the suggestions that came up during the Flood trial actually later made their way into the procedure adopted in professional baseball. Many famous baseball personalities testified at this trial, and the pros and cons of salary arbitration were prominently featured.

Believe it or not, it was the *owners* in baseball who originally proposed that a procedure for salary arbitration be included in the collective bargaining contract between the parties. This historic mistake on the part of the owners took place on February 8, 1973. It is interesting to speculate on why the owners would make such a proposal, after having bargaining power so much in their favor for so many years. Perhaps they felt that this procedure would satisfy the player demands for a greater say in the salary bargaining process and stop them from demanding more freedom to change clubs at will through free agency. Perhaps many owners felt as Bill Veeck did when he noted that arbitration would create a little better relationship between the parties by giving players more of a say in their salary negotiations. Another possibility is that the owners simply made one colossal error in judgment in proposing this system. Maybe this error was made due to poor preparation for negotiations combined with the fact that the owners had little background or expertise in labor relations, whereas the Major League Baseball Players' Association was led by Marvin Miller, a seasoned veteran of many private sector labor wars.

Negotiations over the exact nature of the procedure dragged on for several weeks. Finally, the two sides were able to agree to a compromise proposal and inked an agreement, effective as of February 25, 1973. The initial usage of final offer salary arbitration in professional baseball was scheduled for the months preceding the 1974 championship season (Helyar 1994, 151–170).

THE MECHANICS OF THE PROCEDURE

Though several minor modifications to the salary arbitration procedure have been made over the years, the basic procedure remains pretty much the same as when it was first employed prior to the 1974 championship season. Obviously, the parties may still attempt to negotiate bilaterally to reach an agreement over salary for the ensuing season. As we shall see in the next section of this chapter, the vast majority of salary-arbitration-eligible players do in fact settle on salary terms with their clubs without the need to use the arbitration process.

A basic point to cover is who is eligible for salary arbitration. The actual eligibility rules are as stated in Article VI, F(1) of the Basic Agreement:

F.   Salary Arbitration
The following salary arbitration procedure shall be applicable:
(1)   *Eligibility.* The issue of a Player's salary may be submitted to final and binding arbitration by any Player or his Club, provided the other party to the arbitration consents thereto. Any Club, or any Player with a total of *three* or more years of Major League service, however accumulated, but with *less than six* years of Major League service, may submit the issue of the Player's salary to final and binding arbitration without the consent of the other party, subject to the provisions of paragraph (4) below.

In addition, effective in 1991 and thereafter, a Player with at least two but less than three years of Major League service shall be eligible for salary arbitration if: (a) he has accumulated at least *86 days of service* during the immediately preceding season; and   (b) he ranks in the top seventeen percent (*17%*) (rounded to the nearest whole number) in total service in the class of Players who have at least two but less than three years of Major League service, however accumulated, but with at least 86 days of service accumulated during the immediately preceding season. If two or more Players are tied in ranking, ties shall be broken consecutively based on the number of days of service accumulated in each of the immediately preceding seasons.   If the Players remain tied, the final tie breaker will be by lot (Major League Baseball 1990, 11).

There are three classes of players in professional baseball for the purposes of salary arbitration eligibility. The first class of players are those individuals who have not yet accumulated enough major league service to be able to employ arbitration.   These early career players are not eligible for salary arbitration, and thus they have very little bargaining power when it comes to salary negotiation time. These players are essentially in the same situation that all major league players faced prior to the inception of arbitration and, later, free agency.   That is, these players today face no competition between teams for their services. A prominent feature of this labor market is that each player is bound to the team for which he played in the previous season. Players in this seniority grouping find that their salaries are quite low in comparison to their more senior peers in the major leagues. But, they have some hope for the future. If they can amass more seniority at the major league level, they can then advance to the arbitration-eligible class of players.

The second grouping of players are those who are arbitration eligible based upon the major league service guidelines reprinted previously. These players are referred to as the arbitration-eligible players. Individuals in this grouping do have the right each year to demand salary arbitration if they cannot come to terms bilaterally with the club for which they are employed. The workings of this procedure will be briefly described subsequently.

Finally, the third grouping of major league players are those individuals who have amassed greater than six years of major league service.   Actually, players in this grouping are able to declare themselves to be free agents and negotiate with other teams for their services, much like most workers are able to do in a free market situation. Players in this grouping who file for free agency are also able to accept salary arbitration if it is offered to them by their former club in December of the year in which they become a free agent.

Having explained the three categories of seniority used to define which players are eligible for salary arbitration, it is useful to see how the procedure actually works. As noted previously, very few cases actually proceed all the way to the stage of the arbitration hearing. It is very common for arbitration-eligible players to file for arbitration, thus preserving their rights to use the process if necessary. In practice, however, most filers do eventually settle with their clubs and do not need to actually go before an arbitrator. The process of negotiations works pretty well in most cases. The mere threat of potentially having to go before an arbitrator is usually incentive enough to get both sides talking seriously about settling.

The cases that do proceed all the way to a hearing are regulated by a rather simple set of rules agreed upon through the process of collective bargaining. The most important of said rules are set forth here:

1. The procedure agreed upon by the parties is final offer arbitration. This means that each party at the specified time has to submit one last best offer to the arbitrator. The arbitrator must select either the final offer of the club or the player as the salary for the ensuing season. No compromise arbitration awards are permissible under the rules specified in the collective bargaining agreement. This type of procedure was chosen because it has been shown in previous settings that a final offer procedure tends to encourage the parties to settle on their own and not rely on the process itself for settlements. The results in professional baseball's salary negotiations tend to bear out this assertion. Very few cases proceed all the way to a hearing. Most players and clubs, even where salary arbitration is invoked, seem to be able to settle bilaterally. Final offer arbitration has the advantage of encouraging negotiations, whereas another form of arbitration, which does allow more arbitrator compromise (conventional arbitration), tends to feature a lot of split-the-difference awards. Obviously, if the parties feel that an arbitrator will just fashion a middle ground award, they might actually take more disparate positions in the hopes of "winning" a little bit more from the award fashioned by the neutral.

2. Clear rules as to which players are eligible for the final offer arbitration process are specified in the collective bargaining contract. These rules and categories of players have been described previously.

3. The actual hearings are quite short, and the arbitrator does not explain his or her decision. No rationale for the final position chosen is given. All the arbitrator does is insert the salary figure deemed appropriate into the proper place in Paragraph 2 of the Uniform Player's Contract.

4. Several criteria for the arbitrator to consider are written into the language of the collective bargaining contract. These criteria include the quality of the player's contribution to the club during the past season; the length and consistency of the player's career contribution; the record of the player's past compensation; comparative baseball salaries; the existence of any mental or physical defects on the part of the player; and the recent performance of the club, including league standing and attendance. The rules specify that for players of less than five years of service, the arbitrator is to give particular attention for salary comparison purposes to the contracts of players with Major League service not exceeding one annual service group above the player's annual service group. But the rules also specify that this last regulation shall not limit the ability of a player or his agent to argue the equal relevance of salaries of players without regard to service because of special accomplishments. Of course, in all of these hearings and no matter what type of evidence is presented, it is the arbitrator who ultimately decides what weight to give to the various arguments presented.

5. Arbitrators are chosen jointly by the parties and hearings are held at various sites around the United States. Awards are due within 24 hours of the conclusion of the hearing. No appeal of these awards is possible. The parties may elect to choose other arbitrators in the future if they are not happy with the decision that has been rendered.

THE RESULTS OF THE PROCESS

Just as baseball fans everywhere read their daily newspapers to find box scores and league standings describing their favorite players at work (Will 1990, 1–6), it seems that there has been a lot of interest lately in the results of the final offer salary arbitration process in baseball. Much could be written about individual cases, agents, and arbitrators. My intention, however, is to present some broad macroperspectives on the outcomes of the process, leaving the more micro analyses for another time and paper.

One result that is quite consistent with the theory behind final offer salary arbitration is that the process does tend to have a built-in self-destruct mechanism. That is, very few cases are ever actually heard by an arbitrator. Many if not all arbitration-eligible players do preserve their right to use arbitration by filing to use the procedure at the appropriate time. But, this filing just signals the beginning of the bargaining season. From 1974 through the 1994 round of cases, there had been a total of 375 cases actually decided by an arbitrator. For example, prior to the 1994 season there were 16 cases decided by an arbitrator, six won by the players and 10 won by the owners. But looked at another way, these 16 cases represent around 10 percent of those players who were eligible for arbitration and actually filed their intention to employ the process. What happened to the rest of these players who filed to use salary arbitration? Why did they settle short of going to arbitration? The simple answer is that the mere threat of using arbitration promotes bargaining in good faith. The ultimate result of this bargaining is a large number of settlements, some occurring just prior to the time at which the arbitration hearing is set to begin. Both sides are wary of just what the arbitrator might do after the hearing. Thus, the incentive is to compromise through the negotiations process *prior* to the hearing. If both sides work together and make compromises in good faith, chances are that the difference between them can be narrowed to the point where some type of settlement is quite possible. Each side has to make a calculation as to whether it is better to settle on some compromise position with certainty prior to the hearing or to take the chance on losing (or winning) big at the arbitration hearing. Often players are advised by agents and statisticians, who use modeling techniques to make predictions as to the likelihood of a player winning a particular case. It is through these sessions that the sides typically and gradually move toward a settlement. This has been the case throughout the history of the process of final offer salary arbitration. The largest number of arbitration awards ever was 35 in 1986. The smallest number was nine cases in 1978. Thus, one conclusion we can draw from baseball's 20-year experience with final offer salary arbitration is that the procedure does what many advocates have argued for some time, that is, it gives the parties an incentive to bargain and to try to settle on their own. Anybody who knows anything about labor-management relations will tell you that the best settlement in any matter is one reached by the parties bilaterally, not one imposed by an arbitrator or government intervention. Final offer salary arbitration in baseball has promoted a high rate of self-settlement by the parties over the 20-year period in which it has been used.

One area that seems to be of utmost interest is who wins at salary arbitration cases. This is a tricky question to answer. For what would seem to be a rather straightforward and simple analysis soon turns into a much more complicated matter. The numbers are somewhat surprising and revealing at the same time. This is what has happened in terms of wins and losses over time in the arbitration hearing arena.

The overall results through 1994 indicate 209 wins for the clubs versus only 166 wins for the players involved in salary arbitration. Clubs have won 55.73 percent of the salary arbitration cases heard; players have won 44.27 percent of the cases. One might be tempted to conclude that the owners have done quite well throughout the years at the arbitration table. Who wouldn't like to win more cases than you lose? The plain truth is that no matter what the basic percentage figures might suggest, the actual fact is that the players *never* lose at arbitration. Players "win" at arbitration in three different ways. The first way they win is by simply filing for arbitration. Even if they never have to go through an arbitration hearing, players receive higher salaries than they otherwise would have received if they were not eligible for arbitration. Data on salary increases for players filing for arbitration show that on average, a player can expect to double his salary simply by filing for arbitration. How does this happen? The mere threat of perhaps having to go to arbitration tends to move both parties to negotiate in good faith. The result is often a negotiated salary that is more than twice what the player had earned in the previous season.

The second way a player wins at arbitration is by actually proceeding to the arbitration stage and *losing* the case. It might seem weird to say that a player can "win by losing," but this in fact happens quite regularly. Take the example of a player who had earned $400,000 in the previous season. This player goes to arbitration and demands a salary of $1,000,000 for the ensuing season. The club offers him $800,000 for the next season. After a hearing in which both sides make excellent presentations on the relative merits of their cases, an arbitrator decides for the club. That is, the club wins the case and only has to pay this player $800,000 in the next season. The impact is that the player receives double the salary he had been paid in the previous season. What rational person would consider this to be a loss from the perspective of the player? Several players have noted that going into an arbitration hearing, the only question on their minds is whether they are going to be rich or richer. It has been shown in several studies that losing players at arbitration generally have an increase in salary of at least 50 percent over what they had earned in the previous season (Dworkin 1988, 480–486).

Finally, the player can win at arbitration by actually *winning* his case before the neutral. This, of course, is the situation where the player receives a huge boost in salary over what he had been paid in the previous season. Sometimes these awards have moved players way above peers in the same service grouping. More will be said about this phenomenon in the final section of this chapter. In conclusion, a player stands to gain almost double his salary just by filing for arbitration. Losers at the arbitration table actually tend to wind up with a minimum of a 50 percent increase in salary, whereas winners oftentimes do far better than a doubling of their salaries from the previous season.

CONCLUSIONS AND IMPLICATIONS FOR THE FUTURE

The overriding conclusion to be reached from an exhaustive study of the final offer salary arbitration process in baseball is that it has been a key factor in the meteoric rise we have witnessed in baseball player salaries. Owners in baseball have been burned badly by this system. They have made several key errors over time that have exacerbated their problems in the area of player salary bargaining. A brief listing of these errors is in order at this time.

First, as noted above, it was the owners who first proposed that such a procedure be implemented in baseball. Owners viewed this "carrot" as a good way to keep players from focusing too much attention on the notion of free agency. As things have turned out, free agency also was implemented. Many studies of the baseball players labor market have concluded that both arbitration and free agency have been responsible for the rise in player salaries. It is clear that the owners have fought much harder in recent years to rid themselves of salary arbitration as compared to their efforts to eliminate free agency. The conclusion one must reach is that the high salaries paid to low-seniority players, because of the salary arbitration system, have probably been the foremost factor in explaining why we see baseball players with such high compensation today. Note that in the recent round of negotiations, owners proposed to *eliminate* salary arbitration and to *expand* free agency rights. Why did they do this? Because they realize the mistakes they have made in the past and seek to regain control over players in the early stages of their careers. For if the owners could eliminate salary arbitration, they could return to the days of yesteryear and control the salaries of younger players in their formative years. This would be an effective way of controlling team payrolls.

A second error the owners made was to agree to a procedure that did not contain many restrictions on the arbitration process. Of course, the award had to be either the final offer of one side or the other. But all of the terms, criteria, and procedures described above were the product of collective bargaining. None of these terms had to be included in the contract. The fact that the owners did not insist at the very onset of the bargaining for other restrictions on the procedure was a big mistake. Ever since the inception of the process, owners have been trying to insert some of these restrictions that they failed to suggest or successfully negotiate into the contract from the very beginning. What types of restrictions would have helped the owners? First, restricting the group of players eligible for arbitration would have provided owners with much more control over players in their early years. To the owners' credit, they did achieve some success on this front by changing the eligibility level from two years to two years and approximately 86 days of major league service. It is interesting to note that union leader Donald Fehr received quite a bit of criticism from former union boss Marvin Miller for giving in on this eligibility issue. Second, the owners could have insisted on some sort of arbitration salary cap for players, perhaps something like stating that no player could receive more than double his salary from the previous season through an arbitration award. Other types of restrictions could be suggested as well. The main point is that the owners tended to represent themselves in the bargaining process and they did not in fact have much experience in the process of collective bargaining. Their opponents, on the other hand, were grizzled labor relations veterans who often had the upper hand due to this superior experience factor.

Let me cite just one more example of a major error made by the owners in accepting the original procedure. Owners failed to restrict which seniority groupings arbitrators could make comparisons with when deciding cases. This meant that for a third-year player who may have had fantastic statistics for his previous year *only*, comparisons could be made with *all* other players in baseball. Of course, seniority and performance factors will be built in to the salaries paid to these older players. Perhaps a 10-year veteran has had eight seasons in a row of superior performance. Is it logical to compare this player's salary with the demand made by a player with three years of major league service and only one superior year? The owners tried to remedy this problem by adding language to the collective bargaining contract that said that arbitrators should give particular attention to players *not exceeding* one annual service group above the player's annual service group. This meant in theory that if the player at arbitration was a three-year player, the arbitrator should look at comparative salaries of players not exceeding four years of major league service. This would eliminate the situation described above where an arbitrator would be comparing three-year players with 10-year players. The problem with this new language is that the two sides also added a clause saying that the player or his agent may argue the equal relevance of salaries of players without regard to years of service if *special accomplishments* warrant such comparisons. As just one example, when Pittsburgh Pirates pitcher Doug Drabek went to arbitration in 1991 following his Cy Young Award winning season in 1990, the arbitrator was asked to consider the special accomplishments of the pitcher in the previous season. Drabek, who had a 22-6 season in 1990, did break through this language, and the principle was established that a player could break out of his service grouping in the case of special accomplishments (Hendricks 1994, 242–265). Again, the owners made a nice try. But it did not work. My point is that this type of language restricting the players who could be used for comparison purposes by arbitrators trying to decide cases could have been included in the collective bargaining language from the very beginning. If the owners would have paid more attention to crafting the procedure back in 1973, the problems they have experienced with final offer salary arbitration over the past 20 years probably would have been alleviated substantially.

The final offer salary arbitration system has been very good for the players in professional baseball. These players will not be willing to allow this procedure to be eliminated without receiving something of equal value in return. The owners have been trying to revise the system for some time to no avail. The process of salary arbitration was initially agreed to by the parties through the process of collective bargaining. Although the process has its warts, it has provided an orderly mechanism for the two sides to resolve their salary disputes for 20 years. Given that the procedure was originally the product of the collective bargaining process, the ultimate future of the procedure should also be resolved through this same process, collective bargaining. The parties in baseball have shown an ability to resolve their differences in the past through collective bargaining. The best hope for an improved labor-management climate in professional baseball in the future rests with the process of collective bargaining, *not* through some sort of governmental intervention to resolve the current dispute. My prediction is that the parties will eventually resolve their current difficulties and indeed sign a new collective bargaining contract. I also predict that said contract will feature some salary arbitration procedure. We may see some changes to the current procedures, but salary arbitration has been too integral a part of the labor-management relationship in professional baseball to expect it to simply be eliminated.

REFERENCES

Dworkin, James B. 1981. *Owners versus Players: Baseball and Collective Bargaining*. Boston: Auburn House Publishing Company.
———. 1988. Collective Bargaining in Baseball: Key Current-Issues. *Labor Law Journal* (August): 480–486.
Flood, Curt. 1970. *The Way It Is*. New York: Trident Press.
Helyar, John. 1994. *Lords of the Realm: The Real History of Baseball*. New York: Villard Books.
Hendricks, Randal A. 1994. *Inside the Strike Zone*. Austin, Tex.: Eakin Press.

Kuhn, Bowie. 1987. *Hardball: The Education of a Baseball Commissioner.* New York: Times Books.

Major League Baseball. *Basic Agreement between The American League of Professional Baseball Clubs and The National League of Professional Baseball Clubs and Major League Baseball Players Association, effective January 1, 1990.*

Miller, James E. 1990. *The Baseball Business: Pursuing Pennants and Profits in Baltimore.* Chapel Hill, N.C.: The University of North Carolina Press.

Miller, Marvin. 1991. *A Whole Different Ball Game: The Sport and Business of Baseball.* New York: Birch Lane Press.

Will, George F. 1990. *Men at Work: The Craft of Baseball.* New York: Macmillan Publishing Company.

6

Salary Arbitration in Major League Baseball: A Case of Dog Wags Tail!

William H. Kaempfer

INTRODUCTION

Salary arbitration in Major League Baseball (MLB) is a transitory institution whose time has come and probably gone for good. If arbitration passes from the scene in future labor negotiations there will be few tears shed, however; certainly none at all by franchise owners and probably only one or two by a few players. Owners, usually citing a few specific cases with huge settlements that they lost, blame arbitration for the huge explosion in salaries over the past decade. In particular, whereas owners are more than willing to shell out huge amounts for free agents, they don't like being ordered to pay big salaries beyond their control. Players, on the other hand, see arbitration as an often demeaning process where they must suffer the indignity of having all of their weaknesses exposed before someone who will then pass judgment on their earnings. Moreover, players more often lose than win, and even then the winners are put in the uncomfortable position of playing for a team that thinks that the player is worth considerably less than the salary stipulated by his arbitration award.

But for all of its weaknesses, salary arbitration in MLB is most decidedly not the tail that wags baseball's salary dog. Quite the opposite, the salaries arbitrated for eligible players through this process follow quite closely what is happening to the salaries of players eligible for free agency (Frederick, Kaempfer, and Wobbekind 1992, 29-49). But that defines the very problem that owners perceive with salary arbitration. For owners, players eligible for arbitration are not free agents and should not be paid like free agents. To understand the process, however, it is best to explain the motivations that underlie the behavior of all of the parties involved—owners, players, and arbitrators—and to examine the facts relating to the average outcomes of arbitration over the past decade.

BEHAVIOR OF THE PARTIES IN ARBITRATION

By the time a player's filing for arbitration actually gets to the hearing stage, there are three parties involved in the arbitration decision: the *player* (and his agents and representatives), representatives of the player's *team* management (usually including, among others, the general manager and player personnel director), and the *arbitrator*. The best way to describe or predict the outcome of the arbitration hearing is to understand how these three parties are likely to behave.

Arbitrators are neutral parties, typically lawyers or judges, who are paid to hear an arbitration case and pass judgment. Persons who serve as arbitrators are jointly selected by the Players' Association and the two Leagues (representing the interest of the owners). Presumably, arbitrators enjoy their work and the compensation they receive, and wish to keep their jobs. As such, the decisions that they render, taken as a whole, should not displease the Players' Union or the two Leagues. This implies that arbitrators will try to reach decisions that they hope the players and teams will perceive as fair, but fairness in these cases can mean several things. One interpretation of fairness would be to act in a purely random fashion; that is, the arbitrator could secretly flip a coin in each decision. Though fair—in that players and teams would stand the same chance of winning any case—such an approach would quickly be seen by players and teams as very arbitrary, and the arbitrator would probably not keep his or her job for long. A second interpretation of what is fair would be to rank all of the cases heard in order of the size of the spread between what the player is demanding and what the team is offering. Then rule against the players that are far from their team's offer, but in favor of players who haven't asked for too much more than what the team offers. However, this process presumes that the reason for a large spread lies entirely with the player and not the team. In fact, such a decision rule would give teams an incentive to "low-ball" players with minimal offers in order to make the player's demand seem out of line.

What is probably the best way for an arbitrator to be fair is for the arbitrator to independently arrive at a conclusion of what a player is really worth, and then see which side is closest—player or team. The party who comes closest to the arbitrator's judgment of the true worth of the player wins this baseball version of *The Price Is Right* (Dworkin 1981; Frederick, Kaempfer, and Wobbekind 1992, 29–49).

In fact, players and teams are instructed to provide just the type of information that leads the arbitrator to make this last type of "fair" judgment. The 1973 Basic Agreement allows arbitrators to hear only specific types of evidence, such as player performance and comparative salaries. For instance, suppose there are three left-handed outfielders who play for Kansas City, Philadelphia, and Boston who all have batting averages of around .280 with 15 home runs and about five years of experience, and each of these players has signed a contract for about $1.2 million. Now suppose that a fourth left-handed outfielder with similar statistics files for arbitration asking for $1.8 million when his team has offered $1.0 million. In this case the arbitrator will, out of fairness of trying to pick the offer closest to what he or she believes is the true value of the player under consideration, select the team's offer as closest to the "market" value of the player. On the other hand, if this player had asked for $1.4 million whereas his team only offered $700,000, the player's offer would likely be selected.

What are the objectives of the players and teams in an arbitration hearing? Economic theory says that they will both attempt to maximize the expected value of the outcome of the process. This means that, in the case of a player, he will pay attention not only to the level of his salary request but also to how likely the arbitrator is to choose the player's bid over the team's offer. If the system works as described here, and both the players and the teams know it, players and teams will adopt strategies to try to increase their chances of winning the arbitration case.

There are two ways in which a player or team can try to win an arbitration hearing. First, both parties will present information to the arbitrator that attempts to sway him or her to their side. The most important facet of this information presentation will be to find comparable talent with high (or low) salaries to give the arbitrator a feeling for what the fair value of the player might be. Players will tout their strong points; teams will emphasize weaknesses. This later tendency is what leaves many players highly negative about their arbitration experience—win or lose. They end up feeling underappreciated by their teams.   Second, both teams and players will move their offers closer to what is likely to be seen by the arbitrator as the fair value of the player. Players and teams undertake careful study of exactly what salaries are being paid to other players, either recently signed free agents or arbitration-eligible players who have settled on a contract before a hearing. In this way they can prepare their final offers to try to make the arbitrators more likely to agree with them. In support of this contention is the fact that players who experience salary arbitration hearings in more than one year have significantly smaller spreads between what they ask and what their team bids the second time around. In other words, players tend to learn to try to make an offer that the arbitrator will accept when they repeat the arbitration process (Frederick, Kaempfer, and Wobbekind 1992, 29–49).

ARBITRATION STATS

Baseball fans have an almost universal love of performance statistics. Final offer salary arbitration in MLB gives us yet another opportunity to look into the process and evaluate performance. In this case, though, the competition is not player against player or team against team, but player

against team. Our objective is to reach an educated conclusion about the
pluses and minuses of salary arbitration; but to accomplish this, we don't
have to base our conclusions upon hypothetical conjecture but on the hard
facts of actual outcomes.

The basic "batting average" of salary arbitration that I would like you
to focus on is the bid-ask spread. This spread is the difference between
what a player asks the arbitrator to award and what the team offers.
Figure 6.1 shows the progression of the average salary asked for by
players in all cases that went to arbitration and the average salary bid by
owners. Also included is the average settlement award made by arbitrators
in these cases. Taken by itself, Figure 6.1 looks rather shocking with its
exponential growth of both bid and asked offers. But, of course, this
trend of salaries is simply consistent with what has happened to player
salaries in general in the free agency era. All data have been converted
into 1985 U.S. dollars (*International Statistics Yearbook*, International
Monetary Fund) to remove any exponential growth due to inflation.

Figure 6.1
Ask and Bid in Arbitration: 1974-1994

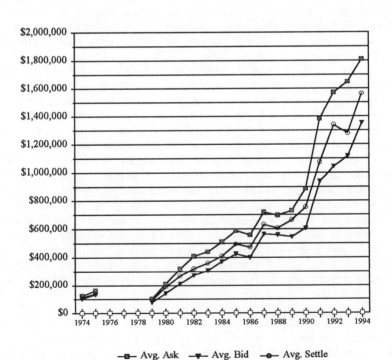

For instance, there seems to be a huge leap from 1990 to 1991 in terms of both what players ask for and what teams offer (they both rose by more than 50 percent). However, in general, baseball salaries soared that year by 37.9 percent from an average of $492,915 in 1990 to $679,887 in 1991. This figure vastly under-states the amount that the amount that salaries actually rose from 1990 to 1991, however. For players who had some ability to negotiate their salary for 1991—that is, excluding rookies and second-year players, many of whom earned the league minimum and free agents who were signed to multiple-year con-tracts before 1990, the rise in salary was probably much greater than 37.9 percent. Even though arbitration award amounts were up more than 42 percent for 1991, arbitration settlements probably lagged behind the general increase for players negotiating new salaries.

Figure 6.2 expands on this concept, showing the spread between what players going through arbitration hearings ask, on average, and what teams bid over the era of "modern" arbitration (1979–1994).

On average, the spread is a 41 percent difference between the two sides (the solid bar). However, there is little evidence of any change in this gap over the years: 1980–1983 and 1990–1993 showed above average spreads, and every other year is below average.

Figure 6.2
Ask-Bid Separation: 1979-1994

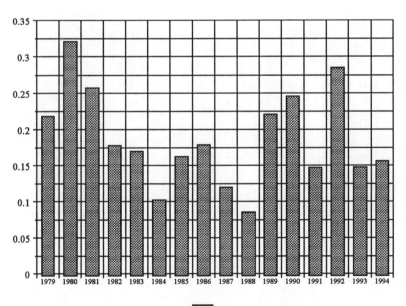

Settle/Bid

Figure 6.3 compares the difference between the judgments made by arbitrators, on average, and the average bids made by teams. This figure shows us that on an average arbitrators make awards that are 19 percent above what teams offer (the solid bar).   Notice two things about this pattern. First, in only six of 16 years (1979, 1980, 1981, 1989, 1990, and 1992) are arbitrators above their long-term average.   Second, whereas arbitration awards are 19 percent above team bids on average, players ask for 41 percent more than teams offer.   In other words, arbitrators are closer to teams in their awards than they are to players.

Is there anything special about the six years in which arbitration awards rose above their long-term average of 19 percent above team offers?   Indeed, these six years are special years for baseball salaries. The first three of the above-average salary years, 1979, 1980, and 1981, come at the beginning of arbitration.   Teams, inexperienced in the ways of this new institution, may not have realized that by trying to offer salaries closer to what the arbitrator would perceive as fair they could raise their chances of winning.

Figure 6.3
Settle-Bid Separation: 1979-1994

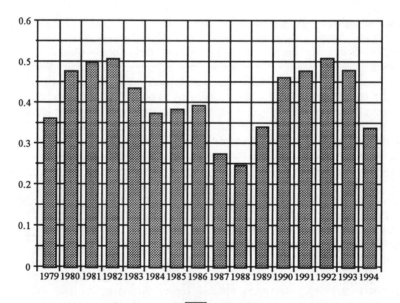

 Ask/Bid

These early years were also during the period when free agency was becoming widely established, and player salaries were beginning to rise rapidly. Arbitration-eligible players had a lot of ground to make up in relative salary terms in the early 1980s.

The second set of years where arbitrators awarded above-average settlements occurred 10 years later in 1989, 1990, and 1992. The important element in these decisions is that they follow shortly after baseball owners were found guilty of colluding against the interests of free agents. In the mid-1980s, grievance arbitrators ruled that baseball owners had illegally colluded to limit their offers to free agents. Interestingly, the response to this among arbitration hearings was very much lower salaries asked by players, lower spreads between teams' bids and players' asked amounts, and settlements much lower than average. In other words, collusion put a chill not only over free agent salaries but also over arbitration, where there was not and could not be any collusion. In light of this past collusion, however, both salaries and arbitration awards were significantly up in the 1989–1992 period. Behavior of salaries open to negotiation through the free agency process strongly impacted what happened to arbitration awards, not vice versa.

THE IMPACT OF ARBITRATION ON BASEBALL SALARIES

Baseball salaries are higher now than pioneers for players' rights like Curt Flood, Andy Messersmith, and Dave McNally ever imagined they would be. But it is important to recall that these three players sought their own free agency, not any kind of arbitration privileges. With the possible exception of the collusion years, each year in the 1980s and early 1990s saw new record salaries being won by players eligible for free agency. Furthermore, a record salary won by a superstar in one year would be gained by a respectable but fairly routine player two years later. Even though salaries awarded in arbitration settlements also rose, these awards surely are not the tail that wagged baseball's salary dog.

Salary arbitration offers a compromise between the old reserve clause system, under which a player had no rights other than to play or not play for the team that owned his contract, and free agency, under which an eligible player can negotiate to play for any interested team. But arbitration only goes part of the way. A player eligible for binding arbitration is still bound by contract to a specific team, but the involvement of an arbitrator—either formally through a hearing or informally because of the threat of an arbitration hearing—allows some of the pressure of the free-agent market to be brought to bear on the player's salary.

The current plans for baseball seem to indicate that the days of salary arbitration are numbered. The likely replacement for arbitration would be to allow all players with more than three years of experience to be eligible for free agency. The relevant question then to ask is if this expanded free agency would cause any change in the rate of increase of player salaries experienced over recent years.

There are three very important features of salary arbitration in baseball that lead me to conclude that free agency for all players with three or more years of experience cannot lead to less-rapid escalation of player salaries. First, in arbitration, teams vie with only one competing offer on salary, the player's own asking offer. As I have argued, the player's asking offer for his services is best calculated based on relevant data like what other, comparable free agents have been getting for a salary on the open market. Players who overestimate their worth will most likely lose their arbitration hearing. Upon the establishment of more-complete free agency rights for players, teams would face competition from all other teams interested in a given player. Furthermore, if one of those teams goes overboard, there is no longer an arbitrator to rule that such an offer is out of line and unreasonable. In free agency, most often the highest bid will win a player's services.

Second, under arbitration, teams tend to win more hearings than they lose, and furthermore, the arbitrated salaries are on average closer to the team's offer than the player's asked for salary. This implies that at the completion of the arbitration process, a team knows that it will have the contesting player under contract, at no more than what the player is asking under arbitration and perhaps even at the team's own offer.

Under a system of free agency, quite a different outcome would prevail. Outside of the years when collusion was present, free agency tends to have players sign contracts with new teams rather than stay put with their old team. This implies that a free agent's past team is also likely to be in the free agent market. Furthermore there are no bounds on salary after the free agency bidding has begun. In addition, free agency might encourage the use of multiyear contracts rather than single-season salary awards. This inflexibility would force owners to continue to pay for players who become unproductive during the course of their contract, instead of being able to release the player or negotiate a more reasonable salary after one season under arbitration.

Finally, under the arbitration system that has prevailed in recent years, if a team felt that a player might get an unacceptable salary from an arbitrator, it had the option of not making a salary offer to a player and declaring him a free agent. In other words, teams were faced with four possibilities for those players with between three and six years of experience who were not currently under contract. They could accept the player's asked for salary (in effect the maximum that they would have to pay); they could make a bid and expect to go to arbitration, knowing that their chances in arbitration were better than even; they could make a bid, and then negotiate before arbitration in order to reach a contract with the player at a salary level somewhere between the player's asked for salary and the team's bid; or they could not offer a contract and make the player a free agent.

It seems clear that simply making all players with between three and six years of experience free agents will not contain salaries in and of itself. For salary growth to be curtailed under free agency, something more must be added to the negotiating process. For instance, during the years when teams clearly were colluding to keep down salaries, they seemed to be successful (although it is hard to tell how long an informal agreement would have stayed in force). A salary cap or some form of salary tax might be even more successful because it would codify the expectations that would be made of teams. However, simply granting free agency rights to all players who would have been eligible for arbitration is not going to cause the growth of major league baseball salaries to slow down.

Note: The author acknowledges the important contributions of David Frederick, Daniel Marburger, Martin Ross, and Richard Wobbekind.

REFERENCES

Dworkin, James B. 1981. *Owners versus Players: Baseball and Collective Bargaining*. Boston: Auburn House Publishing Company.

Frederick, David M., William H. Kaempfer, and Richard L. Wobbekind. 1992. Salary Arbitration as a Market Substitute. In *Diamonds Are Forever: The Business of Baseball*. Paul M.Sommers, ed. Washington, D.C.: The Brookings Institution: 29-49.

International Statistics Yearbook. (various years)   International Monetary Fund.

Stevens, Carl M. 1966. Is Compulsory Arbitration Compatible with Bargaining? *Industrial Relations* 5: 38-52.

USA Today, 1974-1994, various issues.

III

BASEBALL'S QUICK-FIX SOLUTIONS

7

The Salary Cap and the Luxury Tax: Affirmative Action Programs for Weak-Drawing Franchises

James Quirk

Ever since Marvin Miller appeared on the scene in the late 1960s, negotiations between players and owners in major league baseball (MLB) certainly haven't lacked interesting and controversial issues to disagree about, usually at a level just short of actual physical mayhem between the two contending parties. There have been strikes or lockouts over certification of the union, over the reserve clause, and over salary arbitration. The 1994-1995 strike which led to cancellation of the World Series in 1994, was over the owners' demand for a salary cap. By the spring of 1996 the owners had backed away from the salary cap demand in favor of a "luxury tax," which operates by penalizing teams for spending more on player salaries than some prespecified amount. The announced objective of the luxury tax is the same as that of a salary cap, namely, to force something approaching equality on salary expenditures of league teams. No league has actually implemented a luxury tax, but the National Basketball Association (NBA) and National Football League (NFL) already have salary caps in place. In this paper, the effects of such league-imposed regulations or penalties on "excessive" salary expenditures by teams are discussed. A starting point in examining these issues is to look at the recent history of the one league that has had a number of years of experience with a cap, the NBA.

Back in the late 1970s and early 1980s the National Basketball Association was in economic trouble. In 1983 the NBA claimed that 18 of its 23 teams had lost money in the 1981-1982 season. Though there is always a good deal of hyperbole in such statements, still there were some solid facts underlying the report that weak-drawing franchises in the NBA were facing real financial problems. Rumors were that five teams—the Cleveland Cavaliers, Indiana Pacers, Utah Jazz, Kansas City Kings, and the San Diego Clippers—were scheduled to be dropped from the NBA.   (In the event, all five teams survived, but the Kings later moved to Sacramento, and the Clippers moved to Los Angeles.)

The NBA operates under "home team takes all" rules that provide for no sharing of gate or local TV revenues with visiting teams.[1] With the problems facing weak-drawing franchises in the late 1970s, there was a move within the NBA by such teams to change league rules to provide for gate and local TV revenue-sharing. And there was an immediate and clear-cut response from the strong-drawing franchises in the league.

On December 7, 1979, a meeting was held at Club 21 in New York City, hosted by the New York Knicks and attended by representatives of the owners of the five other strong-drawing teams in the league—the New Jersey Nets, Philadelphia 76ers, Boston Celtics, Los Angeles Lakers, and Chicago Bulls. The meeting was intended to develop unified resistance to any change in gate and local TV revenue-sharing rules. By the NBA constitution, approval of a change in revenue-sharing rules required a three-fourths majority of the (then) 22 teams, and the "unholy six" (as they were dubbed by some of the frustrated small-city owners) formed a blocking coalition against such a change. The consequence was that the rules for sharing gate and local TV revenues among teams have remained unchanged in the NBA up to the present day.

Having been rebuffed in their attempt to get some help from their rich fellow league members, the weak-drawing teams and the NBA commissioner's office turned to the NBA Players' Association (NBAPA). The league argued that major concessions were needed from the union to avoid the loss of jobs that would be involved in a down-sizing of the NBA as marginal weak-drawing teams were eliminated. After a typical long, contentious, and difficult negotiation process, the NBAPA agreed to a contract incorporating the novel feature of a salary cap, placing both a floor (53 percent of total revenues) on salary expenditures by the league and a ceiling and a floor on such expenditures by individual member teams.

The salary cap was sold to the union as a device that would equalize talent among league teams, with special benefits for weak-drawing teams that had not been able to compete in the free agent market for players under the old rules. In effect, the salary cap was the NBA's version of affirmative action, with the beneficiaries to be the weak-drawing franchises, and the contributors—the financiers of the cap—to be the players, who gave up a part of the free agency privileges they had acquired through earlier collective bargaining agreements and through successful antitrust suits against the league.

The NBA salary cap went into effect beginning with the 1983–1984 season and has been a part of the league rules since that time. The years under the cap have been the most successful in NBA history, with league revenues and profits skyrocketing. The experience of the NBA did not go unnoticed by owners of teams in the other pro sports. In 1993 the NFL signed a seven-year labor agreement incorporating a salary cap, and the National Hockey League (NHL) and major league baseball have been attempting to talk their player unions into similar agreements—with less success.

On the other hand, the NBA Players' Association has had second thoughts about the cap, and has tried for years to find a way to eliminate it. The union acted to decertify itself and then brought charges against the league, under the antitrust laws, for implementing the cap in the absence of a collective bargaining agreement. The courts rejected the union suit in early 1995 on the ground that it was disingenuous of the union to claim antitrust violations by the league in implementing something that the union had voluntarily agreed to in earlier bargaining. This is truly a classic example of the famous adage "No good deed goes unpunished" and is an object lesson that will no doubt have long-term consequences for collective bargaining in all pro team sports. Ultimately, the NBAPA voted for a new contract incorporating an even stronger version of a salary cap (a "hard" cap), along with higher guarantees on salaries from the owners and sweetened fringe benefits.

The success of the NBA under the salary cap deserves some attention. Between the 1983–1984 and 1993–1994 seasons, attendance at NBA games increased from 10 million to 18 million, with per-game attendance rising from an average of 10,500 to 16,200. TV revenues increased from $60 million in 1983–1984 to $486 million in 1993–1994. Average player salaries went up from $400,000 per player in 1983–1984, to $1.3 million in 1993–1994; the average price of an NBA franchise increased from $12 million in 1983–1984 to $114 million in 1993–1994; and, according to a *Financial World* estimate, each of the 27 NBA teams was making money in 1993–94, as compared to 18 out of 23 losing money in 1981–82.[2] The conclusion seems obvious—what more proof is needed of the beneficial effects of a salary cap on all participants, players as well as owners? Owners, sports writers, and even judges have all used the success of the NBA to argue for the merits of a salary cap.

The facts argue differently—that the salary cap had next to nothing to do with the NBA's success between 1983 and 1995, and that owners and others are committing a "post hoc ergo propter hoc" fallacy in identifying the cap as the cause of that success. As noted earlier, the salary cap was supposed to work wonders for the NBA by equalizing salary expenditures among teams, thus providing better opportunities for weak-drawing teams to acquire star players, adding up to more-competitive balance. But this is not what the data show. The NBA salary cap, as it worked between 1983–1984 and 1993–1994, did not equalize salary costs among teams. In 1993–1994, salary expenditures ranged from a high of $35 million (L.A. Lakers) to a low of $15 million (Dallas Mavericks). Comparable data are not available for 1983–1984, but in 1985–1986, the range was from a high of $9 million (Los Angeles Lakers) to a low of $3 million (Utah).[3] After 10 years of the salary cap, the gap in spending between weak-drawing and strong-drawing teams still persisted.

Has the salary cap acted to increase competitive balance in the NBA? Again the answer is no. Looking at championships or at won-lost percentages, the same answer comes through—there was no significant increase in competitive balance during the salary cap years as compared to the previous years. For example, in the 10 years prior to the cap, the Celtics won three titles, the Lakers won two, and Portland, Golden State, Washington, Seattle, and Philadelphia each won one. During the first 10 years following the cap, the Lakers and Chicago won three titles each, Boston and Detroit won two each. There actually was more concentration of championships after the cap was instituted than before. And a similar story could be told concerning the concentration of won-lost percents among teams. Given the continuing disparity in salary expenditures among teams under the cap, these results should come as no surprise, of course. The predicted effects of the cap on competitive balance simply didn't materialize.

It is natural to ask why the NBA salary cap didn't perform as advertised.   Again the answer is pretty straightforward. Under pressure from the dominant strong-drawing teams in the NBA, the salary cap that was adopted beginning in 1983–1984 was a "soft" cap, one that had a lot of flexibility to it. One provision of the cap permitted the top teams in terms of expenditures at the time-the Knicks, Nets, 76ers, Sonics, and Lakers-to continue to exceed the salary cap, but with frozen salary levels. Any team (including the above five) was allowed to exceed the cap to match another team's offer for one of its free agents.   And, if a team were over the cap and a star player retired, the team was allowed to replace the star by paying someone 50 percent of the retiring player's salary, even if this would violate the cap. These provisions, coupled with the predictable incentive effects of the cap, weakened the cap to the point that in the 1993–1994 season, every team in the league, except Dallas, exceeded the league-announced salary cap of just over $15 million per team!

All of this makes the point that the NBA salary cap was not the factor responsible for the big increases in attendance and TV income for that league between 1983–1984 and 1993–1994, because the cap didn't work to produce more-competitive balance in the league, which is the only way a cap could be expected to increase demand for the sport, and, hence, increase league-wide revenues. The cap did act to increase profits for NBA teams, of course, because the cap did keep a lid on player salaries, which certainly would have gone even further through the roof without it.

If the salary cap didn't produce the booming success of the NBA during the Reagan-Bush and Clinton years, then what did? The answer is that there was a big increase in demand for all of the major pro team sports during the 1980s and early 1990s, both in terms of ticket sales and in terms of TV revenues. The increase in demand was reflected back in the form of skyrocketing player salaries and franchise prices. To illustrate, major league baseball TV revenues went up from $80 million in 1980 to $625 million in 1992, the last year of CBS network coverage of baseball; and the most recent national TV contract continues that general trend.

NFL TV revenues rose from $167 million in 1980 to $1.092 billion in 1994. Major league baseball franchises increased in market value at the rate of about 20 percent per year during the 1980s, and NFL franchises had a slightly larger rate of increase. By 1995 the average baseball franchise was priced at around $110 million, and the average NFL franchise was priced at around $160 million. By way of comparison, in 1983, baseball teams sold for around $20 million each, and NFL franchises in 1983 were around $30 million.[4] No doubt the shift in demand in favor of pro team sports as a whole reflects primarily the basic demographics of the American economy, with the baby boomer generation, the first generation raised on TV, moving into the couch-potato age bracket, with TV-friendly spectator sports being the winners from this population shift.

The 1995 contract negotiated between the NBA and its union is a "hard" cap, comparable to that employed by the NFL. Under an enforceable hard cap, presumably all teams would be required by league rules to keep salary expenditures on players within narrow uniform limits, dropping the various exceptions that were a part of the NBA cap between 1983–1984 and 1994–1995. Assuming that a league can actually enforce a hard cap (a very debatable assumption, admittedly), what consequences can be expected to come from this, and are there any potential problems that a hard salary cap might cause?

To begin with, if a hard cap is enforceable and in fact is enforced by the league, the present pattern of high salary expenditures by strong-drawing teams and low salary expenditures by weak-drawing teams will be converted into a pattern where all teams spend essentially the same amount on player salaries. To the extent that the success of a team depends only on its salary expenditures, an enforceable hard cap would lead to something approaching equal competitive balance within a league. Each team could expect to have a winning season roughly half the time, and a losing season half the time; and league championships would be shared among teams on a roughly equal basis. The historical pattern of domination of league championships by teams located in the strong-drawing areas would end.

But, of course, the success of teams is not determined solely by what they spend on player salaries. Certain general managers and executives are paid six- and sometimes seven-figure salaries because they do a superior job of sizing up players and building a cohesive team. Coaches and managers vary in their ability to get the most out of a roster of players, and their inputs can be critical to a team's success. A salary cap applies only to expenditures on players, so it is to be expected that strong-drawing teams, with more revenue potential than other teams, will be in a better position to hire top general managers and coaches or managers. This will act to offset, to some extent at least, the equalizing effects of the salary cap, so that even though the salary cap is supposed to make all teams equal, strong-drawing teams can be expected to end up "more equal than the rest," even under an enforceable hard salary cap.

Presumably the same sort of argument used to justify a player salary cap could then be used to justify a GM-and coach/manager-type salary cap, although the antitrust implications would be much more chancy. In any event, the most highly touted benefit from the salary cap is an improvement in competitive balance within the league, which should in fact occur under an enforceable hard cap. We will look a little closer at this "benefit" later on.

A related benefit, according to owners, is that a salary cap increases the profitability of weak-drawing teams and hence reduces the possibility both of bankruptcy of such teams and of franchise movements. Owners have been calling "Wolf!" so long about potential bankruptcies that it is hard to believe that anyone takes this issue seriously; but for the record, the last major league baseball franchise to go out of business did so in 1900, when the National League downsized from 12 to eight teams. The old Dallas Texans of the NFL went belly up in 1952, and no NFL team has gone out of business since. In the NBA, the last two teams to go out of business were the Indianapolis Olympians and Baltimore Bullets, both of which died in 1954. The NHL has a more recent fatality—the Cleveland Barons, who went out of business in 1978, when the team was merged with the (then) Minnesota North Stars.

So far as profitability is concerned, *Financial World* 1996 estimates indicate that only three of the 30 NFL teams lost money in 1995, and nine of 28 lost money in 1994. Six of the 26 NHL teams lost money in 1995–96, but about a third of the teams were losers in the two previous seasons. *Financial World* estimated that roughly half of the MLB teams lost money in 1995, and the same would have been true in 1994 even if there hadn't been a strike. All NBA teams were estimated to be profitable both in the 1994–1995 and 1995–1996 seasons. Although the salary cap is certainly a factor in the profitability of the NBA, the data seem to indicate that a cap is no protection against incompetent management; the moves of the Rams from Anaheim to St. Louis, the Raiders from L.A. to Oakland, the Oilers from Houston to Nashville, and the Ravens from Cleveland to Baltimore (Cleveland at least got to keep the nickname "Browns") are all occurring under the newly promulgated NFL hard cap. But, having said that, an enforceable hard salary cap should improve the overall profit picture of a league by holding down salary increases, and weak-drawing franchises should benefit more than strong-drawing ones.

Those are the benefits. What about the downside problems that a salary cap causes? First and foremost, a salary cap creates enforcement problems for the league. Under a uniform salary cap, strong-drawing teams are spending less than what they would if they were free to maximize profits, and, generally, weak-drawing teams are spending more than the amount that would maximize their profits. Thus incentives exist for strong-drawing teams to cheat on the cap, by finding ways of spending more than is allowed under the cap to acquire and retain free agent star players; and weak-drawing teams will try to avoid meeting their mandated cap expenditures. Astute general managers look for loopholes in the rules, and "under the table" payments are not unheard of as well. The NBA's experience under its cap had led to a number of bitter controversies between the league and member teams, most involving payments above specified cap levels by strong-drawing teams. The NFL has only had its cap for two years, and the San Francisco 49ers have already employed one loophole to maintain its stable of star players, by front-loading contracts with payments in the year before the cap went into effect. The Deion Sanders signing by the Cowboys exposes another loophole in the form of signing bonuses. We can predict with virtual certainty that there will be lots of other innovative strategies employed to beat the cap requirements as NFL teams become more familiar with the new rules structure. Thus, the "hard" cap might very well turn out to be an illusion, at least in terms of its impact on the pattern of spending on players by teams.

A more critical enforcement problem arises for players. Under a cap, players are guaranteed a specified percent of total league revenues, but the players have no say in the decisions that determine what those revenues will be. Under the NBA cap, there has already been one prominent instance of underreporting of revenue by a league team, reportedly involving upwards of $100 million, and leading to a confrontation between the union and the league, before the underreporting was corrected. A potentially more important problem than outright cheating in reporting revenue is diversion of revenue away from the league. For example, Ted Turner owns the NBA Atlanta Hawks and the NL Atlanta Braves and also owns the Turner Broadcasting System; the Chicago Tribune Company owns WGN and also owns the Cubs; the Boston Celtics own their own TV outlet; and there are many other similar cases. Because TV revenues received by the league are split with players under cap arrangements, incentives are created for team owners with TV links to sign "sweetheart" contracts between their stations and their teams, shifting TV income from the team to the TV station or network. In turn, this reduces revenues received by the league, and hence the income of players, but profits are not reduced. Even if a team owner is not also a cable or TV station owner, he or she might work out a deal under which said owner sells the TV rights to games at a low price and gets a kickback in low advertising rates on the station for other products he or she is interested in. The potential under a salary cap for an erosion of the revenue to be shared with players is substantial, especially given the increasing importance of TV in the total revenue picture of leagues. This suggests that if salary caps are truly the wave of the future in pro team sports, player unions will be insisting on more say-so in negotiations between the league and its member teams and TV interests, and in other areas as well.

The cap has the possibility of creating major problems within player unions as well. There have already been problems in the NBA involving conflicts between the small group of superstars who earn in the millions per year, and the vast majority of union members who are at the union minimum or not much above it. The superstars are concerned with maintaining their negotiating strength under free agency; journeyman players are concerned instead with raising the minimum salary and with fringe benefits such as pensions and health insurance.

Data from all sports show that, under free agency, the distribution of income among players in a sport has become much more unequal, with the star players taking an increasing fraction of total player income. The boom in pro team sports during the free agency era has been a wave that has lifted all players to higher salary levels, which has helped to dampen potential conflicts within the union up to the present. Nonetheless, in the last NBA labor negotiations, star players publicly opposed the union's agreement to a hard cap but were outvoted by the rest of the players. With an enforceable hard cap, there is a fixed amount of money available to be spent on salaries by any team. The more that is spent to acquire a star player, the less is available to be spent on the rest of the team members. When the boom of the 1980s and early 1990s subsides, as it certainly will, so that allowable salary expenditures stabilize or actually decline, the inherent conflict of interest between stars and garden variety players is bound to intensify. Stars might be what generates revenue in a sport, but union decisions are on a majority vote basis, and every member of the union, whatever his salary, has one vote.

A predictable reaction over time to the salary cap is a move by unions toward bargaining designed to strengthen the economic position of the bulk of their members, even at the expense of sacrifices in the economic position of the superstars. However, the dynamics of a situation like this do not bode well for the survival of player unions. It might be that the hard cap can accomplish what many owners, especially in baseball, have been trying their best to do for years—that is, destroy the player unions.

Finally, let's return to the main perceived "benefit" of a salary cap, namely, an increase in competitive balance in a league by improving the playing strengths of weak-drawing teams relative to those of strong-drawing teams. If the cap is enforceable so that the increase in competitive balance is achieved, this is certainly a benefit to the owners of weak-drawing teams and to their fans, but is it a benefit to fans in general? There are economic arguments to the contrary.

Competitive markets, such as the player market under free agency, allocate resources such as players to their highest valued uses. In a free agency market, as an owner, if a player is worth more to me than he is to the other owners of teams, I will end up with the player because I can bid more for him than any other team can. If a weak-drawing and a strong-drawing team were equal in playing strength, the strong-drawing team should be able to outbid the weak-drawing team in acquiring star players. This is why, under free agency, strong-drawing teams tend to do better on the field than weak-drawing teams do. Moreover, strong-drawing teams are generally those teams located in the larger and/or wealthier metropolitan areas.

Under an enforceable hard salary cap, weak-drawing small-city teams end up with as good teams, on average, as strong-drawing large-city teams. In baseball, this would mean that, on average, the 1.6 million people in the Milwaukee area would have championships as often as the 6.0 million in the Philadelphia area, and half as often as the 19.3 million in the New York City area or the 14.5 million in the Los Angeles area (treating the New York and Los Angeles areas as two-team areas). A more reasonable goal, from an economic efficiency point of view, might be equalizing the average championships on a per-capita basis, rather than on a team basis. Thus it is not at all clear that moving toward equal competitive balance, as under a hard cap, is something that is desirable from the point of view of sports fans in total.

In fact, given the increasing role of playoffs and championships on national TV in league revenues, equal competitive balance carries with it potentially severe financial penalties for a league. A Minnesota-St. Louis World Series does not draw viewers and ad revenue, and bids for TV rights by networks, in the way that a New York-Los Angeles series does—and the same applies to all leagues. If hard caps actually do result in equalizing playing strengths among teams, incentives build up within a league for changing those or other rules to ones that favor the megalopolis teams, simply to increase revenue for the league.

After this extended look at what has gone on and what might be expected to go on under a salary cap, let's turn to the luxury tax currently being considered in baseball negotiations, something that has not yet been implemented in any sport league. In contrast to a salary cap, which specifies the amount that each team in a league spends on salaries, a luxury tax operates by imposing a tax on salary expenditures above a prespecified amount. For example, in the owners' proposal in November 1995, a team would be required to pay a 25 percent tax on salary expenditures exceeding $44 million. There is no minimum salary expenditure mandated under the proposal, so that teams are free to spend as little as they wish, in contrast to the salary cap format. However, the taxes collected by the league (together with a voluntary contribution of 2.5 percent of salaries by the players themselves) would be used to subsidize salary costs for the poorer league teams.

The first point to note is that, other than lump sum taxes, any tax, including the proposed luxury tax, automatically creates incentives for behavior designed to avoid the tax. Contracts can be restructured, salaries can be converted into pensions, players can be placed in lucrative off-field jobs—the possibilities are endless for creative lawyers charged with finding a way to maintain owners of strong-drawing teams in their current dominant and highly profitable situations. This means that there will be an enforcement problem under the luxury tax with respect to strong-drawing teams, just as there has been with salary caps.

And there will be problems with weak-drawing teams as well. We have heard a great deal of rhetoric about welfare fraud, about the negative work incentives that permeate the current welfare system. Under the proposed luxury tax, the haves will be taxed to subsidize the have-nots. This means that have-not teams in effect are taxed on improvements they make, because the better they do on the field and financially, the smaller the subsidy they receive. The tax-subsidy scheme acts to create disincentives for the weak-drawing teams to solve their own problems, in favor of relying instead on handouts from the stronger teams.

Another negative aspect of the luxury tax proposal is that, because there is no mandated minimum salary expenditure for teams, this makes it easier for teams planning a move to dump their high salaried players as they build a case for leaving a city because of "poor fan support" and be subsidized for doing this. The downsizing strategies of teams in the recent past, such as the Montreal Expos, Minnesota Twins, Pittsburgh Pirates, and San Diego Padres, indicates that this is not simply a theoretical notion.

Because no luxury tax has yet been implemented in sports, and because negotiations are still going on in baseball at the time this paper is being written, it is too early to determine just how drastic the changes would be if a luxury tax were instituted in baseball. As the saying goes, "The devil is in the details." The effects of a luxury tax can vary from the one extreme of no change from the situation that holds under present free agency rules in the absence of a tax to the other extreme of an effective hard salary cap. It depends on the level of salary expenditures that triggers the tax, and on the tax rate. Thus, if the salary level at which the tax kicks in is chosen high enough so that no team, acting to maximize profits, would reach that salary level, then the luxury tax leads to no change in salary spending by any team, and hence to no change from the current situation in either competitive balance or in player salaries. On the other hand, if the trigger level for the tax to apply were set at the salary cap level and a sufficiently high tax rate were assigned, then profit-maximizing teams could end up choosing to spend the same amounts that would be mandated under a salary cap. Table 7.1 gives the actual full-season salary expenditures by MLB teams for the 1994 and 1995 seasons, 1994 levels being adjusted to screen out the effects of the 1994 strike.

However, the owners are asking for a six-year agreement with the players. If salaries continued to escalate at 20 percent per year, then half or more of the teams would be in the luxury tax range within two years, and most of the teams would be subject to the tax before the end of the agreement, given the $44 million trigger level. Even at a 10 percent rate of escalation, half the teams would be subject to the tax in three years. Assuming that an agreement is reached by both sides to adopt a luxury tax, there certainly will be tough negotiations on the trigger level, the tax rate, the date for instituting the tax, and the use of tax proceeds to further competitive balance—the details of the final agreement.

Table 7.1
Player Costs by Team, MLB, 1994–1995

TEAM	1995	1994
FULL SEASON **Player Costs***		
New York Yankees	$ 58.0	$ 53.2
Atlanta Braves	54.5	49.4
Cincinnati Reds	52.6	46.4
Chicago White Sox	51.3	45.0
Chicago Cubs	46.9	36.3
Toronto Blue Jays	44.2	47.3
Seattle Mariners	43.2	31.9
Cleveland Indians	41.9	35.5
Colorado Rockies	41.1	26.5
California Angels	40.8	27.5
Baltimore Orioles	40.4	43.4
Texas Rangers	39.1	36.3
Boston Red Sox	39.1	40.7
San Francisco Giants	39.0	47.3
Los Angeles Dodgers	38.0	43.5
Oakland Athletics	36.4	38.7
Houston Astros	35.3	37.1
Detroit Tigers	31.0	46.1
St. Louis Cardinals	30.5	33.2
Kansas City Royals	27.0	45.6
Philadelphia Phillies	26.7	34.9
San Diego Padres	26.1	15.4
Pittsburgh Pirates	23.1	24.1
Milwaukee Brewers	21.6	27.8
Florida Marlins	21.0	21.9
Minnesota Twins	13.8	28.1
New York Mets	13.5	34.6
Montreal Expos	11.5	21.0
MLB Averages	$ 34.1	$ 36.4

* Data from *Financial World*, May 9, 1995, and *Los Angeles Times*, November 29, 1995. 1994 salary costs are those estimated by *Financial World*, assuming that the entire season had been played. 1995 salary costs are calculated from those reported by the Major League Players' Association.

One final note. Owners have been arguing for restrictions on the player labor market from the nineteenth century beginnings of pro team sports right up to the present, claiming that such restrictions are needed to maintain competitive balance in sports. In most cases, the competitive-balance arguments have simply been specious—for example, we now know, both from elementary economic theory as well as from the actual results in baseball, that changing from a reserve clause to free agency has no effect on competitive balance within a league.

In fact, the competitive balance problems that a salary cap or a luxury tax is designed to correct arise in the first place only because of the monopoly nature of sports leagues, along with the peculiar territorial rights that league teams enjoy under existing league rules. The imbalance in drawing potential among franchises can be corrected in large part by expanding the number of franchises in a sport located in the New York, Los Angeles, and Chicago metropolitan areas. This does not occur at present because of the effective veto power against invasion of their territories that is exercised by teams located in those areas.

A real breath of fresh air in pro team sports would result from using the antitrust laws to split up the existing leagues into competing leagues, each free to locate franchises where it wished. This would obviate any need for a salary cap or other kinds of restrictions on the player market, and, as a side benefit, would eliminate most of the subsidies from cities that teams currently obtain by exploiting their monopoly position. Expedients such as salary caps or luxury taxes are poor substitutes for old fashioned marketplace competition.

NOTES

1. In contrast, visiting teams in the NFL get 40 percent of gate receipts, visitors in baseball's American League get 20 percent, and baseball's National League visitors get five percent.   The National Hockey League has rules similar to those of the NBA.   As of 1996 no league provided for sharing of local TV revenues with visiting teams, and all leagues split national TV revenues among all league teams equally.

2. Attendance from *NBA Official Guides* (annual) (Sporting News); TV revenues from *Broadcasting and Cable*; salary figures are from the *New York Times*; franchise prices from James Quirk and Rodney Fort, *Pay Dirt: The Business of Professional Sports Teams* (Princeton, N.J.: Princeton University Press, 1992); profits and franchise prices from *Financial World*.

3.   Salary data for 1985–86 from Quirk and Fort (1992); data for 1993–94 from the *New York Times*.   See Rodney Fort and James Quirk, Cross Subsidization, Incentives, and Outcomes in Professional Sports Leagues,   *Journal of Economic Literature* 33 (September 1995): 1265–1299.

4. Historical figures on TV revenues and franchise values appear in Quirk and Fort (1992). *Broadcasting and Cable* publishes estimates of TV income for each league shortly before the league season, and *Financial World* publishes estimates of revenue, costs, profits, and franchise values for all teams, in an issue that appears in the late spring each year.

8

Increased Revenue-Sharing for Major League Baseball?

Lawrence Hadley and Elizabeth Gustafson

There is widespread sympathy in the major league baseball (MLB) community for increased sharing of revenues between the small- and large-market teams. The primary advocate is Bud Selig, MLB's acting commissioner and owner of the small-market Milwaukee Brewers. He has many supporters. Most importantly, the supporters include all of the owners of small-market teams as well as many owners of teams in medium-size markets. Also, the members of the Economic Study Committee on Baseball (chaired by Paul Volcker) stated that "increased revenue-sharing is warranted" in their December 3, 1992, report (Aaron et al. 1992, 11).

Economists Roger Noll and Andrew Zimbalist have also voiced support for more revenue-sharing. In a study of MLB's financial health released by the Players' Association during the truncated 1994 season, Noll concluded that current revenue-sharing among teams is inadequate. Zimbalist (1992), in his book *Baseball and Billions*, states that the growing importance of local sources of revenue make sharing increasingly important to MLB. Indeed, it appears that just about everybody is in favor of greater revenue-sharing except for the owners of the large-market teams led by George Steinbrenner.

Current arrangements for revenue-sharing in MLB are limited. In the National League, visitors receive $.46 for each ticket sold; in the American League, visitors receive 20 percent of gate revenues. All revenues from national broadcasting are split equally among the 28 teams, but revenues from local broadcasting contracts are almost entirely the property of the home team.

In the summer of 1993 Bud Selig and Richard Ravitch (the owners' chief negotiator in 1993) encouraged the owners to agree on a plan to increase revenue-sharing. However, resistance from the large-market owners led to an agreement in January 1994 that made increased revenue-sharing contingent on the successful negotiation of a salary cap with the Players' Association. Players opposed the salary cap because it is expected to decrease salaries, and this caused negotiations to stalemate indefinitely.

In March of 1996 the owners offered a two-year interim revenue-sharing plan independent of a salary cap agreement. Players, who must agree to the plan before it can be implemented, are expected to find this plan less objectionable. Teams would contribute 22 percent of their ticket, local broadcasting, and stadium revenues after various deductions for expenses to a central pool. Teams with revenues below a certain level would receive money from the pool.

The initial discussion of increased revenue-sharing in 1993 focused specifically on revenue from local broadcasting contracts. Not only is this source of revenue unshared, but it is also a source of growing importance and of growing inequality. As the revenue-sharing talks between the owners proceeded, a subtle but important shift occurred. Sharing local broadcasting revenues between the small- and large media-market teams evolved into the sharing of general revenues between the small- and large-revenue teams. The 1996 plan includes ticket and stadium revenues as well as local broadcasting income.

There are many types of revenues, but the important analytical distinction to be made is between those that are fixed and those that are variable. Local broadcasting revenues are a good example of a revenue source that is typically fixed for the current season. A long-term contract between the local TV media and an MLB team sets a specific payment in exchange for local broadcasting rights. On the other hand, ticket revenues are a good example of a revenue source that is variable within a season. This source is very sensitive to the performance of the hometown team.

Most supporters defend increased revenue-sharing regardless of the type of revenue to be shared. These supporters commonly cite two reasons to justify increased revenue-sharing. First, supporters believe that greater sharing will improve competitive balance on the playing field between large- and small-market teams. Second, they believe it will protect the small-market teams from business failure and bankruptcy. On the surface, these appear to be good reasons. Common sense suggests that increased revenue-sharing will offset some of the inherent advantages of the large-market teams. This must be a good idea?

But sometimes common sense is misleading. Sound economic analysis can demonstrate that increased revenue-sharing is unlikely to alter the competitive balance between large- and small-market teams. It can also demonstrate that MLB teams currently are not at great risk for business failure. And if a few teams were to become at risk at some time in the future, there are preferable methods for dealing with this problem.

SHARING FIXED REVENUES AND COMPETITIVE BALANCE

Consider the first argument for increased revenue-sharing: improved competitive balance. The intuitive idea is that increased revenue-sharing will give small-market teams more money to pay higher salaries and thus hire a greater number of star players. This will lead to a more equal distribution of star players between MLB teams and therefore to greater balance in the competitiveness of small- and large-market teams on the baseball diamond.

Indeed, greater revenue-sharing will give small-market teams more money. But it is unlikely that the small-market owners will use this money to increase their payrolls via the hiring of additional star players. To understand this counter-intuitive argument, we must understand the basic reason that owners hire players.

Our analysis is based upon the proposition that profit is the primary motivation of all owners. MLB is a business, and owners are business executives first. Therefore, a player is hired with the expectation that he will generate profit for the business. This will happen only when the additional revenue from hiring a player is greater than the cost of the player—his salary. By this logic, owners will replace a journeyman player with a star player only if the new revenue generated by that star is greater than his additional salary.

The ability of a star player to generate new revenue depends partly upon the number of other star players on his team and partly upon the size of the market in which his team plays. Other things being equal, a star player will generate greater revenue for teams that play in large cities. But as Professor Fizel noted, a star player will generate less new revenue for teams whose rosters are already well stocked with stars. After all, one more star player added to a team with many other stars is not likely to produce much more excitement, not likely to produce many more team victories, and therefore not likely to generate much additional revenue for the team. In short, a star player is more valuable to teams that play in large cities and/or have few star players on their roster.

When a star player is available (either via trade or free agency), owners will estimate the expected new revenue that would be generated if they were to hire that star. The potential salary bid of each owner will be based on this estimate of new revenue. Other things being equal, the star will accept the highest bid and thus play for the team where he generates the greatest revenue. In this sense, a player's salary is primarily determined by his ability to generate revenue.

If we assume that stars are more valuable to owners in large markets (other things being equal), then we will expect these owners to frequently make higher bids for available stars than small-market owners. Thus, it is logical to conclude that large-market owners will hire more star players in the long run. It is also logical to conclude that this will give the large-market teams a competitive advantage on the playing field in the long run.

Of course, the large-market teams will not get all of the star players. A star's value to these teams decreases as their rosters fill up with other stars. At some point, the value of a star player to some small-market team will be greater than his value to large-market teams with many star players. Therefore, a small-market owner will sometimes outbid the large-market owners for a star player.

Now suppose that large-market owners agree to share local broadcasting revenues with small-market owners. These revenues are based upon long-term contracts, and their dollar values are primarily determined by the size of each local market. They will not change substantially during any given season. They are fixed.

As discussed here, owners' bids are based upon the new revenues that a player is expected to generate. A new star player cannot generate any additional revenue from a fixed source like local broadcasting. In the short run, fixed revenues do not change regardless of the number of stars on the team and regardless of the team's performance. Therefore, owners will not consider fixed revenue sources in making bids for new star players.

By the same logic, large-market owners will not consider any agreements to share their fixed revenues when making their salary bids for available star players. Hiring decisions will not alter the sharing agreements any more than they impact on the revenue source itself. The agreement to share fixed revenues with small-market owners is independent of the number of star players on the team, and it is independent of the performance of the team.

To be sure, the agreement to share fixed revenues will reduce the profits of the large-market owners. Less revenue means less profit. But they cannot replace these profits by cutting back on the number of star players they employ. Indeed, if they respond to the revenue-sharing agreement by releasing star players who generate more revenue for the team than their salary, then they will reduce their profits still further. In short, the profit calculations of large-market owners are not altered by the agreement to share local broadcasting revenue.

The same analysis applies to the hiring decisions of the small-market owners. As a result of the agreement to share local broadcasting revenue, they receive additional revenue. They receive this new revenue regardless of the number of stars on their team and regardless of their team's performance on the baseball diamond. Therefore, the salary bids of these owners will not change because of the sharing agreement.

In summary, the transfer of fixed revenues between large- and small-market teams is completely unrelated to any new revenues that may be generated by hiring additional star players. The impact of the star player at the gate, for example, is the same whether broadcast revenues are shared or not. Therefore, if an agreement were reached to share local broadcasting revenue, large-market owners would have lower profits, and small-market owners would have higher profits, but their decisions to hire star players would be unchanged. Therefore, the competitive balance between large and small-market teams would not be changed. In addition, the salaries of the players are not expected to change. Finally, this same analysis would apply to changes in the sharing of any fixed source of revenue.

SHARING VARIABLE REVENUES AND COMPETITIVE BALANCE

The alternative to increased sharing of fixed revenues is the increased sharing of revenues that are variable in the current season. The major sources of such variable revenues are gate receipts and concession stand revenues, which are both included by the owners in their 1996 proposal to increase revenue-sharing. Variable revenues could be shared more equally by contributing a percentage of them to a central pool or by altering the visitor's and home team's share of gate receipts.

Sharing variable revenues more equally is fundamentally different from sharing fixed revenues more equally. The dollar amount a team must share increases as the success of the team improves. More wins on the baseball diamond generates more variable revenues, which in turn means that more revenue must be shared. Therefore, a more equal sharing of variable revenues will reduce the value of a new star player to large-market owners. These owners do not keep as much of the new revenues generated by the star for themselves. More must be shared with the small-market owners. The result is that the large-market owners' salary bids for star players will be reduced.

With these lower salary bids from the large-market owners, it may appear that the small-market owners will be able to hire more star players and thus improve competitive balance. But the small-market owners also receive less new revenue when they hire a new star because they must also share a greater portion of their variable revenues with the large-market owners. So they also reduce their salary bids! These reduced bids from both the large- and small-market owners offset each other. As a result, no redistribution of star players between large and small-market teams is expected. However, we do expect the players' salaries to be lower because all owners are reducing their salary bids!

The basic reason for this result is that a greater sharing of variable revenues does not change the process by which these revenues are generated. The bulk of the stars currently play on large-market teams because this pattern results in the greatest revenues for all of the owners combined. After an agreement to share variable revenues more equally, the same distribution of star players will still generate the maximum revenues for the combined owners. All will benefit when the total they share is maximized.

The economic process that generates the revenue is not changed just because the revenues are now shared more equally. The relative number of fans and the relative interest in baseball between major league markets is still the same. More equal sharing of variable revenues does not increase the number of fans in Milwaukee and Kansas City, nor does it decrease the number of fans in New York City and Los Angeles. Therefore, the distribution of stars that generates maximum revenue is the same both before and after the agreement to share variable revenues more equally.

Our conclusion is simple. An increased sharing of variable revenues will not alter the distribution of the star players between the small- and large-market teams. Therefore, we expect that the competitive balance between small- and large-market teams will also be unchanged. (For a technical economic proof of these surprising conclusions, see Quirk and Fort 1992, 271-275.)

The only difference between sharing variable revenues and sharing fixed revenues is that players' salaries are reduced when variable revenues are shared more equally. All owners keep a smaller portion of the new revenues generated when another star player is hired. More of the new revenues must be shared, and the salary bids of the owners will reflect only the portion of revenues that they get to keep. For this reason, we expect that all owners would prefer increased sharing of a variable revenue over increased sharing of a fixed revenue.

Of course, players should be opposed to sharing of variable revenues because of the expected reduction in salaries. Because this effect is similar to the expected effect of the salary caps that the players so strongly oppose, we might expect players to also oppose the 1996 owners' revenue-sharing plan, which includes the sharing of variable as well as fixed revenues.

SHARING REVENUE AND BUSINESS FAILURE IN SMALL MARKETS

The second argument for revenue-sharing is the protection of the small-market teams from business failure and bankruptcy. One thing should be clear: An increased sharing of any revenue source has the potential to redistribute profits from the large-market teams to the small-market teams. If so, the market values of the small-market teams will increase, and those of the large-market teams will decrease. Thus, the risk of business failure in the small markets will be reduced. This is true regardless of the type of revenue that is shared more equally.

The reason that increased revenue-sharing alters profits, market values, and risk of failure in small markets is obvious. After increased sharing, small-market teams have more total revenue. As discussed earlier, they are unlikely to use these new revenues to increase their payrolls. In fact, if variable revenues are shared, the downward impact on salaries can be expected to lead to smaller payrolls. Increased revenues combined with no upward change in salary costs must result in greater profits. In turn, greater profits will make these small-market teams more valuable to prospective buyers.

It must be recognized that these expected changes in the market values of small- and large-market teams may redistribute wealth between the owners. Should the redistribution lower the profits of large-market owners, their vigorous resistance to greater revenue-sharing is understandable. They are simply guarding their wealth!

Large-market owners purchased their teams with the expectations of large-market revenues. The prices they paid for their teams reflected these expectations. In other words, they paid "large-market prices" for their teams. Increased revenue-sharing will take away part of the large-market advantage that they purchased and quite possibly part of their wealth. Should the latter occur, the market values of their teams will be reduced.

Few people have much sympathy for the wealth positions of baseball owners regardless of the size of their teams' markets. But if wealth is to be taken from some owners and given to other owners, there must be a reasonable justification. Wealth should not be arbitrarily confiscated and redistributed. The question of reasonable justification revolves around the issue of the current health of MLB, and in particular, the economic health of the small-market teams. Are these teams on the verge of bankruptcy? Do they need financial assistance in the form of increased revenue-sharing?

The popular press has suggested that the economic health of MLB has recently peaked and is now in decline. As a result, many of the small-market teams may be in deep financial trouble. Most often cited in support of this viewpoint is the evidence of declining TV ratings and the reduced values of MLB's two most recent national broadcasting contracts. Low profits are also widely reported by both small- and large-market teams.

But the evidence on profits is not convincing. Reported book profits can easily be distorted, and the suspicion is that such distortions are common practice in MLB (Smith and Norton 93, 1:6). Therefore, book profits are not the best basis for an informed judgment on the financial health of MLB or its particular franchises.

The ultimate test of the financial health of any business is its market value—how much is a buyer willing to pay? If MLB is financially healthy, then the market values of MLB franchises will grow at rates that equal or exceed the growth rates of comparable alternative investments. If MLB is unhealthy, then the market values of its franchises will stagnate or decline.

Between the late 1970s (the early years of free agency) and 1993, the market values of all MLB franchises skyrocketed. One good example is the Baltimore Orioles. This franchise was sold for $12 million in 1979, $70 million in 1988, and $173 million in 1993. The annual compound growth rate from 1979 to 1993 was 21 percent—a rate far exceeding that of most business investments.

The Orioles are not unique. Quirk and Fort (1992, 56) estimate that franchises sold and resold in the 1980s increased in market value at an average annual rate of 23.5 percent. This rapid growth rate makes the reports of low book profits suspect. Owners who have recently purchased a franchise have made a clear statement that MLB is a healthy industry.

Given this evidence on market values of MLB franchises, it is very difficult to justify redistribution of revenue on the grounds of the alleged financial distress of small-market teams. Recent history has demonstrated that there are buyers for these teams who are willing to pay higher and higher prices. If an owner of a small-market team believes that the business is not profitable, it is possible to "cash in the chips" for a handsome capital gain.

Despite this evidence, the owners of the small-market teams have been crying for a long time that their franchises are in deep financial trouble. Escalating salaries due to arbitration and free agency are identified as the cause of this problem. To emphasize their point, all of the owners willingly accepted a prolonged strike in 1994–1995. The stated purpose of the owners is to gain control over rapidly escalating salaries via a salary cap or a self-imposed luxury tax on excessive team payrolls.

Such behavior cannot be ignored. It is possible that certain small-market teams are experiencing financial difficulties. Recently, the Pirates were purchased at a price in the neighborhood of $85 million. This compares unfavorably with the $95 million paid for new franchises (Colorado and Florida) just four years ago. Certainly an organized franchise with players and a minor league system should be more valuable than a new franchise.

If there are financial problems in MLB, it is important to correctly identify the source of these problems. The overall economic health of MLB is probably not the source of the problem. It is unlikely that MLB's financial success over the past two decades has suddenly evaporated. Certainly the players' strike hurt attendance during the 1995 season, but strikes are not the norm. They come to an end. A new labor agreement will be negotiated. Eventually business will return to normal.

Signs that MLB is still healthy include its increased TV exposure via ESPN and the cable superstations as well as the future potential for increased cable TV revenues. Also, the dramatic increase of new stadiums in the 1990s, and the existing plans for the construction of more "baseball only" stadiums indicate a healthy industry in the long run.

The most likely source of any financial problems in MLB is the inability of particular small cities to support teams. This may be true of Pittsburgh, Milwaukee, Montreal, and possibly Kansas City. It does not appear to be true for Cincinnati, which is the smallest market with a MLB franchise. It would also appear that Seattle and San Diego have sufficient populations to support a MLB franchise.

The inclusion of Montreal on the "suspect list" highlights an underlying contradiction. The population of a city is not the only indicator of the city's ability to support a franchise. The local popularity of baseball also counts heavily. Montreal is much larger than Cincinnati, but it is a "hockey town"; Cincinnati is a "baseball town." Perhaps the problem in Pittsburgh (if there is a problem) is the popularity of football and hockey over baseball. In a closely contested National League championship series against the Reds in 1990, the Pirates could not sell all of the available seats in Three Rivers Stadium!

The proper conclusion to draw from all of this is that the financial problems of particular franchises should not be dealt with via increased revenue-sharing. This is a shotgun approach that will impact on many franchises that are not in need of financial assistance. And if it is done strictly on the basis of population, it will miss some of the franchises that may be in need of financial assistance. The inaccuracy of this approach coupled with the capricious transfer of wealth between owners makes revenue-sharing a clumsy and undesirable tool for solving this possible problem.

One alternative solution is the movement of MLB franchises from weak markets to new markets. There are several markets that could currently support new franchises, including Northern Virginia/D.C., Charlotte, San Antonio, and Mexico City. Certainly there are at least 30 markets in North America that can support healthy MLB franchises. Zimbalist (1992, 145–146, 173–175) believes there are at least 36 viable markets and perhaps as many as 42 over the next 10 years. Another possibility suggested by Professor Quirk is to allow expansion teams in large markets that already have a team. This will reduce their effective market size and bring them more into line with the smaller-market teams.

The movement of teams out of weak markets is a far more efficient solution than revenue-sharing because it is particular to the troubled franchise and it avoids arbitrary redistributions of wealth between the owners. In the 1970s, MLB was heavily criticized for allowing teams to move in seemingly random fashion. Loyalty to a city and its fans appeared to be ignored by profit-conscious owners. This criticism caused a reverse reaction in the 1980s and 1990s. Every effort has been made to keep teams from migrating to bigger and better markets. The San Francisco Giants is the latest example of an owner who was convinced to take a lower price from a local syndicate of buyers in order to keep the team at home (and away from Tampa/St. Petersburg).

Other things being equal, team loyalty to the hometown is a good thing. But other things are not always equal. Populations shift gradually over time. If MLB is to be successful, it must follow these shifts. To understand this, consider the retroactive application of a rule forbidding team movement back to 1950. If such a rule had been enforced over the past 45 years, MLB would still have two teams in St. Louis, Boston, and Philadelphia, and there would be three teams in New York City. Clearly, some migration is necessary in the long run.

There are a sufficient number of markets to support the current 28 teams in MLB. The active bidding for the four expansion franchises of the 1990s demonstrates this clearly. If there is insufficient interest to support franchises in Pittsburgh, Milwaukee, and/or Montreal, the optimal solution is to allow these teams to migrate to stronger markets. This approach is clearly better for MLB than subsidizing weak franchises from the pocketbooks of large-market owners. In the long run, MLB revenues will be greatest, and MLB will be strongest if and only if the franchises are located in the biggest and best markets.

CONCLUSIONS

There is little to recommend increased revenue-sharing! Supporters claim that there are two problems that will be solved by greater sharing—competitive balance and the financial problems of weak franchises in small markets. But our analysis concludes that greater revenue-sharing is not the answer to either of these problems. Indeed, these two "problems" may not even be problems. Competitive balance is not perfect in MLB. But it is not clear that perfect equality is the ideal. We estimate that in the 1980s, large-market teams had an advantage of 20 percentage points over small-market teams in the standings (.509 versus .489). This differential is sufficiently small so that a well-managed team in any market can expect to contend for championships with some regularity. Baseball's Economic Study Committee agrees with us that competitive balance is not a problem (Aaron et al. 1992, 18–19).

Even if competitive balance is judged to be a problem, increased revenue-sharing is unlikely to solve it. Our analysis demonstrates that if owners act like profit-maximizing executives, then more revenue-sharing will not lead the small-market owners to increase their payrolls by purchasing more star players.

Only if the small-market owners act like sports fans instead of business executives will increased revenue-sharing alter MLB's competitive balance. Sometimes this happens. The typical case is a new owner of a medium or small-market team. That owner is obviously rich, and is enthused about the prospects of winning a championship with the newly acquired team. For a while, lots of money is spent to hire more star players. The competitiveness of the team improves at the expense of the owner's personal pocketbook. Eventually, good business sense takes over, and many of the stars are unloaded. The long-term process of building a profitable winner from the ground up is begun.

One recent illustration of this phenomenon is Tom Werner and the San Diego Padres. He bought the Padres in 1990 and quickly built a contender. But by 1993, they were "good enough to be expensive, but not good enough to win it all" (Helyar 1994, 538). To the dismay of Padres fans, Werner unloaded most of his star players, and the Padres emerged as the most profitable team in MLB (Ozanian 1994, 50–59). The Houston Astros followed the same road several years earlier. Their success came from unloading their star players in exchange for high-quality prospects.

In the long run, the good business sense of owners is likely to dominate their sports-fan instincts when making their teams' personnel decisions. Therefore, the distribution of star players is likely to reflect the relative sizes of markets regardless of the equality or inequality of the revenue-sharing agreements. Because there is no way to make all of MLB's markets the same size, there is no good way to balance the competition in a perfectly equal fashion. Greater revenue-sharing is unlikely to generate greater balance. And if a few small-market teams find themselves on the verge of bankruptcy, it is better for MLB that they relocate. More-equal revenue-sharing is an inferior tool for dealing with the possible financial problems of a few small-market teams.

Small-market teams can compete! They often follow a different strategy than the large-market teams. Rather than hire a team of highly paid stars, small-market teams look to develop young prospects. The recent experiences of the 1990 Reds and the 1991 Twins prove that this strategy can produce a winner. At the other extreme, the New York Mets and Chicago Cubs have often proved that a team full of highly paid stars does not always produce a contender. To quote Peter Pascarelli, "Who is running a franchise matters much more than where the franchise is located" (Pascarelli 1994, 15).

REFERENCES

Aaron, Henry et al. 1992. *Report of Independent Members of the Economic Study Committee on Baseball* (December 3).

Helyar, John. 1994. *Lords of the Realm: The Real History of Baseball.* New York: Villard Books.

Ozanian, Michael K. 1994. The $11 Billion Pastime: Why Sports Franchise Values are Soaring Even as Team Profits Fall. *Financial World* (May 10): 50-59.

Pascarelli, Peter. 1994. Who Says Small Markets Should Keep Their Teams? *The Sporting News* (July 18): 15.

Quirk, James, and Rodney Fort. 1992. *Pay Dirt: The Business of Professional Team Sports.* Princeton, N.J.: Princeton University Press.

Smith, Timothy K., and Erle Norton. 1993. One Baseball Statistic Remains a Mystery: The Real Bottom Line. *The Wall Street Journal* 1 (April 2):6.

Zimbalist, Andrew. 1992. *Baseball and Billions: A Probing Look inside the Big Business of Our National Pastime.* New York: Basic Books.

9

Whither Baseball after the Strike of 1994?

James D. Whitney

As the baseball world slid farther away from the canceled World Series of 1994 and closer to an uncertain starting date for the 1995 season, owners appeared determined to implement a new player-compensation system. They proposed a modest amount of revenue-sharing between large- and small-market teams but only in conjunction with either a salary cap or a payroll tax set at very high rates. Players were equally determined to refuse a salary cap of any sort or any payroll tax high enough in their view to be functionally equivalent to a cap on salaries.

George Bernard Shaw supposedly once said, "If you laid all the economists in the country end-to-end, they still couldn't reach a conclusion." But when it comes to the present labor-management strife in baseball, there is a considerable amount of agreement among economists to the effect that in this dispute, baseball owners are right about the problem they face, but baseball players are right about the remedy. More specifically, the complaint on the part of owners that small-market franchises tend to face particular economic difficulties in the market for free agents is a complaint consistently backed by economic research. However, the owners' proposed remedy of a salary cap or luxury tax finds little support among economists. For over 25 years, economists have been recommending revenue-sharing among the owners themselves as sufficient to address the big-market/small-market disparity while avoiding the bad side effects of a salary cap. That remedy remains sufficient today.

Fans appear alienated from the entire affair, far removed from what they see as a high-profile dispute between some very rich workers and their even richer employers. Ironically, a large proportion of the working-class sports fans have expressed more hostility toward the players than toward the team owners who employ them. Fans see the players as a privileged lot who earn fantastically high salaries at their expense just to play a game that countless others would play for free. But fans do have a stake in the outcome of the dispute. For fans, greater revenue-sharing could be a step forward for baseball, but a salary cap or its equivalent could mean two steps back.

Baseball owners date their woes to the advent of free agency, ushered in with the 1976 season and culminating in 1994 with the eighth work stoppage since 1972. Team owners have criticized free agency ceaselessly as a cause of higher ticket prices, a threat to competitive balance, and—a new item on their list—an impediment to the owners' "right to cost certainty." These criticisms of free agency do not fare well under close scrutiny. The only clear and indisputable consequence of free agency is the stratospheric rise in player salaries. In 1976 the average player salary was just over $50,000. Adjusting for inflation, the equivalent salary in 1994 would have been slightly under $135,000. Players have done considerably better: Without their season-ending strike, they would have earned an average salary of $1.2 million in 1994.

The perception that rising salaries should translate into higher ticket prices is commonplace, understandable—and incorrect. It is also the longest-running lament of team owners: St. Louis owner August Busch lectured his players about the dire consequences of escalating player salaries back in 1969, well before the advent of free agency itself. That salaries and ticket prices should be closely linked seems sensible. But consider, for example, the case of Los Angeles Dodger baseball tickets. Between 1976 and 1994, while the average player salary rose from $50,000 to $1.2 million, Dodger tickets rose from an average price of $3.51 to $9.20, outpacing inflation by just three cents.[1] As advertised, Dodger baseball remains "the best buy in town." Ticket prices may vary at stadiums near you. Teams with small seating capacities have experienced upward pressure on ticket prices because of the sharp increase in fan attendance during the years of free agency. Likewise, teams that have improved their performance under free agency may have raised ticket prices to cash in on their fans' appreciation of their better-quality product. But ticket-price arguments based on the popularity or success of baseball teams under free agency illustrate the benefits of free agency, which is hardly what team owners have in mind when they try to use ticket-price evidence to criticize free agency.

The apparent link between salaries and ticket prices breaks down because baseball's former system affected only salaries, not ticket prices. Under the reserve clause, team owners could, with impunity, pay players less than they were worth in a free market. And that's just what they did. Some of the stories are shocking compared to what we see today. The Chicago White Sox earned the name "Black Sox" before they threw the World Series in the scandal of 1919; they got the name because team owner Charles Comiskey decided to make players pay for laundering their own uniforms, which they refused to do. Comiskey relented, paid for the laundry, and then took the money back out of the players' World Series bonuses. An extreme case, perhaps, but the exploitation of players under the reserve clause was systematic: Near the end of the reserve-clause era,

Gerald Scully (1974) published a study on just how underpaid baseball players were, reporting that players were paid only 10–20 percent of the money they earned for their employers. Even now, 45 percent of major league players, those with less than three years of major league service, labor under a reserve clause, and they account for just nine percent of total player salaries, earning an average just 10 percent as much as veteran players entitled to free agency (Aaron et al. 1992, 15).

But the reserve clause was not matched by any corresponding obligation of team owners to hold down ticket prices. Fans see the best baseball talent the world has to offer. That was true before free agency, and it is still true now. But is has also always been the case that one reason owners have been in the baseball business is to make money, so they have consistently charged fans as much as the market will bear. All free agency has done is introduce competition into the players' market, so now owners do have to pay players their market value, sharing more of the profits they have earned all along with the players they hire. Free agency does not mean higher ticket prices unless you think owners are more likely to charge us high prices to pay to someone else rather than to put the money into their own pockets. Nothing in the way we think about how business people behave suggests that should be true.

Consider the following scenario as an example. You own the San Francisco Giants, and Barry Bonds decides to play for your team. The Giants win more ball games. Fan support surges. You find that you can raise ticket prices and get richer, that is, until you reach $12 a ticket. Beyond that, fans stay home and your gate receipts drop. Learning this information, you have two choices: Charge what the market will bear and appear greedy, or don't and appear foolish. Depending on the agreement between you and Barry Bonds, you can pocket the extra income or pass it along to him. With the reserve clause, you keep it. With free agency, you don't. But fans pay full value either way.

The lack of a link between player salaries and ticket prices matters now because what hasn't gone up under free agency is not likely to come down with a salary cap. By and large, free agent salaries have come out of the pockets of team owners, and any salary rollback under a cap or luxury tax will return to exactly the same place. Fans should not expect to see a penny of it.

The owners' demand for "cost certainty" is the latest and lamest complaint on their list. Uncertainty pervades our own lives and livelihoods: from farmers who face uncertain weather to pharmaceutical firms who face uncertain experimental results, from Wall Street investors who saw the prices of their stocks collapse in October 1987 to Southern California homeowners who watched their home prices drop for half a decade after 1989. In pursuing cost certainty, team owners are pursuing the sort of financial security that the rest of us don't have, even though baseball owners are in a better position to cope with uncertainty than most of the rest of us. What distinguishes the owners' situation is that their uncertainty is generated entirely by the parties now lodging the complaint. The owners create their own costs by bidding against each other for star players.

The timing of the owners' complaint about cost certainty is also ironic, because the upward trajectory of player salaries may be on the verge of easing now that the broadcast revenue that financed some of the bidding wars has dropped. League expansion may ratchet up salaries for a while longer, but baseball management presumably took the impact of the expansion on salaries into account when charging the Colorado Rockies and Florida Marlins $95 million apiece as an entry fee.

The strong suit of the owners is their concern with competitive balance: the possibility that free agency will ultimately divide major league baseball into "have" and "have not" teams based on market size. So far, there is no evidence of less competitive balance during free agency than there was before it.

Nor does there appear to be any imminent threat to the financial viability of baseball franchises. Despite escalating salaries, franchise values rose sharply after the advent of free agency. The recent reduction of national broadcasting revenues has taken a toll, but expansion teams still ponied up $95 million apiece to enter the National League in 1993, and the small-market Giants fetched a $100 million price by buyers committed to keeping the team in San Francisco (Ozanian 1994, 54).

But as the data in Table 9.1 reveal, there are considerable revenue disparities between teams. The $56.2 million paid out in player salaries by the Toronto Blue Jays in 1993 exceeded the total revenues earned by 13 of the other major league teams. And nine teams paid more in salaries than the $43 million in total revenue received by the Pittsburgh Pirates. The greatest good for the greatest number suggests that it might not be inappropriate for teams in large markets to win championships more often than teams in small markets. Although it is difficult to know at what point revenue and salary discrepancies become "too great," it is certainly plausible that the sport as a whole flourishes best with exciting games and pennant races and that a case can therefore be made for promoting the competitive viability of small-market franchises.

Recommendations by economists that sports leagues address the financial disadvantages faced by small-market teams through more-liberal revenue-sharing arrangements date back 25 years. Baseball currently has exceedingly stingy revenue-sharing provisions. In football, visiting teams receive 40 percent of gate receipts. In baseball, visiting teams get just 20 percent of gate receipts in the American League, and as little as 46 cents per ticket (less than five percent) in the National League. Ironically, increased revenue-sharing would do more than just improve the financial viability of small-market teams; it would also serve to hold down player salaries. If the San Francisco Giants have to share 40 percent of the increased cash-flow they get from signing Barry Bonds, they clearly have a reduced incentive to pursue him so aggressively. Revenue-sharing should be increased for gate receipts and extended to include local broadcast revenues as well.

Table 9.1
Baseball Statistics: 1993

TOTAL PLAYER SALARIES					
Franchise	Franchise Rank	Revenue (million dollars)	Salaries as Revenue	Salaries as Percent	Salary Rank
NY Yankees	1	$ 107.6	$ 54.2	50.4	2
Toronto	2	88.4	56.2	63.6	1
Chicago Cubs	3	82.8	45.7	55.2	6
Baltimore	4	81.3	33.8	41.6	18
New York	5	80.8	46.0	56.9	4
Los Angeles	6	79.7	41.6	52.2	11
Atlanta	7	79.0	53.6	67.8	3
Chicago	8	78.8	41.3	52.4	13
Boston	9	77.5	45.2	58.3	7
San Francisco	10	69.1	42.3	61.2	10
St. Louis	11	64.8	24.8	38.3	22
Philadelphia	12	61.1	36.7	60.1	15
Houston	13	60.5	34.7	57.4	17
Texas	14	60.3	41.6	69.0	11
Oakland	15	60.1	37.8	62.9	14
Detroit	16	55.6	43.6	78.4	9
California	17	53.8	28.2	52.4	20
Cincinnati	18	52.9	45.9	86.8	5
Colorado	19	52.2	16.6	31.8	27
Kansas City	20	51.7	44.1	85.3	8
Seattle	21	50.7	35.3	69.6	16
Minnesota	22	48.9	30.9	63.2	19
Cleveland	23	48.8	18.5	37.9	25
San Diego	24	47.7	12.2	25.6	28
Milwaukee	25	46.3	27.8	60.0	21
Montreal	26	46.2	16.8	36.4	26
Florida	27	44.9	24.1	53.7	23
Pittsburgh	28	43.0	23.7	55.1	24
League Averages		$ 63.4	$ 35.8	56.5	

Source: Financial World, May 10, 1994.

Revenue-sharing has become more urgent in the present environment of lower national television revenues. The decline is one factor in the increase of player salaries as a share of total revenues from 46 percent in the late 1980s to 56 percent in 1993.[2] Even more important, national television revenue is subject to perfectly even revenue-sharing among teams, so its decline forces small-market teams in particular to look elsewhere for compensation.

The appeal to team owners of a salary cap or its equivalent as a rider to revenue-sharing is obvious. Estimates by economist Henry Aaron (1992, 9) indicate that a 15 percent salary rollback, which is about what the owners proposed in their 1994 offer, would result in a windfall gain for team owners that would add an average of $38 million to the franchise value of each team, a 40 percent boost to the average value of franchises sold between 1989 and 1992.

But for the remaining interested parties—that is, baseball fans and players—tacking a salary cap onto revenue-sharing is not only unnecessary but counterproductive. In 1993 the salaries of 22 of baseball's 28 teams were outside the owners' proposed band restricting salaries to between 84 percent and 110 percent of the league average. A salary cap is a formula not just for salary restraint but for salary compression. Moreover, a salary cap will likely amount to a direct assault on free agency and the increased player mobility that has accompanied it. Surprisingly perhaps, therein lies the rub for fans.

Some fans have lamented the increased mobility of players under free agency and might view this reduction in mobility as a benefit of the owners' proposal. But this makes free agency a scapegoat: Free agency simply requires team owners to express their appreciation with their checkbooks instead of contract shackles. True, the Pittsburgh Pirates lost Barry Bonds to free agency, but there was scant public mourning over his departure. The small-market Minnesota Twins, in contrast, retained Kirby Puckett. And even the tightfisted management of the San Diego Padres held onto Tony Gwynn.

More often, player mobility under free agency has been one of the system's principal benefits. The California Angels demonstrated that teams cannot build from the ground up with free agents. However, the judicious signing of free agents can turn teams around or round them out: The assistance provided by free agent Terry Pendleton in catapulting the 1990 last-place Atlanta Braves to a National League pennant in 1991 illustrates the point.

Free agents have also afforded baseball some of its most dramatic moments in recent years: free agent Reggie Jackson hitting four home runs in four consecutive swings for the New York Yankees in the 1977 World Series; free agent Jack Morris pitching a shutout for the small-market Minnesota Twins in game seven of the 1991 World Series to set the stage for local hero Kirby Puckett's tenth-inning home run; free agent Kirk Gibson, in the bottom of the ninth inning, hitting a two-out, two-strike, two-run home run for a Los Angeles Dodger victory in the first (and possibly decisive) game of the 1988 World Series; and free agent Mike Davis drawing a two-out walk off control expert Dennis Eckersley to extend the inning for Kirk Gibson. For every Gibson success there is a Darryl Strawberry failure, but that mix of exhilaration and frustration, anticipation and hindsight is part of the excitement generated by free agency.

A reasonable interpretation of the long-running stalemate is that large-market franchises tied revenue-sharing to a salary cap or equivalent in order to put themselves in a fail-safe position. Either the players accept a cap, and the large-city teams finance at least part of the revenue they share through reduced salaries, or players don't accept a cap, and the large-market teams can use player resistance as an excuse to abandon revenue-sharing. This interpretation provides an additional good reason for ending baseball's antitrust exemption. The exemption aids team owners in enforcing restrictions on franchise relocations, restrictions that insulate big-market teams and lock other teams into markets too small to support them. The potential threat of franchise relocation by small-market teams might make large-market teams more amenable to more-liberal revenue-sharing.

In theory, owners can buy and sell player contracts as easily as they can hire and fire players, and they did just that under the reserve clause. Connie Mack made his money by selling off players he developed with the Philadelphia Athletics. Yankee manager Casey Stengel routinely raided the Washington Senators for talent. And Red Sox owner Harry Frazee kept his theater productions afloat by selling Babe Ruth to the Yankees. But the pace was much slower before free agency. Management was sloppier. Teams stagnated for years, even big-market teams. In the Ken Burns baseball documentary series, the 1950s and 1960s were rated baseball's golden era, the era of legends such as Willie Mays, Mickey Mantle and Henry Aaron. The series narrator pointed out how ironic it seemed that fan attendance plummeted during the same era. But baseball during those years was less a game than a clinic. Two great continuities of the era were that the Yankees would finish first in the American League and the Cubs and Phillies would battle for the cellar of the National League. The sport was in the doldrums, and lackluster fan interest continued into the 1970s. The American League responded by adopting the designated hitter rule in 1973. One sportswriter even proposed that baseball switch to a tennis-style format: win a game by winning two out of three three-inning sets.

Then came free agency, and during a time span in which the population of the country grew by 16 percent, baseball attendance surged by 84 percent overall, or by an average of 55 percent per team.[3] Coincidence perhaps, but fans may find out otherwise if the owners prevail. Free agency has, after all, made baseball a year-round sport, extending much of baseball's strategizing and second-guessing into the off season. It has also increased the speed of hope, because a team coming off a lousy season is not doomed to field a lousy team again the following year. Free agency helped launch teams like the Atlanta Braves and Minnesota Twins from last place to first place in successive seasons—both in the same year (1991), and both for the first time in baseball history.

The owners' original plan for revenue-sharing plus a salary cap is a case in which half a loaf is better than the whole. A salary cap threatens to have a stultifying effect on exactly the kind of revamping and fine-tuning that have added to the excitement of baseball in recent years. It could turn teams into rather boring clones of each other, no team very much stronger than any other team, no team a clear champion for a year. But the owners may yet succeed in their objective of imposing a salary cap or its equivalent in the form of a prohibitive payroll tax. After all, players have accepted a cap at 64 percent of revenue in football and 54 percent of revenue in basketball. And with a 1994 median salary of $410,000 even many baseball players might see themselves as coming out ahead by chopping up a fixed salary pool in a way that steers more of the $1.2 million average salary in their direction.

But if the players can stand firm and persuade owners to proceed with revenue-sharing but scrap the salary cap, then fans could emerge the biggest winners from the 1994–1995 strike. Otherwise, the next Ken Burns baseball retrospective may reflect back on the free agency years as the true golden era of baseball.

NOTES

1. Player salary data for 1976: Major League Baseball Players' Association for 1994: *New York Times*. Dodger ticket price data for 1976: *The Official Baseball Dope Book*, 1976; for 1994: Los Angeles Dodgers published ticket price information.

2. Data source for 1980s: Aaron et al., 1992, 14; for 1993: Ozanian 1994, 52.

3. Data source: *World Almanac and Book of Facts*, various issues.

REFERENCES

Aaron, Henry et. al. 1992. *Report of Independent Members of the Economic Study Committee on Baseball* (December 3).

Aaron, Henry. 1992. *Supplemental Statement: Report of Baseball Study Committee* (December 3).

Major League Baseball Players' Association. 1985. Average Salaries in Major League Baseball, 1967–1986, (January 2). Mimeo.

New York Times. Various issues.

The Official Baseball Dope Book. St. Louis: The Sporting News. Various issues.

Ozanian, Michael K. 1994. The $11 Billion Pastime: Why Sports Franchise Values are Soaring Even as Team Profits Fall. *Financial World* (May 10):. 50–59.

Scully, Gerald W. 1974. Pay and Performance in Major League Baseball. *American Economic Review* 64 (December): 915–930.

World Almanac and Book of Facts. New York: Press Publishing Co. Various issues.

IV

THE ANTITRUST ISSUE

10

Why Baseball's Antitrust Exemption Must Go

Bruce Johnson

Of all the labor disputes to rack major league baseball (MLB) in the last 100 years, none can match the bitterness, destructiveness, and longevity of the 1994-1995 strike. Naturally, after the trauma of a World Series canceled for the first time since 1904, most fans want a scapegoat to kick. Some take aim at the owners' money-grubbing, shortsighted stubbornness. Others condemn the players' greedy, myopic inflexibility. Many blame both sides for caring more about their selfish interests than for the fans or the national pastime itself. As President Clinton said, the whole thing was a dispute among a few hundred people over a few billion dollars.

It's certainly hard to defend either side—both are greedy and stubborn. As a fan, I'm disgusted with the players and the owners. But as an economist I recognize that the centrifugal economic forces tearing the game apart are far larger than either the owners or the players. Until those forces are counteracted, we're likely to see the threat of strikes or lockouts every time the collective bargaining agreement comes up for renewal.

Baseball's problems arise from two, mutually reinforcing factors that predate anyone involved in the game today. First, the major leagues suffer from a fundamental design flaw that places too few teams in huge markets such as New York and too many teams in small markets such as Milwaukee. Second, the Supreme Court has exempted baseball from the antitrust laws. Baseball will never rectify the design flaw voluntarily, but if Congress were to lift the antitrust exemption, natural market forces would realign the major leagues and mitigate the underlying tension generating MLB's labor strife. Perhaps the best evidence for the effectiveness of eliminating the antitrust exemption is that players and many owners would hate to see it happen—despite the labor tranquility it would bring.

BASEBALL'S DESIGN FLAW

Since 1953, MLB has expanded its numbers from 16 teams to 28, and has seen 10 franchises move to new cities. The guiding principle behind the expansion and realignment seems to be to put one team in each major league city. The very largest metropolitan areas can have two teams each. As a result, at one extreme, New York has just two teams for its 19 million people, giving the Yankees and Mets an average fan base of 9.5 million each. At the other extreme, the Kansas City Royals and the Milwaukee Brewers have only about 1.6 million people in their home metro areas. Clearly, the Mets and the Yankees have a much larger potential market to tap than do the Royals and Brewers.

In the economics of professional sports, market size is everything. More fans translates directly into more money. In a bigger city, a team can sell more tickets at higher prices. The Brewers collected about $17 million from ticket sales in 1993. The Yankees, with a much larger fan base, took in $30 million even though Yankee Stadium stands in the Bronx, one of the nation's most infamous slums (Ozanian 1994, 52).

As lopsided as ticket revenues are, TV and radio really kill the Brewers in their economic competition with the Yankees. In 1993, from national and local TV and radio contracts combined, the Brewers collected about $21.5 million. Meanwhile the Yankees received $63 million from the media. The difference arose almost entirely from the Yankees' $40 million local cable TV deal (Ozanian 1994, 52).

The Brewers can never hope to catch the Yankees in media revenue. The Milwaukee metro area simply cannot match New York's potential audience, so Milwaukee TV stations cannot charge advertisers New York prices for commercials during Brewers games. Even if the Brewers broadcast their games in every media market in Wisconsin, their potential audience would only reach about five million.

Overall, the Yankees take in more than twice as much money as the Brewers each year. Neither the Yankees nor the Brewers are aberrations. All across the major leagues, teams in large cities tend to collect substantially more revenue than teams in small markets, even when large-market teams share their cities with other teams. None of the small-market teams such as Milwaukee, Cincinnati, or Pittsburgh can hope to compete on the bottom line with their rivals in New York, Chicago, or Los Angeles. They simply don't have enough people. It's an economic fact of life.

The disparity in market size, not the bad blood between owners and players, is the fundamental source of the labor strife undermining the game today. Very simply put, the richest teams in the biggest markets set the salary scale, making it extremely difficult for a small-market franchise to field a competitive team and still turn a profit.

Consider the sad—for Pittsburgh fans—case of the Pirates. In 1990 and 1991 Bobby Bonilla and Barry Bonds led the Pirates to two division titles and the best winning percentage in the National League. Yet as soon as Bonilla became eligible for free agency, the Mets lured him to New York for about $6 million per year. A year later, the San Francisco Giants seduced Bonds with an even higher salary.

It's not just that the Mets had the money and the Pirates did not. Bobby Bonilla was worth more in New York than in Pittsburgh because more people in New York were willing to pay to watch Bonilla play, both in the flesh and on the tube. The number of potential fans Bonilla could pull through the turnstiles and to TV sets in New York exceeds the entire population of Pittsburgh!

The only way for small-city teams to keep stars like Bonilla and Bonds is to pay big-city salaries. They can't afford to do so, but sometimes must. Three years before players become free agents, they become eligible for salary arbitration. In baseball's final offer arbitration, the arbitrator compares the team's salary offer and the player's salary demand to the salaries paid comparable players on other teams, including those in the biggest markets. He chooses the proposed salary closest to those of comparable players, with no regard to the economic impact on the team. Even if Milwaukee and other small-market teams never hire a free agent, binding arbitration forces them to pay big-market salaries.

True, owners in big cities moan and groan about exorbitant player salaries. Of course they do—they're only human. As profitable as it was for the Mets to pay Bobby Bonilla $6 million per year, they would have made even more if they could have paid him $4 million, or better still, $400,000. Only the teams in small markets cannot afford the $6 million salaries.

Teams in small markets have always had a hard time keeping stars because the best players have always been worth more in the largest cities. However, in the reserve clause era, before 1976, teams in small markets could benefit from the discrepancy. If the reserve clause were still in place, the Pirates might have sold Bobby Bonilla to New York for millions of dollars. Both teams would have been better off financially with Bonilla in Shea Stadium. Bonilla would have had no choice in the matter except to retire or play for the Mets for a few hundred thousand dollars a year.

Before free agency, small-market teams made a lot of money selling players to bigger markets. Connie Mack, whose Athletics shared Philadelphia with the Phillies, sold off such stars as Jimmie Foxx and Al Simmons. After they moved to Kansas City in the 1950s, the Athletics served as a virtual farm team for the Yankees, sending Roger Maris, Ralph Terry, and Bobby Shantz to New York. The St. Louis Cardinals, under Branch Rickey, developed many players in their farm system who went on to successful major league careers after Rickey sold them off.

In effect, the reserve clause resulted in a sort of revenue sharing between big and small markets. But free agency has killed that golden goose for small-market teams. When players move from small to large cities, their old teams no longer benefit.

And that's what caused the strike. The poor teams wanted a revenue-sharing scheme to replace the reserve clause. The rich teams resisted the idea but, recognizing the financial bind of the poor teams, proposed first a salary cap and then a payroll tax, both of which would force players to take substantially lower pay. In effect, the players would pay for the revenue- sharing, much as they did before 1976. But the players would have no part of it, and the great strike of 1994–1995 ensued.

Certainly the destructiveness and length of the strike owes much to the intense acrimony and distrust owners and players so obviously feel toward each other. But the oxygen feeding this fire was the economic gap between teams in big and little markets. Unless that gap can be bridged, baseball faces a future of continuing labor strife.

In most other businesses, natural market forces would eliminate the tension between small and large markets. But as long as MLB "enjoys" an exemption from antitrust laws, the market's corrective forces will be blocked.

BASEBALL'S ANTITRUST EXEMPTION

Some days even Hall of Famers screw up. Bob Lemon walked ten batters in one game. Tris Speaker was caught stealing three times in one game. Reggie Jackson struck out five times in one game.

As in baseball, so in law. One of America's greatest jurists, Oliver Wendell Holmes, had one of the all-time worst days in Supreme Court history in 1922 when he wrote the opinion in *Federal Baseball Club of Baltimore v. National League et al.* Ruling that baseball is not interstate commerce, Justice Holmes and the rest of the Court's starting nine said major league baseball is not subject to the Sherman Antitrust Act. The decision made no sense in 1922. Today, when the average player earns more than $1 million per year, the average franchise is worth more than $100 million, and MLB's total annual revenues approach $2 billion, the notion that baseball is not interstate commerce is ludicrous. Yet, several times since 1922, the Supreme Court has declined to rescind the antitrust exemption. In 1972 the Court charged an error to the Holmes team but said that Congress, not the Supreme Court, must correct it.

As Red Barber, the late, great play-by-play announcer for the Brooklyn Dodgers might have said, Justice Holmes's decision would seem to put MLB team owners in the catbird seat. Unfettered by the rules restricting other businesses, such as pizza parlors, grocery stores, or football teams, baseball teams appear perfectly placed to rake in the profits.

Many of them have indeed prospered, but ironically the catbird seat looks more and more like an electric chair. The antitrust exemption has set MLB's basic design flaw in concrete, with perhaps fatal consequences for the game. The exemption short-circuits the market's natural corrective forces that would otherwise close the gap between baseball's rich and poor teams.

The key to understanding the problem lies in understanding the difference between restaurants and baseball teams. Imagine what would happen if all of greater New York had only two pizza restaurants, one in the Bronx and one in Queens. People would line up for blocks to wait for tables. The restaurants would need huge fleets of cars to handle home deliveries. With no competition and high demand, a pizza meal would be pretty expensive.

Those pizza restaurants would earn a fortune—for a while.   Soon, clever entrepreneurs, and even some not-so-clever ones, would open pizzerias all over town. The new restaurants would force pizza prices and profits down, and pizza lovers would have many more options to satisfy their cravings.

Competition would destroy the monopoly power of the two original pizza restaurants. If a group of pizzerias tried to prevent competition, whether through collusion or coercion, they'd be violating the Sherman Act. If found out, they and their managers could be convicted of a felony, fined, and the managers imprisoned. That's not the only reason the pizza business in New York is competitive, but it doesn't hurt.

Now look at the New York baseball market. The Yankees in the Bronx and the Mets in Queens have the biggest metropolitan area in North America all to themselves. The Yankees in 1993 had the largest total revenue in the major leagues, and the Mets had the highest in the National League (Ozanian 1994, 52). They make large profits, too—a fact reflected in the estimated market values of the two teams: In 1994 the Yankees were the most valuable team in the American League, the Mets the most valuable in the National League.

Which brings us back to restaurants. If the Yankees and Mets played by the same rules as restaurants, they'd soon have plenty of competition. Teams like the Brewers or the Pirates might well decide to quit Milwaukee and Pittsburgh in favor of New York. The Mets and Yankees wouldn't make $25 or $40 million a year from local broadcasts for long because, with the Brooklyn Brewers and the Meadowlands Pirates, the competition to sell broadcast rights would drive the fees down. Ticket revenues would fall, too, as fans in New York could choose among four rather than two teams.

The effects of increased local competition in New York would extend far beyond the Hudson River. More teams would mean fewer fans per team.   Paying $6 million for a single player would no longer make economic sense. The salary scale throughout the major leagues would fall because New York teams would face markets effectively no larger than those of teams in much smaller cities.

But that won't happen. The Yankees can block any American League team and the Mets can block any National League team from settling within 75 miles of their home fields. Nor could a new league easily invade New York because the majors, through their own rosters and their minor league farm systems, control almost all the talent in America good enough to play professional baseball. The antitrust exemption may even allow the majors to legally blacklist for life any player in the majors or minors who jumps ship to play in an upstart league. Not many would willingly take such a chance.

So the giant metropolitan areas of New York, Los Angeles, Chicago, and San Francisco have only two teams each. Baltimore and Washington, together about the size of the San Francisco metropolitan area, have only one team between them. It is unlikely that Kansas City, Milwaukee, Cincinnati, or any of the other small cities in the majors will ever grow to rival the large metropolises. So is baseball doomed to a permanent division into the haves and have-nots, the bigs and the smalls? Yes, as long as MLB can flaunt the antitrust laws.

If MLB were to lose its antitrust exemption, it could no longer prevent teams from moving to more-lucrative markets that happen to be claimed by another team. The National Football League (NFL), which must obey the antitrust laws, tried and failed to stop the Raiders from moving to Los Angeles in 1982, previously monopolized by the Rams. The court ruled that the NFL's efforts to keep the Raiders in Oakland violated the Sherman Act. Because NFL teams share equally in all league media revenues, and they share ticket revenues much more equally than do baseball teams, football teams have less incentive than baseball teams to relocate. Lured by more-lucrative media money in bigger cities, several baseball teams would surely move if they were allowed.

After the dust settles from franchise relocation, New York and Los Angeles might have four or five teams each, Chicago three, Baltimore/Washington two. The major leagues could then expand, putting some teams back in smaller cities. With so many more teams fighting for market share in the biggest cities, teams in small cities could compete on the balance sheet as well as the diamond.

Sure, some small cities might lose their teams for good. Milwaukee, for instance, has a tough time supporting the Brewers, just as it had a hard time supporting the Braves and the franchise that eventually became the Baltimore Orioles. Those teams both quit Milwaukee earlier in the century. Even with three or four or five teams in New York and Los Angeles, Milwaukee might have trouble competing with the big boys. But some small cities will find keeping their teams easier. The breakup of the big market monopolies might be a lifesaver for franchises in Cincinnati or Seattle.

Without the antitrust exemption, big cities might get more teams even if existing teams stay put. No upstart league has challenged MLB since the Federal League folded in 1915, partly because major and minor league players must face the threat that an MLB blacklist would be found legal under the antitrust exemption. With a large pool of talent to draw upon, new leagues might spring up, placing teams in New York and the other large markets. Even with the exemption, the proposed United League hoped to begin play with teams in New York, Los Angeles, and the Baltimore/Washington area. If Congress lifts the exemption, the survival prospects of ventures such as the United League would improve a great deal.

Modern fans who began to follow the game after the 1950s might summarily dismiss the possibility of having multiple teams in some cities. They should not. Before 1953 half of all major league cities had more than one team, and New York had three. Not until the Browns (now Orioles), Braves, Athletics, Dodgers, and Giants moved out of their shared cities for new homes did that pattern change. The expansions of the 1960s, 1970s, and 1990s for the most part continued the new tradition of one team per city.

Even with three teams, New York was the most lucrative of all baseball markets, and its teams could buy the best players. From 1949 through 1956, all eight teams that won the World Series, and six of the teams that lost it, came from New York. The area could have easily supported more than three teams, as it certainly could today. Even though the balance on the playing field is more even today, the economic balance is still lopsided.

With the removal of the antitrust exemption, the natural market forces that regulate virtually every other industry would be unleashed. Teams would move to more-profitable locations, some of which happen to be occupied already. The tensions between small-market and large-market teams would diminish, or vanish altogether, because the large markets would effectively be so much smaller than they are today. If the market size for all teams were about the same, player salaries would fall to a level all teams could afford. All teams would find profits just as easy, or just as hard, to come by. There would be no pressure for revenue-sharing, or for salary caps.

Whether the complete removal of baseball's antitrust exemption would cure baseball's ills remains to be seen. But as long as major league baseball circumvents the market's natural, competitive forces by hiding behind the antitrust exemption, the national pastime will remain locked in a three-way struggle among rich teams, poor teams, and players. The prospects for long-term labor peace will be grim indeed.

REFERENCE

Ozanian, Michael K. 1994. The $11 Billion Pastime: Why Sports Franchise Values are Soaring Even as Team Profits Fall. *Financial World* (May 10): 50-59.

11

Preserve Baseball's Antitrust Exemption, or, Why the Senators Are out of Their League

William F. Shughart II

INTRODUCTION

When the upstart Federal Baseball League began play in 1914, the owners of the established National and American League teams aggressively tried to hold on to their players and fans. They bought up some of the new clubs, and they induced others to withdraw from the league. The actions the majors took to limit the Federal Baseball League's market opportunities ended in a private antitrust lawsuit, filed by the league's sole surviving franchise, that eventually wound its way to the Supreme Court. The Court's 1922 decision in *Federal Baseball Club of Baltimore* v. *National League*[1] carved out an exemption for baseball from the Sherman Antitrust Act of 1890, section 1 of which declares illegal "every contract, combination in the form or trust or otherwise, or conspiracy, in restraint of trade or commerce among the several States." In those innocent times of nearly a century ago, the justices held that big league baseball was not "commerce" within the meaning of the law.[2]

Baseball's antitrust exemption has been reconfirmed by the courts at every opportunity since.[3] Perhaps because of the deference accorded to the game by its status as the "national pastime", baseball's favorable treatment under the antitrust laws is unique among the professional sports.[4] There are, however, a large number of other industries and activities to which the courts or Congress have granted antitrust law exemptions over time, including banking, insurance, farmers' and fishermen's cooperatives, labor unions, political lobbyists, and, of course, "amateur" athletics.[5]

No one nowadays would argue seriously that Major League Baseball (MLB) is not commerce.[6] With franchise fees in excess of $100 million and player salaries not far behind, the big leagues obviously *are* big business. Coupled with fans angered by labor disputes, threats by owners to move their teams to larger markets, and defections of their local sports heroes to free agency, stratospheric numbers such as these seem to cry out for action of some sort before the game is forever destroyed.

The strike that ended the 1994 season was nearly the final straw. Threats have often been made before to scrap baseball's antitrust exemption, usually as part of a city's last ditch effort to keep its franchise from moving to greener pastures. But the demands for action became more urgent as the 1995 season approached. The players' union, fans, and sports columnists across the country called on Congress to play antitrust hardball to get the owners back to the bargaining table. Hearings were in fact held on the "National Pastime Preservation Act," a bill sponsored by New York's Senator Daniel Patrick Moynihan, among others, that would have brought MLB within antitrust's reach.

Amidst a great deal of uncertainty, spring training opened only slightly behind schedule in 1995. While most teams were inviting nonunion "replacement players" to camp, the Major League Baseball Players' Association (MLBPA) continued to press Congress for antitrust action in the hope of persuading the owners to withdraw the salary cap demand that remained the major obstacle to resuming play. Utah's Senator Orrin Hatch, an opponent of proposals to do away with baseball's antitrust exemption altogether but apparently believing that it would help force a settlement, introduced legislation in February 1995 to deny the owners the ability to assert the exemption for matters related to labor disputes. The strike ended before Congress could act, thereby moving baseball's antitrust exemption off the front burner for the time being. But the amount of money at stake, the large number of fans and local officials forced to live with the constant fear that their team will pull up stakes, and the resentment harbored by the losing cities when baseball's barons intermittently entice them with offers of expansion franchises mean that questions about the appropriateness of exempting the national pastime from the antitrust laws will surely be raised again.[7]

This essay aims to put this controversy to rest once and for all by arguing not only that baseball's antitrust exemption should be preserved, but that it should be expanded to include all other professional team sports as well. The argument stands on two legs. One is that those who support applying the antitrust laws to major league baseball are wrong to assume that the individual teams comprising a professional sports league can be thought of in the same way as the individual firms comprising an ordinary industry. In sports, the fundamental unit of analysis is the league, not the team, and for this reason antitrust is not an appropriate policy tool for regulating the business of baseball. Second, even if antitrust policy could in theory be effectively brought to bear in resolving baseball's perceived problems, as a practical matter the antitrust enforcement authorities and the courts cannot be trusted to apply the laws in ways that would improve the game or enhance the welfare of its fans.

ANTITRUST AND SPORTS

The antitrust laws are the basis of a public policy supposedly intended to strike at anticompetitive business practices that lead to lower production, higher prices, and diminished consumer welfare. These anticompetitive business practices can in theory be undertaken by a single firm—a monopolist—acting unilaterally or by two or more rivals who agree among themselves to act in concert so as to approximate the output and pricing decisions of a single firm. In any case, antitrust policy rests on the premise that private markets often cannot be relied on to produce results consistent with the economist's textbook model of "perfect competition," which assumes that a market is served by such a large number of firms that no one of them acting alone can influence industry output or price.

A Concise History of Antitrust

American antitrust policy emerged at the end of the nineteenth century in response to the growth of the great "trusts" that came to dominate industries like railroading, oil refining, steel production, and meat packing. Under the leadership of "robber barons" with names like Rockefeller, Carnegie, Gould, and Armour, the trusts were created by establishing holding companies to buy up the shares of many of the formerly independent rivals in these basic industries. The trust's manager was then charged with the responsibility of coordinating members' production and pricing decisions so as to increase their joint profits. The standard historical view is that centralized decision-making by the managers of the trusts yielded smaller outputs and higher prices for consumers than would have been the case with free and open competition, each firm making its own production and pricing decisions independently of its rivals.[8]

Agricultural interests were particularly vocal in their opposition to the trusts and lobbied Congress to intervene. Farmers, it is said, saw themselves being squeezed between the falling prices they received for their own produce on the one hand and, on the other, the rising prices they paid for manufactured articles and the ever higher railway rates they were charged for shipping their crops and livestock to market. These complaints crystallized into the populist Granger and Alliance movements, which targeted the great industrial trusts as the leading source of the farmers' troubles. The passage of the Sherman Act, the first major American antitrust law, is thus seen as an important victory for agrarian interests over the forces of industrial monopoly.

Whether popular history rings true or not (and there are substantial doubts that it does),[9] antitrust is less concerned nowadays with the possibility of anticompetitive acts by large, single-firm monopolists popularly exemplified by the great steel and tobacco trusts of a century ago. This change in focus is based on a recognition that examples of private monopoly are exceedingly rare, especially so in a highly competitive global economy; that vigorous enforcement of the merger provisions of the antitrust laws can, at least in theory, prevent monopolies from being created in the first place; and, most important, that under open market conditions worries about the possible anticompetitive effects of one firm's unilateral actions are as a rule misplaced.

Antitrust has accordingly turned more of its attention in recent years to collusive agreements. In markets served by only a "few" large firms, each seller knows that its own pricing and output decisions will have a direct impact on the sales and profits of the others. The producers in such markets are interdependent, and recognizing their interdependence, they may be tempted to agree, either explicitly or implicitly, not to compete as vigorously as otherwise. Through various devices such as assigning exclusive geographic sales territories to particular sellers or adopting uniform price lists, the coconspirators can mutually limit their production and thereby increase their prices and profits at consumers' expense.

The run-up in world crude oil prices orchestrated by the members of the Organization of Petroleum Exporting Countries (OPEC) cartel during the early 1970s is a classic example of the consequences of collusion. Representatives of the member oil-producing countries, which controlled a substantial fraction of the world's proven reserves, were able for a time to create an artificial shortage of crude oil by collectively agreeing to limit their production. Drivers in those few countries like the United States that did not allow gasoline prices to rise proportionately and clear the market faced long lines at the pump and rationing by waiting.

McBaseball?

By ferreting out and sanctioning such price-fixing agreements among domestic producers, antitrust action can in theory maintain competitive market conditions, with all the benefits thereby implied for consumers. Herein lies the conventional wisdom for bringing the antitrust laws to bear on major league baseball. Clubs are "firms" from this point of view, big league baseball is the relevant "industry" or "market," and the national pastime's unique antitrust exemption has made it possible for the owners of these otherwise independent rivals to collude openly, collectively determining the number of teams in the league, the locations of franchises, the length of the regular season, and so on. The welfare consequences of collusion for the game's fans are thought to be essentially the same as those imposed on gasoline and heating oil customers during OPEC's heyday.

This analogy is false, however.[10] Although it is true that professional baseball franchises have separate names, separate owners, and separate balance sheets, in no meaningful sense are they independent business entities. Baseball franchises are *interdependent* in a quite fundamental way. In baseball, the relevant unit of analysis is the *league*, which from April until October competes for fans with a large number of other sports and entertainment events, both live and televised. No one club has anything to offer to this marketplace (except perhaps an old-fashioned barnstorming tour playing a haphazard schedule against local amateur or semipro teams) outside a league format with a mutually agreed to regular season schedule, a playoff system, and a World Series championship. The Detroit Tigers may have a separate identity for tax purposes, but they cannot produce much of anything of value unless they are a member of the American League and thus have access to a schedule of American League opponents.[11]

The interdependence fostered within the framework of a professional sports league confronts the owners of the individual teams comprising it with a peculiar economic problem. Clubs may compete against each other on the field, but off the field, they have no interest in running their rivals out of business. And because of this peculiarity, sports leagues have evolved elaborate systems of controls over such matters as player selection and compensation, revenue sharing, the number and location of franchises, and franchise ownership arrangements.

These control systems serve to help resolve a point of potential conflict between team owners. The welfare of a league is at a maximum when "competitive balance" prevails. Balance of this kind enhances attendance and television ratings across the league, making all teams better off financially than they would be under a situation of one- or two-team dominance and generally uninteresting competition between teams. By contrast, the welfare of Microsoft Corporation or any other ordinary firm is at a maximum when it succeeds in monopolizing its market by driving all effective competition from the field.

Put another way, a professional sports league is a joint venture of individual team owners. As in all other cases of jointness and shared responsibility, controlling free-riding is the basic economic challenge. If competitive balance is the key to a league's success in competition with its rivals in the entertainment market, franchise ownership will be carefully monitored and controlled. The incentive to limit free-riding would seem to explain the prevalence of provisions in league constitutions and franchise contracts requiring careful review of who can invest in league franchises, how many franchises there are, where the franchises are located, and so on. In these ways incumbent owners stand guard against the possibility that one of them will radically reduce the quality of his or her team by hiring cheap, low-quality players and losing lots of games, all the while sharing in the league's revenues from national television contracts and other jointly produced income sources.[12]

The recently held fire sale of San Diego Padres players, partly but not wholly based on the expectation that the league would soon adopt a salary cap, shows that free riding cannot be avoided entirely. The control systems adopted collectively by the owners do however help keep opportunistic behavior of this sort to its cost-effective minimum.

In many ways, then, the purposes and effects of the provisions included in the constitutions and franchise contracts of professional sports leagues are not fundamentally different from the restrictions imposed on franchisees by franchisors in more-ordinary industries. Control of free riding and quality assurance ("competitive balance")—and not the creation or extension of monopoly power—are the relevant considerations. Competition is not reduced in any meaningful sense when McDonald's limits the number of franchises it sells, determines where the franchises will be located, and exercises control over the business decisions of its franchisees by requiring them, among other things, to successfully complete an intensive training course at the company's "Hamburger University," to follow a cookie-cutter business operating plan, to purchase many of their inputs either from McDonald's Corporation directly or from lists of authorized suppliers, and, perhaps most important, to put some of their own capital at risk. Such restrictions, which purposely limit rivalry between McDonald's franchisees (*intra*brand competition), help promote *inter*brand rivalry between McDonald's franchisees as a group and the franchisees of Wendy's, Burger King, Kentucky Fried Chicken, Pizza Hut, and a host of other competitors in the market for fast food.

Though the courts have recently begun to recognize the efficiency benefits of exclusive territories and other restrictive provisions commonly included in franchise contracts, the history of antitrust policy in the United States suggests that the enforcement agencies and the courts get it wrong more often than not.[13] Even it this were not true, though, antitrust is simply not an appropriate policy tool for capping skyrocketing player salaries, for protecting the owners and fans of small-market clubs (including "historic" baseball franchises), or for forcing MLB to expand at more than a snail's pace.

ANTITRUST STRIKES OUT

Threats by at least some members of Congress to enact legislation repealing baseball's long-standing antitrust exemption, coupled with the owners' staunch opposition to it, represent tacit admissions that the sport generates substantial monopoly rents (profits). This conclusion is supported unequivocally by the whopping fees the backers of expansion clubs stand willing and able to pay for the right to field new major league baseball franchises. Some commentators have suggested that the owners of professional sports teams are driven more by the love of the game than by the love of profits (Demsetz and Lehn 1985), and, of course, the owners themselves have an interest in pleading poverty, especially when it is time to renew a stadium lease or to renegotiate a star player's salary. But it is highly unlikely that large numbers of otherwise successful businesspeople routinely pay franchise fees in excess of $100 million for the right to lose money.

Support for removing baseball's antitrust exemption is based on the idea that replacing collusion with competition between the National and American Leagues would eliminate the owners' existing monopoly rents. Competition would limit the owners to earning no more than a normal return on their investments by redistributing income from them to the players, to the television networks, and to other outside interests, including the backers of professional baseball franchises in cities that do not now have teams but think that they could support one (Quirk and Fort 1992, 298).

The Salary Cap and Expansion Controversies

Player salaries and league expansion are at the heart of the debate over baseball's antitrust exemption. Baseball's professional athletes, who are represented by a labor union that is itself exempt from the antitrust laws, clearly think that they would be major beneficiaries of legislative repeal of the *Federal Baseball Club* decision.[14] During the 1994–1995 strike, Donald Fehr, the executive director of the MLBPA, in fact said that his members would return to work immediately if such a law were passed.[15]

There is no doubt that removal of baseball's antitrust immunity would in the short run redistribute some of the game's monopoly rents from the owners to the players. Rather than triggering an immediate increase in salaries, which, after all, have in general been market determined since the era of free agency began in the late 1970s, this redistribution would work prospectively by allowing the players to avoid the imposition of a leaguewide salary cap that threatens to limit future pay increases. Antitrust charges, which raise the stakes in contract disputes considerably by providing for the recovery of treble damages, could be brought against the owners to prevent them from displaying a united front in labor negotiations. The MLBPA would thereby be free to bargain with the owners of one team, in much the same way representatives of the United Auto Workers selectively bargain with Chrysler, Ford, or General Motors, to hammer out contract language that would then serve as a model for subsequent negotiations with other teams.

The reasoning used by the owners to justify their salary cap demand has admittedly been quite weak (Goff and Shughart 1994). Central to the owners' position on this issue is the idea that "small market" teams in cities like Milwaukee and Pittsburgh cannot possibly compete for the skills of premium players when forced to bid against deep-pocket clubs located in New York, Chicago, and Los Angeles. The financial advantages enjoyed by the teams in big-city markets, with large population bases that generate lots of viewers for televised games and sellouts at the ballpark, require limits on player salaries in order to preserve the economic viability of teams in smaller cities. Otherwise, so the argument goes, the small-market clubs will be left in the unenviable position of choosing between bidding for free agents, thereby inflating their payrolls far beyond their revenue-producing abilities, or resigning themselves to being perennial cellar dwellers.

The owners have also argued that a salary cap is essential to maintaining competitive balance across the league. Without it, they say, the big-city clubs will use their deep pockets to stockpile all the best and brightest players, thereby positioning themselves to be pennant contenders year in and year out. This argument falls flat in the face of evidence showing higher turnover among baseball's championship teams since the onset of limited free agency in the mid- 1970s. It also fails as a matter of economic logic. Not all of the top free agents will be signed by the team with the deepest pockets. The third or fourth best shortstop in the league, for instance, is worth more—and will therefore be paid more—playing for a smaller market team than collecting splinters riding the pine in the Big Apple or the Windy City.

Whereas it is illogical to argue that a cap on players' salaries is essential to maintaining competitive balance, control over the number and location of franchises is critical to the game's welfare. Indeed, other than the players' obvious interest in securing an important advantage at the bargaining table, league expansion lurks in the background of the debate over baseball's antitrust exemption. The key argument here is that without their antitrust shield, the owners would move much more quickly to accommodate currently unfilled demands for new MLB franchises.

Professional sports league rules generally require that a three-fourths majority of the incumbent owners approve transactions involving either the sale of a new franchise or the movement of an existing one. Moreover, because each franchise is granted an exclusive right to the game within a designated geographic area around the team's home field (the exclusive territories overlap in the cases of two-team cities like New York and Chicago), until very recently owners could unilaterally veto expansion into their own territories.[16] Collective decision-making of this sort, it is alleged, slows the expansion process considerably as the incumbent owners drag their feet in order to protect existing monopoly rents.

Supporters of this idea point to the existence of a number of major metropolitan areas that have seemingly been bypassed by major league baseball. Some evidence in this regard is provided in Table 11.1, which, along with information on selected Canadian cities, shows the numbers and types of major professional team sports franchises located in the 40 largest U.S. metropolitan areas as well as two smaller markets. As can be seen, Washington, D.C., Phoenix, and Tampa are the only U.S. cities among the 25 largest metropolitan statistical areas without a major league baseball franchise.[17] (Washington's case is somewhat special in the sense that the Baltimore Orioles are located nearby, and perhaps because of this the Washington Senators have twice moved to new markets, once to Minneapolis-St. Paul and once to Arlington, Texas.) These cities have been particularly vocal in their complaints about baseball's slow expansion pace, but there are a number of other urban areas with populations of a million or more that could possibly support new professional baseball franchises. Denver, whose Rockies drew four million fans during their first season in the National League, serves as an example to backers in areas of similar size of the obvious pent-up demand for big league baseball.

Table 11.1
Major League Markets in the United States and Canada

	Population		Major League Franchises					
	#	Rank	NL	AL	NFL	NBA	NHL	Total
New York	19,34	1	1	1	2	2	3	9
Los Angeles	14,53	2	1	1	0	2	2	8
Chicago	8,240	3	1	1	1	1	1	5
Washington	6,742	4	0	1	2	1	1	5
San Francisco Oakland-San Jose	6,253	5	1	1	2	1	1	5
Philadelphia	5,893	6	1	0	1	1	1	4
Boston	5,455	7	0	1	1	1	1	4
Detroit	5,187	8	0	1	1	1	1	4
Dallas-Fort Worth	4,037	9	0	1	1	1	1	4
Houston	3,731	10	1	0	1	1	0	3
Miami	3,191	11	1	0	1	1	1	4
Seattle	29,710	12	0	1	1	1	0	3
Atlanta	2,960	13	1	0	1	1	0	3
Cleveland	2,860	14	0	1	0	1	0	2
Minneapolis	2,539	15	0	1	1	1	0	3
San Diego	2,498	16	1	0	1	0	0	2
St. Louis	2,493	17	1	0	1	0	1	2
Pittsburgh	2,395	18	1	0	1	0	1	3
Phoenix	2,238	19	0	0	1	1	0	2
Tampa	2,068	20	0	0	1	0	1	2
Denver	1,980	21	1	0	1	1	0	2
Cincinnati	1,818	22	1	0	1	0	0	2
Portland	1,793	23	0	0	0	1	0	1
Milwaukee	1,607	24	0	1	0	1	0	2
Kansas City	1,593	25	0	1	1	0	0	2
Sacramento	1,481	26	0	0	0	1	0	1
Norfolk	1,443	27	0	0	0	0	0	0
Indianapolis	1,380	28	0	0	1	1	0	2

Table 11.1 (continued)

	Population		Major League Franchises					
	#	Rank	NL	AL	NFL	NBA	NHL	Total
Columbus	1,345	29	0	0	0	0	0	0
San Antonio	1,325	30	0	0	0	1	0	1
New Orleans	1,285	31	0	0	1	0	0	1
Orlando	1,225	32	0	0	0	1	0	1
Buffalo	1,189	33	0	0	1	0	1	2
Charlotte	1,162	34	0	0	1	1	0	2
Hartford	1,158	35	0	0	0	0	1	1
Providence	1,134	36	0	0	0	0	0	0
Salt Lake	1,072	37	0	0	0	1	0	1
Rochester	1,062	38	0	0	0	0	0	0
Greensboro	1,050	39	0	0	0	0	0	0
Memphis	1,007	40	0	0	0	0	0	0
Jacksonville	907	46	0	0	1	0	0	1
Green Bay	180	N/A	0	0	1	0	0	1
CANADA								
Toronto	3,893		1	0	0	0	1	2
Montreal	3,127		0	1	0	0	1	2
Vancouver	1,603		0	0	0	0	1	1
Ottawa	921		0	0	0	0	1	1
Edmonton	840		0	0	0	0	1	1
Calgary	754		0	0	0	0	1	1
Winnipeg	652		0	0	0	0	1	1
Quebec	646		0	0	0	0	1	1
Total			14	14	30	27	26	111

A large measure of the support for revoking major league baseball's antitrust exemption in fact comes from the members of Congress who represent cities and regions with hunting for franchises. Legislative repeal of the *Federal Baseball Club* decision would, by weakening the owners' collective grip on franchise location decisions, facilitate team movement and expansion into areas where fans have long been denied a big-league team of their own.[18] This sword has two edges, though. Politicians representing existing big-league cities generally favor retaining baseball's antitrust exemption in order to keep clubs in place. Thus, conservative Republican Representative Henry Hyde, chairman of the House Judiciary

Committee, found himself agreeing—perhaps for the first time ever—with liberal Democrat Senator Carol Moseley-Braun, a fellow member of Illinois congressional delegation, that legislative intervention in this case would constitute "blatant favoritism" in behalf of baseball's labor union.[19]

The essence of the expansion controversy is that some business decisions that are profitable for the owners of one professional sports franchise may not be profitable for the league as a whole. Hence, although the backers of new major league baseball teams in some franchise-less cities are undoubtedly justified in perceiving personal profit opportunities in the team movement and league expansion activity that would follow the repeal of the game's antitrust exemption, the long-run consequences of loosening incumbent owners' control over the entry and location of franchises are lower league profits, lower player salaries, and lower fan interest.

These conclusions follow from recognizing once again that a professional sports league is a joint venture among the owners of the individual teams comprising it. Under current league rules, expansion is undertaken only when the amount the backers of a proposed new franchise are willing and able to pay for exclusive territorial rights is sufficient to compensate the existing owners for the losses they will sustain on account of adding another member to the league. The costs the incumbent owners bear when the league expands come in a number of forms. Most obviously, entry reduces each team's pro rata share of jointly produced league revenues such as those generated by national television contracts and sales of officially licensed MLB products. Travel budgets may be increased by the necessity of rearranging regular season schedules and, perhaps, realigning the league's divisions to accommodate the new member while preserving traditional rivalries.

Most important, though, expansion dilutes the quality of play throughout the league as athletic talent is spread more thinly (Scully 1995, 30–31). If fans value the absolute level of athletic talent fielded by sports teams and not just the competitive balance between them, then league revenues will decline as more teams are added to it.[20] Although the adverse revenue impact of declining quality of play may be partially offset by local fan interest in the new teams, it is also true that fans may be less loyal in a post-exemption era when players and teams can move more freely.

In short, expansion tends both to reduce the size of the league revenue pie and to serve smaller slices to each member of it. Downward pressure on league revenues translates into lower profits for owners and lower compensation for players. Ironically, then, though repeal of baseball's antitrust exemption promises to forestall a cap on salaries for the time being, big-league players will be worse off in the long run as the competitive market forces unleashed by the entry of new teams and new players reduce baseball's profits and pay to normal levels.[21] Given the lower quality of play and the higher turnover of players and teams thereby implied, it is not at all clear that baseball's fans will be better off. Indeed, the short-run benefits for players and expansion cities may well be purchased at the expense of the national pastime's long-run well-being.

What is to be made of the existence of a number of cities that apparently could support a big-league franchise but do not now have one? One possibility is that baseball's owners are simply exploiting their collective market power, restricting output and raising price like any other ordinary monopolist. This conclusion is reinforced by the fact that with many major league teams playing in publicly owned stadiums, there are obvious strategic advantages from having a few cities available to which clubs could potentially move. Such alternatives increase the credibility of threats to relocate a franchise, thereby allowing the owner to extract additional concessions from municipal authorities (Quirk and Fort 1992, 299).

Another possibility is that it is not now collectively profitable for major league baseball to expand beyond 30 teams. That is, even though the owner of an expansion club in, say Washington, D.C., could expect to make a profit based on the revenues and costs associated with exploiting an exclusive baseball franchise in that city, entry is not profitable when its impact on the rest of the league is taken into account. In other words, because baseball's owners can extract in the form of a franchise fee the present discounted value of the new franchise plus compensation for whatever losses the existing teams sustain when a new team is added, one must conclude that the league has already expanded into all locations consistent with the objective of joint profit maximization. Under this interpretation, backers in baseball-less cities must await further market growth or some other change in the underlying determinants of the optimal league size before expansion into their areas becomes worthwhile.

The debate over baseball's antitrust exemption is at bottom debate over who shall have the right to determine which of these two possibilities is the most likely explanation for the observed number and location of big-league franchises. Whose judgment should be trusted? That of baseball's owners, of whom whatever else has been said, have never been accusd of making less money when they could have made more? Or that of antitrust bureaucrats, lawyers, and judges, who frequently seem unable "to distinguish between competition and monopolizing" (Peterman 1975, 143)?

Antitrust Is Anticompetitive

Baseball and other professional team sports are classic examples of an industry structure known as "bilateral monopoly," wherein a single buyer of a product or service—in this case a league acquiring the skills of talented athletes—deals with a single seller of that product or service—a players' union. Unlike competitive labor markets, in which the forces of supply and demand create and enforce a single wage rate, in bilateral monopolies the firm and union negotiate within a range of wage rates that are mutually acceptable. The wage that ultimately emerges from the collective bargaining process depends on the relative negotiating strengths of the two sides. Wages will be closer to the upper end of the range when the seller has the upper hand; they will be closer to the lower end when buyers have the advantage.

Disputes between buyer and seller are part and parcel of bilateral monopoly. Although it is true that revoking one side's antitrust immunity will tip the balance in favor of the other, the experiences of professional hockey and football suggest that repealing baseball's antitrust exemption will not guarantee labor peace. What, then, do those who support repealing the *Federal Baseball Club* decision hope to accomplish? A temporary redistribution of baseball's monopoly rents from owners to players? A 40-team league? A third chance at a baseball franchise for our nation's capital so that federal bureaucrats and members of Congress are no longer forced to drive to Baltimore to see a game?

Answers to questions such as these are critically important in light of antitrust's systematic failure to promote competitive market conditions elsewhere in the economy. Though a survey of antitrust's failings is well beyond the scope of this essay, suffice to say that the weight of the evidence points to the conclusion that law enforcement activities in this area tend to protect not the interests of consumers but rather those of politically powerful special interests (McChesney and Shughart 1995).

The four-year-long antitrust investigation of Microsoft Corporation provides a recent example in this regard. Under the terms of a 1948 liaison agreement between the Federal Trade Commission (FTC) and the Justice Department's Antitrust Division (DOJ), the two agencies divide the antitrust enforcement market between themselves. Various industries are allocated to a particular agency—the oil industry "belongs" to the FTC and the steel industry to the DOJ, for example—and the other agency agrees not to compete in investigating any antitrust matter involving that industry.

Antitrust enforcement history was made in the summer of 1993, however, when the Justice Department began investigating Microsoft Corporation, arguably America's most successful company of the last decade. The FTC had been investigating Microsoft for three years, and its staff was eager to initiate legal action against the firm for alleged monopolization. Among other things, the commission's attorneys maintained that Microsoft had unlawfully foreclosed the market opportunities of rival software companies by entering into contracts with substantially all major manufacturers of personal computers that granted substantial discounts to them in return for agreeing to preload Microsoft's MS-DOS™ and Windows™ on all of their PCs. (More specifically, the computer manufacturers were required to pay a royalty to Microsoft on each PC shipped whether or not MS-DOS™ was actually bundled with it.) But the commission itself twice refused, on split votes, to issue a complaint. Following the FTC's second refusal to sue Microsoft, the Justice Department requested the FTC's files and began its own inquiry.

The FTC's investigation was in one sense unexceptional, exemplifying an historically familiar story of unsuccessful firms appealing to government for antitrust action that will handicap a highly successful rival. The investigation had centered particularly on the lack of success experienced by DR DOS™, marketed by Novell, Inc., a product that competed head-to-head with Microsoft's MS-DOS™. But the FTC's action was more interesting at another level: The Commission's failure to vote out a complaint was almost surely politically driven. President Clinton had not yet named a new chairperson of the Commission, and most of the commissioners voting on Microsoft were said to be seeking the nomination. But no one could discern the White House's position on the Microsoft matter. "Part of the commissioners' problem," one observer said at the time, "has been trying to divine what the administration wants to do" (Taylor 1993, 16)

The commission's inaction disappointed the droves of rival firms' lobbyists and lawyers who had patrolled the corridors of the FTC's headquarters building for months in hopes of getting a complaint against Microsoft. As their hopes faded, Microsoft's competitors turned to Congress. The DOJ's intervention in the Microsoft investigation occurred only after calls from Capitol Hill to Anne Bingaman, President Clinton's Assistant Attorney General for Antitrust. As the *New York Times* reported, "Because Ms. Bingaman's request for the FTC documents followed prodding by two senators, her action "does appear to have taken on a bit of the political aspect," Mr. [Charles] Rule said.   But if it's political, it's also bipartisan. Sen. Howard Metzenbaum (D., Ohio), chairman of the Senate Judiciary Committee's antitrust subcommittee, and Sen. Orrin Hatch, the ranking Republican on the full committee, both have urged Ms. Bingaman to examine the Microsoft case" (Davidson 1993, B8).[22] The *Times* did not report, though other publications did, that Novell's headquarters is located in the State of Utah, whose voters sent Orrin Hatch to the U.S. Senate. Utah is also the home of WordPerfect, Inc., whose closest competitor in word processing software is Microsoft Word™.

The Microsoft investigation illustrates how the rivals of highly successful firms can, working through their political representatives, use antitrust processes to subvert competitive market forces. Unfortunately for consumers, the Microsoft case is not an isolated incident in antitrust policy's long and checkered history. It follows that baseball fans should not look to the law enforcement authorities and the courts to protect their interests in present or future disputes between owners and players.

CONCLUDING REMARKS

Baseball is not an ordinary "industry" made up of "firms" with cute names like Braves, Cardinals, Tigers, and Yankees. In sports the fundamental unit of analysis is the league, not the team, and because of this antitrust is not an appropriate policy tool for regulating the business of baseball. Hence, there are good reasons beyond simple deference to judicial precedent (*stare decisis*) for continuing the antitrust exemption granted to the sport nearly 75 years ago. Indeed, because controlling free-riding among team owners is a problem common to professional sports leagues, the exemption should be expanded to include other major sports so that the owners of these teams too have broad discretion to collectively promote the on-field competitive balance needed to remain viable in a highly competitive sports and entertainment market.

In the short run, revoking baseball's antitrust immunity would redistribute income from existing owners to the players and to the backers of professional baseball franchises in cities that do not now have teams but think that they could support one. Herein lies the special-interest basis for legislative repeal of the *Federal Baseball Club* decision. The sport's active players and fans in cities hunting for franchises would gain by loosening the incumbent owners' collective grip over pay and franchise-location decisions. However, the uncontrolled entry of new teams (and perhaps new leagues) would in the long run dilute the average quality of play and put downward pressure on team revenues and player salaries. Hence, even though bringing baseball within antitrust's reach might force a solution to the sport's present woes, the victory would at best be temporary.

NOTES

Note: Thanks to Dan Marburger and Fred McChesney for helpful comments and to Tim Greer for able research assistance. Any remaining errors are my own.

1. *Federal Baseball Club of Baltimore, Inc.* v. *National League of Professional Baseball Clubs et al.*, 259 U.S. 200 (1922).

2. Writing for a unanimous Supreme Court, Justice Oliver Wendell Holmes reasoned that the transport of players across state lines "is a mere incident" to the business of conducting baseball exhibitions, which "although made for money would not be called trade or commerce in the commonly accepted use of those words" because "personal effort, not related to production, is not a subject of commerce." See *Federal Baseball Club of Baltimore, Inc.* v. *National League of Professional Baseball Clubs et al.*, 259 U.S. 200, 209 (1922). Dissenting in *Flood* v. *Kuhn*, 407 U.S. 258 (1972), at 287, Justice Douglas would later call this a "narrow, parochial view of commerce." Justice Kenesaw Mountain Landis, the Chicago federal judge first assigned to hear the case, subsequently resigned to become commissioner of major league baseball.

3. The controlling precedents are *Toolson* v. *New York Yankees, Inc.*, 346 U.S. 356 (1953) and *Flood* v. *Kuhn*, 407 U.S. 258 (1972). In both cases, the Court admitted that baseball's antitrust exemption is an "aberration," but one that had survived too long to be overruled. Moreover, because the "inconsistency and illogic" is of such long standing it must be remedied "by the Congress and not by the Court." See *Flood* v. *Kuhn*, 407 U.S. 258, 284 (1972).

4. In *The Washington Professional Basketball Corporation, Inc.* v. *The National Basketball Association, et al.* 147 F.Supp. 154 (S.D.N.Y. 1956), the court held that the NBA's attempt to block the purchase of the defunct Baltimore Bullets represented an unlawful conspiracy under the Sherman Act. Justice Douglas later stated flatly that "basketball . . . does not enjoy exemption from the antitrust laws." See *Haywood* v. *National Basketball Association*, 401 U.S. 1204, 1205 (1971). Then, in *Radovich* v. *National Football League et al.* 352 U.S. 445 (1957), a player blacklisting case, the Supreme Court ruled that the business of professional football is subject to the antitrust laws (Scully 1989, 27). Indeed, to avoid having *Federal Baseball* and *Toolson* cited regularly by defendants in other fields of business seeking to shield themselves from antitrust liability, in its *Radovich* decision the Court specifically limited the exemption established by those precedents to "the business of organized baseball." See *Flood* v. *Kuhn*, 407 U.S. 258, 279 (1972). The Professional Sports Telecasting Act of 1961 did provide a limited antitrust law exemption to the member clubs of professional sports leagues permitting them to pool their television broadcasting rights for the purpose of negotiating national TV contracts. The legislation also expressly exempted the merger of the National and American Football Leagues from antitrust scrutiny.

5. The courts have generally declined to interfere with the National Collegiate Athletic Association's (NCAA) broad powers to regulate college sports in the United States. In 1984, however, in a suit brought by the University of Oklahoma and the University of Georgia in behalf of the members of what is now known as the College Football Association, the Supreme Court ruled that in reserving to itself the exclusive right to negotiate television broadcasting contracts and in limiting television appearances by member institutions, the NCAA had overstepped the bounds of its authority by engaging in what amounted to an unlawful restraint of trade. But in writing for the Court's majority, Justice John Paul Stevens actually endorsed many of the NCAA's other restrictions, including those relating to the recruitment and payment of players, because of their importance in helping to "preserve amateurism" and maintain "competitive balance" in intercollegiate athletics. See *National Collegiate Athletic Association* v. *Board of Regents of the University of Oklahoma et al.*, 468 U.S. 85 (1984). For criticisms of the Courts view, see Gary Becker (1985) and William F. Shughart (1990).

6. "Baseball is today big business that is packaged with beer, with broadcasting, and with other industries. The beneficiaries of the *Federal Baseball Club* decision are not the Babe Ruths, Ty Cobbs, and Lou Gehrigs." *Flood* v. *Kuhn*, 407 U.S. 258, 288 (Justice Douglas dissenting) (1972).

7. Indeed, in the 20 years between *Toolson* and *Flood* v. *Kuhn*, 50 bills relating to baseball's antitrust exemption were introduced in Congress. Interestingly, the few of these that passed one chamber or the other would have expanded, not restricted, the antitrust exemption—at least inso-

far as it related to the reserve system—to other professional league sports. See *Flood* v. *Kuhn*, 407 U.S. 258, 282 (1972).

8. For a contrary perspective, supported by evidence that the production of manufactured goods in the industries dominated by the trusts was expanding faster than the economy as a whole (and that prices in most of these industries were consequently falling faster than the general level of prices), see Thomas DiLorenzo (1985).

9. George Stigler (1985), for one, considers the standard account of the origins of antitrust to be "gravely incomplete." Similar doubts are raised more recently in a number of the contributions to McChesney and Shughart (1995).

10. The following discussion is based in part on Fleisher, Shughart, and Tollison (1989).

11. "At the foundation of the business of one of these [baseball] leagues—in its primary conception—is a circuit embracing seven different States. No single club in that circuit could operate without the other members of the circuit, and accordingly in the very beginning of its business the matter of interstate relationship is not only important but predominant and indispensable." See *Federal Baseball Club of Baltimore, Inc.* v. *National League of Professional Baseball Clubs et al.*, 259 U.S. 200, 201 (Briefs for Plaintiff in Error) (1922).

12. The major professional sports differ considerably in the extent to which live gate receipts are shared by the home and visiting teams. For major league baseball, the mutually agreed-to formula provides for an 80-20 split in the home team's favor in the American League, whereas visiting teams in the National League receive 46 cents; it is 60-40 for the owners of NFL teams. Professional basketball's and professional hockey's home teams keep 100 percent of the live gate. National television revenues are generally shared by professional sports league members on a pro rata basis.

13. The leading precedent is *Continental T.V., Inc.* v. *GTE Sylvania, Inc.*, 433 U.S. 36 (1977). In the face of a declining market share in retail television sales, Sylvania had in 1962 phased out its wholesale distribution network and instituted a plan of selling directly to a smaller and more select group of franchised retailers. In the process, Sylvania designated Young Brothers, a San Francisco retailer located nearby one of its previously most successful dealers, Continental T.V., Inc., as one of its new exclusive franchisees. No longer authorized to carry Sylvania products, Continental sued, alleging that Sylvania's network of exclusive retail territories constituted a per se violation of the Sherman Act. The Supreme Court disagreed, however, deciding that Sylvania's actions had "no pernicious effect on competition." Indeed, it was the majority's opinion that such "restrictions help promote interbrand competition by allowing the manufacturer to achieve certain efficiencies in the distribution of his products."

14. Section 6 of the Clayton Act of 1914 expressly immunizes labor unions and their members from antitrust liability when "lawfully carrying

out" their "legitimate objectives." Strikes, boycotts, and other activities employed in the course of disputes "concerning terms and conditions of employment" are specifically exempted by Section 20 of the same law. In *United States* v. *Hutcheson*, 312 U.S. 219 (1941), the Supreme Court held that these two Clayton Act provisions, along with the Norris-LaGuardia Act's language prohibiting employers from obtaining injunctive relief in labor disputes, combined to shield the lion's share of union activities from the antitrust laws. Recognizing that it would be capricious to exempt labor union activities intended to force employers to the bargaining table without also exempting the agreement that resolves the dispute, the Supreme Court has also conferred a "limited non-statutory exemption" on the collective bargaining process itself. *Connell Construction Co.* v. *Plumbers Local 100*, 421 U.S. 616 (1975). See Areeda (1981, 110–112) for more details.

15. Political Hardball, *Sports Illustrated*, 21 November 1994, 14.

16. Recent court decisions have voided provisions in league constitutions giving individual team owners the power to veto expansion into their own territories, substituting supermajority (usually three-fourths of the owners) voting rules. See, for example, *Los Angeles Memorial Coliseum Commission* v. *NFL*, 468 F.Supp. 154 (C.D. Cal. 1979), 726 F.2d 1381 (9th Cir. 1984), 791 F.2d 1356 (9th Cir. 1986). The fact of the matter is that in spite of these court rulings, expansion can be blocked by one or at most a few league members (Quirk and Fort 1992, 300).

17. Perhaps to defuse opposition to the antitrust exemption, it was announced recently that major league baseball would expand into the latter two cities.

18. According to the *Washington Post*, Republican Senator John Warner offered to withdraw his support for a plan to repeal baseball's antitrust exemption in return for the promise of an expansion franchise for Northern Virginia. Senator Warner's vote was evidently not needed (Lipton and Maske 1995, B1). The story continues on page B7 with the headline, "Antitrust Could Hold Key to Virginia Baseball Team."

19. Political Hardball, (1994, 16).

20. Evidence that sports fans care about the absolute quality of play can be found in comparisons of attendance figures at minor league and major league contests, which typically differ by a factor of 10 or more.

21. Superstars will continue to be paid a premium that reflects the fact that some athletic talents are in short supply. Athletes are no different than other entertainers in this regard. In general, though, competition will reduce the size of this premium and, moreover, will drive the pay of average players down to levels approximating their opportunity cost (i.e., the value of their skills in the next best alternative employment opportunity). See Scully (1995, 30).

22. Charles Rule is a former Assistant Attorney General for Antitrust.

REFERENCES

Areeda, Phillip. 1981. *Antitrust Analysis: Problems, Text, Cases*, 3rd ed. Boston: Little, Brown and Company.

Becker, Gary S. 1985. College Athletes Should Get Paid What They Are Worth. *Business Week* (September 30): 18.

Davidson, Joe. 1993. U.S. Considers a Second Probe of Microsoft. *New York Times* (August 2): B8.

Demsetz, Harold, and Kenneth Lehn. 1985. The Structure of Corporate Ownership: Causes and Consequences. *Journal of Political Economy* 95 (December): 1155–1177.

DiLorenzo, Thomas J. 1985. The Origins of Antitrust: An Interest-Group Perspective. *International Review of Law and Economics* 5: 73–90.

Fleisher, Arthur A. III, William F. Shughart II, and Robert D. Tollison. 1989. Ownership Structure in Professional Sports. In Richard O. Zerbe, Jr., ed. *Research in Law and Economics* Greenwich, Conn.: JAI Press. 12: 71-75.

Goff, Brian L., and William F. Shughart II. 1994. Small Market is Big Farce in Salary Cap Battle. *Detroit Free Press* (December 18): 8E.

Lipton, Eric, and Mark Maske. 1995. Aide Says Warner Cut Deal for Baseball Team. *Washington Post* (February 23): B1.

McChesney, Fred S., and William F. Shughart II, eds. 1995. *The Causes and Consequences of Antitrust: The Public-Choice Perspective.* Chicago: University of Chicago Press.

Peterman, John L. 1975. The Brown Shoe Case. *Journal of Law and Economics* 18 (April): 81-146.

Quirk, James, and Rodney D. Fort. 1992. *Pay Dirt: The Business of Professional Team Sports.* Princeton, N.J.: Princeton University Press.

Scully, Gerald W. 1989. *The Business of Major League Baseball.* Chicago: University of Chicago Press.

———. 1995. *The Market Structure of Sports.* Chicago: University of Chicago Press.

Shughart, William F. II. 1990. Protect College Athletes, Not Athletics. *Wall Street Journal* (December 26): 6.

Stigler, George J. 1985. The Origin of the Sherman Act. *Journal of Legal Studies* 14 (January): 1-14.

Taylor, Stuart Jr. 1993. Will FTC Break Microsoft Corp.'s Near-Monopoly? *Legal Times* (July 19): 16.

United Nations. 1994. *1992 Demographic Yearbook.* New York: United Nations Publishing Division.

U.S. Department of Commerce, Bureau of the Census. 1993. *Statistical Abstract of the United States 1993.* Washington, D.C.: USGPO.

V

THE FUTURE OF BASEBALL

12

The Stadium Mess

Rodney Fort

INTRODUCTION

Previous essays in this volume have shown just how it is that arrangements among Major League Baseball (MLB) teams help small-revenue market teams and, consequently, the league itself to prosper. (Another useful resource, but of a technical nature, is Fort and Quirk [1995].) Another important element in the survival of teams is the stadium deal. Indeed, as detailed below, the maintenance of individual team market power by MLB facilitates lucrative stadium deals. In another league, this has become so important that the NFL now has a special stadium fund in order to help the stadium have-nots.

That the stadium deal has become as important a part of operating revenues as ticket sales or local TV broadcast contracts cannot be denied. One popular source, the annual survey of team values in *Financial World*, lists the value of the stadium arrangement alongside other revenue sources. Every team in trouble demands a new stadium arrangement, if not a new facility. Saviors of financially troubled teams, since Peter McGowan bought the Giants, have announced that the stadium arrangement requires immediate attention. Unlike football, a tribute to the ability of MLB teams to extract increasingly lucrative stadium deals is that there has not been an MLB team actually exercise its threat to move since the Senators left Washington for Texas in 1972. Even the Giants, after quite a few years of failing to obtain public support, now have it and are about to finalize plans for a new stadium.

Although cooperative ventures between MLB owners and local governments are becoming more commonplace for new stadiums (a useful review of public involvement and dubious economic benefits is in David Swindell [1996]), current stadiums nearly all are entirely publicly owned.

But just as typically, MLB tenants enjoy nearly complete authority over the flow of revenues from such facilities. The usual observation is that stadiums become albatrosses around the necks of taxpayers, and a fair reading of the scholarly work in the area suggests just such a conclusion. The goal of this chapter is to explain just how this happens.

The stadium issue involves substantial amounts of public money. Benjamin Okner (1974) analyzed 30 publicly-owned facilities (out of the 53 total publicly-owned in 1970-1971) and found that 25 lost money, with subsidies to six of them exceeding $1 million. He put the total subsidy at somewhere near $23 million ($59 million in base year 1982–1984 dollars). Quirk and Fort (1992) estimated the subsidies to 25 publicly-owned facilities (out of about 65 total publicly-owned for 1989) to range from $511,000 to $42.2 million. They put the total subsidy at about $500 million ($405 million in base year 1982-84 dollars). Based on these estimates, subsidies appear to have increased about sixfold in about 20 years. With current stadium costs nearer to $300 million, it is reasonable to expect that the size of these subsidies will continue to increase.

The discussion in this chapter starts by showing how it can make perfectly good sense for a local community to be happier subsidizing a stadium, even to the point of building it and handing it over to the team owners, than they would be forgoing a stadium and its benefits altogether. But there are two sources of problems along the way. First, by virtue of its monopoly power, MLB artificially restricts the number of teams competing for public stadiums. This stacks stadium negotiations in favor of existing MLB teams, and subsidies will be larger than if there were competitors seeking public subsidies. The second problem area appears when basic economics runs into local politics. Stadium decisions are made by elected officials, and the usual logic of collective action leaves every reason to believe that subsidies will be too large and paid by many who could care less about MLB. Thus, others who have blamed MLB market power for the current stadium messes are only partly correct (Fort and Quirk 1996; Ross 1989, 1991; Zimbalist 1992). Some thoughts on how these problems might be turned around appear in the conclusions.

THE COMMON SENSE OF STADIUM CONSTRUCTION SUBSIDIES

It can make very good sense for a community to fund a stadium either totally or in part. Typically, public involvement is thought to make sense if no private operator will be able to make enough money to make a go of it. This, in turn, depends on the revenues that a private operator can capture. The usual revenue sources include ticket and concession prices and fees for personal seat licenses, parking, and television rights. These revenue sources stem from benefits provided to direct consumers of stadium outputs. If these revenues prove sufficient, a private operator will find it profitable to provide the stadium. If not, then the public may be able to find justification for providing a subsidy or build the stadium itself. But there must be other benefits that are generated that justify such a decision. Otherwise, the public is in no better position than the private operator.

The first type of benefit that a private operator may not be able to capture is the economic impact generated beyond the stadium confines. Just as an anchor store in a mall will draw customers and, subsequently, new businesses around it, so will a stadium; pre- and post-game entertainment, restaurants, and lodging facilities. From the public funding perspective, it is important that this be *new* economic activity and not just relocation of activity that would have happened anyway somewhere else in the political jurisdiction. Unless a private operator can buy the land around the stadium, as must any mall operator or as Wayne Huizenga has in mind for his Florida sports/business complex, these are values that will not be captured by the stadium operator. But other mechanisms, such as taxes and user fees, are available to local governments that will allow part or all of these values to be collected and put toward covering the costs of providing the stadium.

The rest of the benefits provided by stadiums and their MLB tenants usually are referred to as "intangible" benefits in public debates. But they need not necessarily be intangible in the sense that some of them can be measured. One step removed from direct economic impacts are the so-called economic development benefits, that is, the value of being identified as a "major league" location. According to Wisconsin State Representative Marlin Schneider (*The Sporting News*, October 16, 1995, p. 5), "Without the Brewers, without the Bucks, without the Packers, we ain't nothing but another Nebraska." From the private operator's perspective, it is difficult to collect on this type of benefit that flows from stadium provision for two reasons. First, it is difficult to measure. One method would be to compare cities that are similar in other ways except that some have MLB teams and some do not and look at their growth rates. But there usually is not time for this type of evaluation, and even if a measurement is found, the second problem is just who should be charged over a potentially large geographic area, and how much, for the benefits they received. But these difficulties are less of an impediment to local governments collecting via taxes.

Finally, and much more difficult to measure, are the day-in and day-out benefits to members of the local community who may never even attend a game. There is, after all, a sports page in every local paper. When the local MLB team does well (or otherwise), it is the talk of the town even among those who may never attend a game. That these types of benefits are difficult (at best!) to measure does not render them beside the point or small in magnitude. Indeed, it is just this type of sentiment upon which the foundation of the demand for MLB is built and that leads each local citizen to make a decision about supporting subsidies to current MLB teams. Again, private operators cannot collect on these benefits provided by a stadium, but local government can.

The upshot of all of this is as follows. There will be revenues that a potential private operator can collect, but other benefits will be generated by a stadium and its MLB tenants for which a private operator can collect nothing. Even though revenues may prove insufficient for private operation, a public operator, with a broader ability to capture benefits through taxes or other collection mechanisms, can provide a subsidy that would make the stadium financially viable. Through a combination of pricing and other revenue-collection techniques that covers costs, the local community may find itself better off with a subsidized stadium and its MLB tenants than if there were no stadium at all.

Put another way, even if the best that publicly operated stadiums can do is operate in the red, they may well be worth it to local residents. Stadiums and their MLB tenants provide many benefits that cannot be measured strictly in terms of the revenues captured by stadium operation. If benefits enjoyed by those not party to stadium operation are large enough, subsidies are justifiable. Of course, the final decision about whether public money actually is spent on stadiums rather than other pressing social needs depends on how policymakers compare public desires for stadiums to these other activities.

Interestingly, public decision makers will find themselves facing many of the same thorny issues that would confront a private operator. A prime example of current interest is the "personal seat license," an off-shoot of the long-standing "donation" seating approach in college sports. The potential users of the stadium, of course, prefer their costs to be as low as possible and have reacted negatively to personal seat licenses (especially since, unlike the college sports case, they are not tax deductible!). But public operators must investigate all revenue possibilities, just as would a private operator, if they are going to economize on more general subsidy sources. If public operators can coordinate a "stadium builder" donation, or a one-time charge for lifetime rights to purchase season tickets, or a corporate sponsorship fee that also contains rights to buy season tickets, with the pricing policy of the MLB team tenant, then a stadium can become a viable proposition. At least, using these mechanisms, the subsidy from other public sources can be reduced.

Thus, if a private operator cannot make a go of it and the untaxed benefits from a stadium and its MLB tenant are in excess of the losses incurred by public operation, local residents may find that a subsidized stadium is worth it. But this statement also sets the boundaries for public involvement. Though it can be worth it for local governments to consider partial or total funding of a stadium or arena, the pricing and tax mechanism choices must be carefully chosen. It is crucial that users get to keep some of their excess willingness to pay under the price/seat license/tax combination that makes a public stadium financially viable. As a preview for the next section, if the collections exceed the benefits or if part of the subsidy is collected from those who receive no benefits, then the stage is set for a costly social result and opposition to the subsidy.

HOW STADIUM ARRANGEMENTS TURN MESSY

It is time to push the nice theory of the last section face-to-face with reality. Two factors practically guarantee that the price/seat license/tax combination that minimizes the public stadium subsidy will not come to pass. First, the subsidy negotiations between local governments and MLB teams occur in a setting where MLB artificially restricts the number of teams. Without any competing potential tenants, the current MLB tenant is in an advantageous bargaining position. It should be expected that the team will take advantage of this circumstance, driving subsidies up.

But, even if there were a large number of competing tenants, the second problem is that decisions are made by elected officials. Even a basic understanding of the political decision process recognizes that elected officials respond to constituency groups. Some groups will not like the size of the subsidy in the first place and will argue that it can be reduced if prices at the stadium are raised. The result is that fewer fans attend, they are less happy about it, and team owners will demand another round of subsidy concessions. In addition, elected officials may not collect the subsidy from users of the stadium and other beneficiaries, engendering hard feelings on the part of many taxpayers who could care less about MLB. Thus, contrary to views cited in the introduction, there is more to the current stadium mess than MLB market power alone.

But it is important to see how market power contributes to the stadium mess. Consider a world of competing major leagues. In such a world, teams in each league would be in competition over financially viable host cities. The result would be multiple bidders for the stadium services provided by any given locality. If one team pushed its host too far in its stadium subsidy demands, there would be another team bidding for the host city by accepting a lower, competitive subsidy. It is reasonable to expect that this type of competitive discipline would make the type of behavior currently observed by MLB teams a thing of the past.

The National Football League (NFL) provides somewhat a case in point. Through a combination of past antitrust actions and owner preferences, teams seem willing to move at the drop of a hat; they are willing to compete for different locations. This means that a given NFL host community can find a replacement for its current tenant, without waiting for expansion, if stadium negotiations go sour. The owner of the Rams has already filled a hole in St. Louis; the current Seahawk and Buccaneer owners appear willing to fill the hole in Los Angeles. Thus, when there is competition, cities have been able to cut overly-demanding NFL owners loose and find another team. In MLB, on the other hand, with its antitrust exemption and owners unwilling to replace an owner who threatens to move, cities have paid dearly and more often. In the absence of competition, a local government must deal with its current tenant or   lose a team   and hope it can compete in the next expansion round. Clearly, this leads to stadium subsidies in excess of the minimum amount that it takes to make a stadium viable.

Turning to how the incentives confronting local elected officials contribute to the stadium mess, subsidy critics will deplore its size. Even if support for the stadium is widespread, there can be any number of competing uses for the money. Observers of local politics would suggest that those with the most political clout will decry the subsidy when a possible redistribution away from stadium subsidization will further their other preferred causes. If politically potent enough, these groups can get their way—prices go up and the subsidy falls, freeing up money for other purposes. But when prices rise, revenues fall, and MLB team owners argue for even more. But with rising prices and a higher subsidy, popular support for the stadium declines.

It should be noted that subsidy supporters typically shoot themselves in the foot by overstating the value of the stadium. They typically chalk up the entire amount of economic activity to the stadium. But if a truck driver delivering popcorn to the stadium would deliver something else of lower value in town if the stadium were not there, it is only the marginal decline in activity that can be attributed to the stadium. If restaurants and bars move from the perimeter of town to downtown in order to be closer to the new stadium, this may represent no change in economic activity in the local jurisdiction. The proper measurement is value over and above economic activity that already would have occurred without the stadium. Detractors have a field day with consulting reports that dramatically overstate the benefits, and the public feels misled.

In addition, each side argues in offsetting ways about the "intangible" benefits of the stadium. Important progress is being made on analytical approaches to so-called "intangible" values in the area of contingent valuation, and as noted above, at least there are comparable situations that could be examined. But this never is done, partly because of the short-fuse ultimatum strategy employed by MLB owners and partly because there is a chance that the analysis would reveal that these values are small. Again, voters are left with nothing but rhetoric; supporters play up the intangibles, and detractors minimize the importance of such benefits.

In the typical way of local politics, then, the stage is set. Detractors emphasize only the costs, supporters overstate the benefits, and voters are left with little in the way of anything on which to decide. The results have been mixed, for baseball. Votes against stadiums for the White Sox and, only until just recently, the Giants and the failure of a stadium referendum in Seattle suggest a decline in support for subsidies. Nonetheless, contrary signals have arisen in Milwaukee and Cincinnati—both cities have approved new stadium construction.

And there is more. The idea in the last section was that users could be charged the extra costs of operation and government could collect a tax that would just make the stadium worth it. But the actual choice of tax mechanisms does not match this subsidy-minimum prescription. The variety of mechanisms ranges from hotel taxes, which collect from some MLB fans and non-fans alike, to more sales taxes and bond issues guaranteed out of the general fund. None of these taxes meets the suggestions of the last section, but politicians appear reluctant to impose such concentrated costs on sports fans. Apparently, they enjoy some political potency.

In summary, the market power position of the MLB tenant, coupled with the workings of the local political process, is destined to increase stadium subsidies above their minimum requirements. The MLB team is the only game in town, and the political support for its presence is practically guaranteed. Prices rise, or taxes rise, out of line with the original willingness to pay in order to satisfy MLB owners who threaten to move their teams if the subsidy does not increase. As a result, fewer people enjoy any difference between what they are willing to pay and what they have to pay. Losses from stadium operation increase, and taxes rise. Support for the stadium subsidy declines. Theoretically, the case where public operation can be worth it is clear. But there is little hope that the stadium situation will be anything but a mess given the market power position of MLB tenants and the political incentives of decisionmakers.

CONCLUSIONS

Given the description here, the verdict must be that stadium subsidies for MLB teams have not been worth it, to date. The superior bargaining position of MLB teams, derived from the fact that they are the only game in town, plus the political incentives that rule the decision, generate event prices and subsidies that are higher than required to cover stadium costs. However, that local stadium subsidies have ended up to be too large does not detract from the central idea that such subsidies can make sense. One needs to examine what would happen if events were priced to cover operating costs and taxes were used to cover the remaining fixed costs and debt service. If there is a combination that generates revenues to cover all costs, and enough benefit remains to engender public support, then public subsidies can make sense.

Many have argued that it is market power that is to blame, and they are partly correct. If there ever were competing major baseball leagues, the balance of power would swing away from a particular MLB team toward sports fans and other taxpayers. But observations about the political process and stadiums lead one to be less hopeful even if competition did occur. As long as politics rules the decision process, the outcome will not approach the lowest possible subsidy unless that is what the prevailing interest groups can obtain. It is more likely, and more typical, that vigorous opponents obtain price increases aimed at reducing the subsidy and political incentives lead to taxes on people who do not benefit at all from the presence of the stadium and its tenants.

But it does remain true that, after a stadium is in place, matters can be made better by injecting a healthy dose of subsidy-reducing competition into the process. Calls for antitrust intervention are not new, but the times may well be changing in favor of antitrust approaches. There is widespread dissatisfaction over the recent absence of the MLB playoffs and World Series, increased Congressional scrutiny of MLB expansion, and active state and local intervention into the recent moves of teams in the NFL. The time may be ripe for active antitrust enforcement of the classical variety, or a removal of MLB's antitrust exemption through Congressional intervention. On this point, Rivkin's (1974, 408) early view of the chances for antitrust enforcement in sports may well prove prophetic: "To the extent that organized athletics can maintain public respect, there will be little incentive on the part of either courts or Congress to force professional sports to conform to norms of behavior somewhat arbitrarily drawn from less noble realms of economic activity. On the other hand, whenever abuse of public confidence is clearly perceived and unambiguously substantiated, the barrier to external regulation will tend to fall away."

If nothing is done to encourage economic competition in MLB, the most reasonable prospect is more of the same. It seems these days that every city wants a sports team. The direct economic activity, eventual contribution to development, prestige, and civic pride associated with an MLB team's presence are proclaimed throughout the land. However, given the tight control over expansion by MLB, the quantity of baseball teams demanded exceeds the quantity supplied. In order to get a team, cities strive to prove themselves worthy by building a new stadium or renovating an old one. The best-known example is Tampa Bay-St. Petersburg, which spent (by some reports) $165 million on the SunCoast Dome in a failed attempt to obtain one of the expansion teams that began National League play in 1993 as the Rockies and the Marlins. The citizens of the area also failed to attract a team from among the White Sox, Mariners, and Giants but eventually were awarded the Devil Rays, which will begin play shortly. But at what cost? And at what cost into the future? Should the current mix of MLB market power and political incentives continue on into the future, the citizens of the area might well wish they had never been granted the franchise in the first place.

REFERENCES

Fort, Rodney, and James Quirk. 1995. Cross-Subsidization, Incentives, and Outcomes in Professional Team Sports Leagues. *Journal of Economic Literature* 33 (September): 1265–1299.
———. 1996. Introducing a Competitive Environment Into Professional Sports. Department of Economics Working Paper. Pullman, Wash.: Washington State University.

Okner, Benjamin A. 1974. Subsidies of Stadiums and Arenas. In Roger G. Noll, ed. *Government and the Sports Business.* Washington, D.C.: The Brookings Institution.

Quirk, James, and Rodney D. Fort. 1992. *Pay Dirt: The Business of Professional Team Sports,* Princeton, N.J.: Princeton University Press.

Rivkin, S. 1974. Sports Leagues and the Federal Antitrust Laws. In Roger G. Noll, ed. *Government and the Sports Business.* Washington, D.C.: The Brookings Institution.

Ross, Stephen F. 1989. Monopoly Sports Leagues. Minnesota Law Review 73: 643-761.

――――. 1991. Break Up the Sports League Monopolies. In Paul D. Staudohar and James A. Mangan, eds. *The Business of Professional Sports.* Champaign, Ill.: University of Illinois Press.

Swindell, David. 1996. Public Financing of Sports Stadiums: How Cincinnati Compares. *Policy Insight.* Dayton, Ohio: The Buckeye Institute.

Zimbalist, Andrew. 1992. *Baseball and Billions: A Probing Look inside the Big Business of Our National Pastime.* New York, N.Y.: Basic Books.

13

Baseball in the Twenty-First Century

Andrew Zimbalist

Baseball is more resilient than Richard Nixon and more durable than the Energizer Bunny. Try as it might, it cannot self-destruct. It will be around at least as long as the automobile. The question is not whether it will survive but in what form it will survive. Will it continue to ignore its mass fan base? Will it persist in blackmailing U.S. cities to provide new stadiums with multiple, novel revenue-generating accoutrements and concessionary leases? Will it be disrupted by work stoppages every four to six years? Will Major League Baseball (MLB) continue to benefit from its presumed blanket exemption to the country's antitrust laws? How fast will MLB expand? Will there be a salary cap, a luxury tax, salary arbitration or additional revenue-sharing? And so on. Without engaging the tools or vernacular of futurology, I will address a sample of these questions in this essay.

THE PRESUMED ANTITRUST EXEMPTION

Because most of the issues posed above will be shaped by MLB's antitrust exemption, it is logical to begin here. The starting point, however, must be to acknowledge some ambiguity in MLB's present circumstance. The last legal opinion proferred on this judicially conferred exemption was in August 1993 in *Piazza* v. *MLB*, when U.S. District Court (Pennsylvania) Judge Padova interpreted the Blackmun decision in *Flood* v. *Kuhn* (1972) to mean that only baseball's reserve clause (and not its cable television deals, franchise-location decisions, relations with the minor leagues, etc.) was exempt from the antitrust laws. This interpretation remains to be tested.

Assuming that the blanket exemption is upheld in the courts, is there any reason for Congress to modify or eliminate it? Anyone familiar with the history of the 1994–1995 work stoppage will answer this question in the affirmative. The Players' Association has long argued that the exemption prevents the baseball players from defending themselves in court if the owners unilaterally implement new labor market policies in restraint of trade. This vitiation of players' defenses has compelled more-frequent recourse to the strike weapon.

This is not just idle theory. In the spring of 1994, Don Fehr, head of the players' union, went to the owners and said that if the owners would pledge not to implement a salary cap during the next off-season, the players would pledge not to go on strike during the season. The owners were not interested. Fehr then went to the U.S. Congress and appealed repeatedly for a repeal of that aspect of the exemption dealing with labor market restrictions. Such a repeal would allow the baseball players, as had the football and basketball players before them, to take the owners to court if they attempted to institute a salary cap outside of a collective bargaining agreement. Fehr pledged to Congress that if this limited repeal were enacted, the players would abstain from striking during the 1994 season. By a close vote, the limited repeal bill failed to make it out of the Senate Judiciary Committee.

Of course, the repeal of the exemption would not guarantee labor peace in baseball; nothing short of a true partnership between players and owners could accomplish a stable labor peace. But a repeal or partial repeal would humble the owners a bit (possibly excepting Marge Schott) and give the players a concrete option other than a strike. Work stoppages would be less frequent. Further, lifting baseball's antitrust immunity would facilitate the formation of a rival league *inter alia* by making minor leaguers, the best alternative source of player talent, available to be drafted by a new league. Competition for MLB, something it hasn't had since 1914–1915, could only help. Among other things, it would promote expansion, and large metropolitan areas like Atlanta, Boston, or Washington/Baltimore may get a second team and larger areas like New York may get a third team. There could be no better solution for concerns about competitive balance.

Unfortunately, the U.S. Congress, which has been holding periodic hearings on baseball's anomalous exemption since 1951, is less concerned with reason and sound public policy than it is with political expediency. The issue is raised by members of Congress who are looking for a favor from MLB; after their parochial interests are attended to, the issue hibernates—until the next time. If the exemption is to be narrowed or lifted, it will have to be done in the courts.

EXPANSION AND PLAYER QUALITY

Some sportswriters have argued that however salutary it might be for stimulating fan interest in new geographical areas or promoting better competitive balance, expansion would cause talent dilution and ultimately reduce fan interest. Although it is true *by definition* that expansion will engender talent dilution, it is false that this will diminish fan interest.

In fact, the opposite will occur. To understand why this is so, it is necessary to explain the phenomenon of talent compression.

As demonstrated in Table 13.1, in 1995 the population-to-player ratio was 50 percent higher than it was in 1903, the beginning of the modern era of professional baseball. That is, a 50 percent smaller share of the U.S. population is playing major league baseball today than at the beginning of the century. Further, new groups have entered the game. Before 1947 no African-Americans played in the major leagues, and there were few Latin ball players. Today these two groups comprise over 35 percent of major leaguers. Moreover, the population today is healthier, more physically fit, and better trained in baseball-specific skills through the expansion of youth league baseball as well as the sophistication of high school and college baseball. Because major league ball players are a smaller fraction of an increasingly prepared population, the difference between today's best, average, and worst players is much smaller than it was 20 or 40 years ago. Unlike track and field records, which are based strictly on individual prowess and improve gradually over time, baseball performance statistics are the result of the balance of competing forces. Baseball's annual hitting and pitching records not only have not improved over time but with one exception they have not even been approached in recent times. The one exception dates back to 1961 and is tainted by an asterisk in the minds of most fans. There is no more compelling evidence of talent compression than a review of batting and pitching records and their dates of accomplishment. (See Table 13.2.)

Similar to today's batters, the great batters of yesteryear faced many strong pitchers, but they also faced a steady diet of weak pitchers not enjoyed by today's players. Likewise, the great pitchers of yesteryear faced many strong batters, but they also faced large numbers of weak batters.

Because the inequality among the players was greater during baseball's earlier years, the strong players were better able to take advantage of their weaker opponents and set baseball's long-standing records. With rare exceptions, the only yearly record that is challenged by today's players is stolen bases, and this accomplishment is more a function of individual prowess than it is an outcome of competing forces. In any event, it is this compression of baseball talent that today results in historical records not being challenged, and any baseball fan knows that this detracts from the game's excitement. Expansion would attenuate this problem, and the resulting absolute dilution of talent would be so negligible as to be imperceptible.

Table 13.1
Baseball Players and Population

Year	Major League Players	U.S. Population	Population/ Player
1890	480	63 million	131,250:1
1903	320	80 million	250,000:1
1995	700	263 million	375,000:1

Table 13.2
Performance Records

Category	Player	Year	Category	Player	Year
Batting Average			Doubles		
.424	Hornsby	1924	67	Webb	1931
.420	Sisler	1922	64	Burns	1926
.420	Cobb	1911	64	Medwick	1936
RBIs			Runs		
190	Wilson	1930	177	Ruth	1921
184	Gehrig	1931	167	Gehrig	1936
183	Greenberg	1937	163	Ruth	1928
Home Runs			163	Gehrig	1931
61	Maris	1961	ERA		
60	Ruth	1927	1.01	Leonard	1914
59	Ruth	1921	1.04	Brown	1906
58	Greenberg	1938	1.09	Johnson	1913
58	Foxx	1932			

THE BURDEN OF SALARY ARBITRATION

Salary arbitration is perhaps the most misapprehended among the institutions of baseball's labor market. Owners have claimed that salary arbitration forces them to pay for the sins of the most extravagant owner and that, despite a small majority of decisions made that select the owner's rather than the player's last offer since salary arbitration's inception, the owners always lose. These claims are misleading. The first claim overlooks the fact that if an owner does not want to live with an arbitration award, the player can be released. The only difference in outcomes between this and free agency is that there is no draft pick compensation if the player is cut loose. Not only is the value of a draft pick in baseball small, but the owner in arbitration retains the advantage of not having to bid against other owners. The second claim—that the owners lose, whether the arbitrator rules for one side or the other, because the player's salary always goes higher—ignores the context. From the early 1970s through 1994, baseball salaries were on a steady upward climb for all players, arbitration eligible or not. This impressive spurt in salaries was a product of the rapidly growing revenues in the sport and the phenomenon of catch-up as baseball's labor markets became more open. Further, arbitration eligibility occurs for players between two-plus and six years of service, a career span that is almost invariably associated with rising performance expectations for continuing players, and players whose cases reach the final arbitration stage generally have faster rising performance indicators than those who settle. Thus, the relevant question is not whether a player's salary goes up after arbitration, but how much it goes up relative to the player's performance. The suggestion that the owners go higher on their arbitration bid to avoid having the arbitration decision go against them and, therefore, the outcome is weighted in favor of the player, ignores the built-in symmetry of the process—that is, players lower their final bid in order to avoid losing the arbitration decision.

The real problem with salary arbitration is not related to the setting of salaries at all. Rather, it is in the process. By making the owners argue against the value of a player, it not only creates bad blood between ownership and the players, it prevents the owners from properly promoting the sterling athletic abilities of the world's top baseball players. In the arbitration case between the New York Yankees and Pat Kelly during the 1995–1996 off-season, Kelly's agent argued that the player possessed a popularity with the fans that went beyond his on-field statistics. The agent adduced as evidence the choice of *Yankee Magazine* to put Kelly's picture on the cover of one its issues. The lesson to ownership is clear: promote only those players who have reached free agency or whom you want to develop as trade bait. The National Basketball Association (NBA) has not had to worry about the salary implications of promoting its up-and-coming stars.

REVENUE-SHARING AND COMPETITIVE BALANCE

At the level of theory and in a world of certainty, there is little reason to believe that increased revenue-sharing from rich to poor franchises will alter the allocation of player talent across teams. This is because a player's value to a team is determined by the player's abilities, the other players on the team, and the economic characteristics of the team's market. It is not determined by how much money the owner has in his or her pocket. If Barry Bonds generates $10 million in revenues in San Francisco and this is known with certainty, then Peter Magowan should offer him anything up to this figure to play for the Giants.

The rub, of course, is that Bonds' worth is not known with certainty, nor is that of any other player. Indeed, with talent compression it is more difficult for the top players to stand out consistently, and the uncertainty of player performance is further compounded by pressure from media coverage and big money as well as more-frequent injury. Thus, uncertainty is a major factor and should not be assumed away by any analyst endeavoring to make sense of the game's economics.

After uncertainty is admitted into the equation, it becomes apparent why greater revenue-sharing could help promote competitive balance. Owners with only marginally profitable franchises will be less willing to incur the risks of paying out big salaries than owners with handsomely profitable franchises. If an expected superstar doesn't play well, then small-city franchises may face the prospect of appreciable losses. The owner of such a team, other things being equal, will be more risk averse, and the tendency will be for the superstars to go to the rich teams. Greater revenue-sharing would help provide a cushion to absorb some of the risk.

Naturally, revenue-sharing will not guarantee a more equal allocation of player talent. Some owners, a la Tom Werner, may simply decide to free ride, always a danger in team sports leagues when a sizable share of revenue is invariant to performance. However, just like the salary caps in the NBA and National Football League (NFL) have minimum as well as statutory maximum payrolls, it may be desirable to make revenue-sharing in MLB contingent upon meeting a minimum payroll standard. Alternatively, if a luxury tax on salaries is imposed and some of the collected revenues are shared with low-income clubs, then the tax might also be levied on payrolls that fall below a stipulated level.

Even with a contingency on revenue-sharing, the magnitude of the redistribution effect on competitive balance is uncertain. Nonetheless, baseball is not yet suffering from serious competitive imbalance. Although in normal times all of MLB's franchises are potentially profitable, the strike in 1994 and 1995 created serious losses in at least one-third of baseball's less advantaged teams. Together with growing inequalities from stadium revenues and other sources, the need to provide greater financial aid to these teams became pressing, and MLB finally agreed to introduce more revenue-sharing. The plan announced in Spring 1996 reportedly will provide between $3 and $5 million to the poorest clubs. Though this plan will help deal with short-run cash-flow problems, the longer-run significance may be that this policy signals the beginning of greater ownership cooperation and cohesion. It is the absence of this cohesion that has been at the root of most of the game's problems over the last 20 years.

FOOTLOOSE FRANCHISES AND MUGGING THE METROPOLIS

The last time a major league baseball team moved was in 1972. Contrast this with the NFL, which has seen the Rams, the Raiders, the Browns—and perhaps the Seahawks and Oilers—move in the last two years. Clearly, some of MLB's franchise geographic stability is connected to its antitrust exemption, and NFL Commissioner Paul Tagliabue has been pleading in Congress for lawmakers to grant football a similar immunity. MLB's immunity, under the leadership of acting Commission Bud Selig, enabled it to prevent Bob Lurie from moving the San Francisco Giants to Tampa Bay, but it hasn't prevented Bud Selig from threatening Milwaukee and Wisconsin that without a new stadium the Brewers would move to Charlotte. Even though the antitrust exemption may reduce the amount of litigation in baseball, it does not address the root cause of the problem, namely, the artificial scarcity of franchises. The fact that the NFL, the NBA, the National Hockey League (NHL), and MLB are monopoly sports leagues enables them to limit the supply of teams in their leagues below the effective demand for such teams from economically viable cities. This excess demand to host a professional sports team leads U.S. cities to compete against each other.

The tendency of sports teams to seek more-hospitable venues has been exaggerated in recent years by the advent of new stadium technology. This technology replaces the cookie-cutter stadiums of the 1960s and 1970s with single sport constructions that maximize opportunities for revenue generation from luxury suites, club boxes, concessions, catering, signage, parking, advertising, and theme activities. Depending on the sport and the circumstance, a new stadium or arena can add anywhere from $10 million to $40 million in revenues to a team's coffers. In fact, the economics of new stadiums can be so alluring that demographically lesser cities (e.g., Memphis, Charlotte, Jacksonville) with new stadiums can begin to compete with larger cities with older stadiums. Thus, the new stadium technology creates new economically viable cities and, thereby, exacerbates the imbalance between supply of and demand for sports franchises.

This imbalance, in turn, leads cities imprudently to offer the kitchen sink in their effort to retain existing teams or to attract new teams. The cities build new stadiums costing in excess of $200 million plus infrastructural expenditures and debt service obligations that often double the cost of the project. Furthermore, when the state government is involved in financially supporting the effort, it generally requires the approval of parallel pork projects elsewhere in the state to secure the necessary votes in the legislature. Frequently, the stadium lease is on such concessionary terms that the city cannot even cover its incremental debt service with rent and other stadium revenues. The public ends up paying for the stadiums, only to generate millions of extra revenue that inevitably is divided between higher player salaries and ownership profits.

This line of reasoning applies to all the professional team sports leagues, but it applies most forcefully today to the NFL for two reasons. First, the NFL relies less on regular ticket sales for revenue than the other sports because each team only plays between 8 and 10 home games each year. Smaller cities can fill a stadium of 60,000 eight times a year with relative ease. Further, in contrast to basketball, baseball, and hockey where less than 25 percent of total revenues are shared among the teams, in football this proportion rises above 75 percent. Thus, there are more potentially viable cities in professional football.   Second, because NFL teams must share 100 percent of their television, licensing, and marketing revenues as well as 40 percent of their gate, NFL teams have a powerful incentive to maximize stadium revenues, which are not shared at all. Although it might trouble Jerry Jones and some other owners, the NFL would be well served by sharing 40 percent of all stadium revenues.

It is a common perception that sports teams have an economic impact on a city that is tantamount to their cultural impact. This is wrong.   In most circumstances, sports teams have a small positive economic effect, similar perhaps to the influence of a new department store. First, individual sports teams are not big business. The average MLB team prior to the 1994–1995 work stoppage grossed $65 million. Compare that to the 1993 Effective Buying Income (EBI) for the metropolitan limits of St. Louis of $21.1 billion. An average MLB team would account for 0.3 percent of   St. Louis' EBI, 0.6 percent of Jacksonville, Florida's EBI, and just 0.05 percent of the EBI of the metropolitan limits of New York City. The average NFL franchise also has gross revenues of around $65 million, the average revenues in the NBA are approximately $50 million, and those in the NHL are closer to $35 million. In terms of permanent local employees, sports teams employ between 50 and 120 full-time workers, along with several hundred low-skill and low-wage, part-time and temporary stadium or arena personnel.

Second, economic studies have shown that most public stadiums and arenas do not cover their own fixed and operating costs. Operating and debt service deficits mean that city or state governments will have to levy additional taxes.   Higher taxes, in turn, discourage business in the area and reduce consumer expenditures, setting off a negative multiplier effect.

Third, virtually all independent economic research has confirmed a diminutive or negligible economic effect from the relocation of a sports team in a city.   For instance, Robert Baade and R. F. Dye (1990) looked at nine cities over the period 1965–1983 and found no significant relationship between adding a sports team or a new stadium and the city's economic growth.   In fact, they found that in seven of the nine cities, the city's share of regional income declined after the addition of a sports team or the construction of a new stadium.   Baade (1994) recently updated and expanded this study to include 48 metropolitan areas over a 30-year period (1958-1987) and found that in no cases did a new stadium have a statistically significant, positive economic impact on the city's growth and in three cases it had a negative impact.   Mark Rosentraub (1996) studied Indianapolis, which put forth an integrated sports development strategy in conjunction with a downtown redevelopment initiative.   The city was fortunate to be able to leverage only $436.1 million of its own funds to attract a total of $2.8 billion in private and public monies.   That is, the city paid less than one-sixth of the total bill. Rosentraub's study found that although the number of sports-related jobs increased, sports was too small a component of the local economy to have an appreciable impact.   Indeed, most of the employment growth was in low-wage services, and Indianapolis's share in the total county payroll actually declined from 1977 to 1989.   Economist Roger Noll and I are editing a book that includes several additional case studies that reach the same conclusion.

Fourth, dozens of studies have been performed by consulting firms under contract with the affected city or team.   Predictably, most of these studies have concluded that there would be a substantial, positive impact from adding a sports team.   The main methodological problem with these studies is that they do not account for or do not sufficiently account for the difference between new and diverted (or gross and net) spending. People have only so much income that they will spend on leisure and entertainment activities.   If they go to a ball game, it generally means that they are not spending the same dollars locally to go to the theater, to the movies, to a concert, to dinner, to rent a video, and so on.   That is, the dollar spent at the sports event usually replaces the dollar spent elsewhere in the local economy.   The net spending impact is nil.   The main source of net spending is out-of-town visitors to a ball game.   With a few exceptions, such as Baltimore or Denver, this number is usually small for professional sports teams. It consists primarily of the visiting teams and out-of-town media.

These same studies also tend to make favorable assumptions about the size of the area being impacted, the share of executive and player salaries remaining in the local economy, the interconnections between the sports team and the rest of the city's economy, and the terms of stadium financing as well as conditions of its lease.   Depending on the assumptions made, one can get wildly different estimates.   For instance, two studies were made about the impact of the Colts on the Baltimore economy in 1984.   One study found an impact of $30 million, and the other an impact of $200,000. The former estimate is wildly unrealistic, but even at such a level the benefits would have to be weighed against the costs of constructing, financing, and possibly maintaining a new stadium.

There have been at least two promotional studies on the economic impact of Camden Yards, one by the state Department of Business and Economic Development and the other by the Department of Fiscal Services. The former estimated benefits at $110.6 million with 1,394 jobs created and the latter at $33 million with 534 jobs created. Using a modest project cost estimate of $177 million, the cost per job created is $127,000 in the first study and $331,000 in the second. These estimates should be contrasted with the cost per job created of the state economic development program of $6,250 per job. Further, Camden Yards benefited from being part of the harbor redevelopment, from absorbing Washington, D.C. (the seventh largest media market in the United States) by its location off the interstate in south Baltimore, from being the first example of its architectural genre, and from housing a successful ball club.

Mayors, under pressure not to lose a city's historical franchise and cajoled by local contractors, unions, lawyers, hotel, restaurant, and real estate interests—among other political powers—tend to look favorably upon new stadium construction. They invoke images of city grandeur and new corporate headquarters moving to town. Although it is conceivable that some cities are on the threshold of recognition and a sports team could lift them over the hump, such an effect is highly speculative, and there is no case where it has actually taken hold in a significant way. Moreover, corporate relocations rarely occur to cities whose fiscal situation is deteriorating.

To the extent that (a) a new stadium is a central element of an urban redevelopment plan and its location and attributes are carefully set out to maximize synergies with local business and (b) the terms of its lease are not negotiated under duress and are fair to the city, then the city may derive some modest economic benefit from a sports team. The problem, however, is that these two conditions rarely obtain when dealing with monopoly sports leagues. Cities are forced to act hastily under pressure and to bargain without any leverage. Properly reckoned, the value of a sports team to a city should not be measured in dollars but appreciated as a potential source of entertainment and civic pride.

The last several years have witnessed the emergence of a movement for cities to resist the demands placed upon them by the monopoly sports leagues. Peter Magowan, owner of the San Francisco Giants, has floated a proposal to privately fund the construction of a new park in the downtown area. Some new financing schemes, such as PSLs and the sale of naming, concession, and pouring rights, can yield a substantial share of private financing, especially in cities attempting to attract a team for the first time. The 1986 tax reform, which eliminates the use of tax exempt bonds for stadium projects when more than 10 percent of the bond service is covered by private sources (e.g., stadium rent or luxury box income), has encouraged sweetheart stadium leases, instead of promoting its manifest purpose of reducing private appropriation of municipal privilege. It would be prudent for both teams and cities to anticipate that for aesthetic and economic reasons the Camden Yards/HOK design may begin to wear thin. The cookie-cutter stadiums of the 1960s and 1970s received enthusiastic reviews when they were built. Today they are scorned. The same fate awaits the old-fashioned ball park design of the 1990s. In short, the politics and economics of stadium financing are shifting, and it would behoove MLB to design a coherent and farsighted strategy to deal with the new environment and avoid the anarchy of franchise movements that the NFL has experienced in recent years.

CONCLUSION

After a prolonged spurt of rapid growth and escalating franchise values during the 1970s and 1980s, the baseball industry has leveled off in the 1990s. All industries advance in cycles. In spite of itself, MLB is poised to stage a remarkable recovery. Baseball has lost some relative ground in its popularity ratings with football and basketball, but it is still the national pastime and it still reigns supreme in the summertime. The Fox Network not only rescued MLB from the nightmare of The Baseball Network, but it has brought an aggressive, positive outlook to its promotion of the sport. Meanwhile, both the owners and the players' union seem to have been sufficiently chastened by the debacle of the 1994-1995 work stoppage that they have agreed to keep their dirty laundry in the closet and they have realized the crucial importance of their cooperation. Baseball still suffers from arrogance, neglect of its fan base, poor management, disunity among the owners, and gentrification, but as long as the magnates can keep the game on the field and slowly learn their lessons, the game has a bright future.

REFERENCES

Baade, Robert. 1994. Stadiums, Professional Sports, and Economic Development: Assessing the Reality. *A Heartland Policy Study* (April).

Baade, Robert, and R. F. Dye. 1990. The Impact of Stadiums and Professional Sports on Metropolitan Area Development. *Growth and Change.* (Spring): 1–14.

Rosentraub, Mark. 1996. Does the Emperor Have New Clothes: Sports and Economic Development. *Journal of Urban Affairs* 18 (April): 23-31.

14

Concluding Remarks

Daniel R. Marburger

Work stoppages have accompanied baseball's collective bargaining agreements for nearly 25 years. The 1994–1995 strike is significant not as a single event but for symbolizing the struggles that have competed with box scores for print space in the sports pages. Neither the resumption of a new season nor a new collective bargaining agreement will bring peace to baseball. History has shown that, at best, labor agreements provide the fans with a brief respite as the two sides gear up for the next battle. Readers of *Stee-rike Four!* have undoubtedly noted that economists are not in agreement on every issue confronting the game. Nonetheless a common theme is interwoven between the essays—baseball's status as a cartel. Understanding this theme is the key to grasping baseball's problems and looking toward its future.

The historical perspective detailed in the first chapter explains the mutual distrust rooted in the national pastime. In reviewing this history, several observations are worthy of note. First, whereas Major League Baseball's (MLB) work stoppages began when Marvin Miller became executive director of the Players' Association, his retirement did not usher in an era of labor peace. To the contrary, one lockout and two strikes followed Miller's retirement, the latter of which spawned the premature end of the 1994 season.

Similarly, the turnover rate in the players' union is extraordinary relative to most industries. Relatively few baseball players have careers that span two collective bargaining agreements, and only a privileged few extend into three or more agreements. All of this suggests that baseball's labor problems cannot be tied to the militancy of individual players or union executives.

Nor can the problems be traced to the stubbornness of individual owners. Turnover among owners is almost as fast paced as the players. Only a fraction of the current owners were around during the 1981 strike, and even a smaller number owned franchises prior to the beginning of free agency (Quirk and Fort 1992, 391–409). The same can be said of John Gaherin, Ray Grebey, and all of the other labor negotiators who have passed through baseball's revolving door throughout the years. Labor problems and infighting among owners are not a result of personalities but of the structure of the sport itself.

THE PRODUCT

To understand the source of the problem, let us first answer the following question: Major league baseball brings in $2 billion per year. Just what are the consumers buying?

The popular assertion is that the players are the product. Such a pronouncement, however fashionable, is incorrect. If MLB did not consist of games and league standings but merely of individuals displaying their ample skills (i.e., taking batting practice, shagging fly balls, and demonstrating their speed on the basepaths), the industry would quickly die of fan disinterest.

Neither are the teams the product. Although Atlantans pour through the turnstiles to watch their beloved Braves, the presumption is that a game will be played against another club. Absent the competition, the stands would be barren.

Professor Shughart's essay reveals the essence of baseball's "product." In short, the national pastime is a unique blend of tangibles and intangibles. Fans are attracted by the competition between teams, with a winner and loser emerging from each game.

But the product is much more than a collection of individual games. Records are kept of the number of contests won by each team. At season's end, the league declares one of the clubs to be the "World Champions."

Because the image of baseball is indelibly tied to the legitimacy of its games, rules are created to appropriately discern the best teams from the worst teams. Each team must be seen as expending considerable effort to win. Similarly, the players must possess skills that are worth the price of a ticket, that make the title "World Champions" defensible.

This mix of tangibles and intangibles suggests that teams need players, players need teams, and teams need opponents. Given that no single player, team, or owner stands to earn a nickel absent the other ingredients, one would expect major league baseball to constitute the perfect recipe for labor peace and cooperation among owners. Why does precisely the opposite appear to persist?

BASEBALL: A CARTEL WITH REDEEMING QUALITIES

The answer has been implied throughout the essays. Several authors have labeled major league baseball as a cartel. A cartel is an agreement between firms to band together as if they were a single business.

In most industries, cartels have no redeeming impact on consumers. The Organization of Petroleum Exporting Countries (OPEC) is a prime example. During the 1970s, OPEC restricted the supply of oil and agreed to charge a significantly higher price.

In contrast to OPEC, baseball's cartel provides an enormous benefit to the consumer. Absent the cartel, there would be no product. The Yankees cannot attract interest in their team unless they can persuade the Boston Red Sox to stage a game at their ballpark. Of course, the Red Sox have no incentive to help another firm earn some fast bucks; as a condition for playing the game, the Sox will either insist on a reciprocal game at Fenway Park or that the Yankees agree to give the Red Sox a share of the receipts. All of this necessitates the formation of a cartel.

Given the need for cooperation among franchises, the cartel must establish rules to promote the overall product. Although these rules are constructed to benefit the collective enterprise, not all of them enhance the short-term profits of individual franchises.

Baseball's early days are rife with examples of the divergence between club and league interests. In the late 1800s, several owners bought into multiple franchises. They immediately capitalized on the incentive to transfer their best players to the team that drew the biggest crowds. Some owners freely lent their stars to competitors with whom they were shareholders. "Home" games were often played on the road if the competitor's ballpark was likely to draw larger crowds than the home field.

Not surprisingly, these actions were harshly criticized by the fans and media. Nonetheless, despite damaging the image of the league, few doubt that the strategies enhanced individual owner profits. In time, however, the will of the league prevailed, and joint ownerships were banned (Seymour 1960).

Similar restrictions appear in other professional sports. Player sales are explicitly banned in the National Football League (NFL) (Quirk and Fort 1995, 1282). The rationale for the policy is puzzling at face value, considering that Professor Fizel suggested that player sales benefit both the buying club and the selling club (otherwise why would they consummate a deal?).

Perhaps the rule reflects the league's concern that player sales will damage the legitimacy of the NFL product (Daly 1992, 18). Fans want to believe that their favorite club and its opponent are striving to win, and selling off star players for a quick buck doesn't exactly further that image. Clearly, former baseball commissioner Bowie Kuhn fostered this belief when he barred the sales of Vida Blue, Joe Rudi, and Rollie Fingers in 1975.

Kuhn's contention that player sales damage baseball's image is not the relevant issue here. Details on player sales in baseball history are rather sketchy, leaving plenty of room for disagreement among economists and healthy debate among fans.[1] The salient point is that the objectives of the league do not always go hand in hand with those of individual franchises. When conflicts of interest arise, the league must protect the overall enterprise from the perverse incentives of its individual members. (As I recall, this was once the rationale for hiring a baseball commissioner.)

Not all cartel rules are fan-friendly. Just as most cartels profit by keeping the public hungry for more, many of the essayists accuse MLB of purposefully slowing expansion to a snail's pace to instill competition among cities for franchises. The fierce intercity competition results in taxpayer-financed ballparks and cozy sweetheart leases. If baseball's cartel unambiguously serviced consumer demand, megamarkets such as New York and Los Angeles would likely have at least one more team, and other large metropolitan areas such as New Orleans and Buffalo might also sport franchises. Tampa Bay might have dusted the cobwebs from its SunCoast Dome long ago.

MLB's regionalized broadcasts of the 1995 League Championship games were another example of a policy that was good for the league and bad for the fans. In contrast to televising all playoff games nationwide, the 1995 format called for all playoff games to be played at night (when ratings and advertising revenues are higher) and broadcast regionally. In this manner, the league could attract more revenue, but the fans were denied the opportunity to watch all of the games.

The negative aspects of baseball's cartel caused Professor Johnson and several other essayists to call for the elimination of baseball's antitrust exemption. The exemption currently gives the league carte blanche freedom to act in its own best interests, even if those interests are not beneficial to the consumer. Absent the exemption, individuals could challenge acceptability of league policies that subvert the best interests of the consumers. One result could be more franchises in untapped markets.

LEAGUE POLICY: MAKING THE CARTEL WORK

Despite its negative elements, we must return to the reality that the cartel is necessary to provide the fans with a product. Understanding that it takes two teams to create a game, the cartel must design policies not only to promote the legitimacy of its games but also to protect the financial viability of each individual franchise.

Although present-day concerns regarding the financial condition of individual franchises are considered by several essayists as dubious, they cannot be ignored in formulating league policy. In baseball each team spends the off-season wheeling and dealing to improve its roster. Conceivably, each club can enter into the season with a better team than the year before. Nonetheless, because each game produces a winner and a loser, one team will finish the year in last place. Despite the fact that its roster is loaded with individuals of extraordinary talent, the last-place team will be labeled a "bad ball club," and its attendance (and revenues) invariably slide accordingly.[2] Competition among franchises produces not only winners and losers on the field but on income statements as well.

All of this makes for a rather perplexing situation. The image of the game hinges on the perception that each club is striving to win. From this perspective, competition among baseball franchises for the best players is desirable for the cartel. At the same time, however, baseball needs to assure that economic competition between teams does not drive the weaker franchises into extinction. Balancing these two objectives is the responsibility of the cartel, which must promote the former while avoiding the latter.

Several essayists recommended adding teams to the more lucrative markets as a means of achieving economic balance. Clearly, if baseball's megamarkets supported more teams, individual franchises would be less able to profitably drive salaries beyond the reach of teams in smaller markets. This would benefit the game all around, not only by protecting the financial stability of small-market clubs but also by reducing the need for "artificial" restraints such as revenue-sharing and salary control. Greater balance in revenue potential might even improve competitive balance.

Don't hold your breath until baseball initiates such a strategy, however. MLB is no more likely to place a new team in an existing market than McDonald's is to locate two franchises on the same block. Economic competition between regional franchises means lower ticket prices (heavens!), less-lucrative broadcast contracts, and a host of other implications that drain the wealth of the collective enterprise. If baseball is to promote itself as a viable financial entity, its members must come to an agreement on some other internal policy.

THE CHEATING PROBLEM IN CARTELS

The Owners

Revenue-sharing. This brings us back full circle. Why does an industry so reliant on cooperation between franchises breed such well-documented infighting among owners? The answer can be traced to the "cheating" problem that is commonplace in cartels. To the extent that the best interests of a club do not necessarily coincide with the those of the league, after an agreement has been reached among members of a cartel, individual members soon discover that they can benefit by breaking the rules.

Again OPEC serves as the ideal model. Despite its success in driving up the price of oil in the 1970s, individual members of the cartel recognized that they could increase their wealth by producing and selling oil that exceeded their assigned quotas. In time, cheating on the production quotas became widespread, and the glut of oil drove prices downward.

Similar incentives are pervasive in professional sports. To illustrate, the NFL rules require the equal sharing of national broadcast and merchandising revenues between franchises. Clearly, the edict implies a recognition that the franchises are partners first and competitors second; that no team stands to benefit unless other franchises are financially sound.

Despite this rationale, Dallas Cowboys owner Jerry Jones grabbed the headlines in 1995 by negotiating his own merchandising deals with Nike, Pepsi, and American Express in flagrant violation of NFL policy (Forest, Hoffman, and Schiller 1995, 54). The NFL sued Jones for $300 million, claiming that he had no right to revenues that were not to be shared under league rules. Jones countersued for $750 million, using antitrust legislation as his weapon (Weisman 1995, C1).

A significant irony in Jones's actions, and more importantly, his defense of such actions, is that the 1995 National Football Conference (NFC) Championship Game, which packed Texas Stadium wall to wall with Cowboy fans, was played against the Green Bay Packers, the poster-child among all professional sports franchises as one that could not exist without leaguewide revenue-sharing. However, as with any cartel, as long as the other members keep Green Bay afloat, the less revenue Jones shares with other clubs, the more he profits.

In reflecting on the NFL/Jerry Jones rivalry, the perspective of Professor Shughart in supporting baseball's antitrust exemption becomes clear. Rather than label baseball a "cartel," he argues that the franchises do not constitute "firms" at all, because it takes two teams to create a game. Because the league, rather than the individual team delivers baseball's "product," MLB must have the final say in dictating policy.

From this perspective, allowing individuals to sue MLB on antitrust grounds gives members the freedom to milk the benefits of the league and then turn around and defy its rules. Should the courts consistently rule against the league and in favor of the individual, club owners will be able to choose which rules they will follow and which they will not. Cheating on the cartel is not only easier, it is encouraged.

The difficulties in getting baseball's owners to agree on a revenue-sharing plan are founded on similar grounds. Despite the fact that each team relies on its partner franchises to produce games, any rule that calls for a sharing of the wealth is viewed as a sacrifice.

Several issues compound this problem. First, as Professors Hadley and Gustafson pointed out, large-market owners paid large-market prices to obtain their franchises in the first place. The premium was based on the assumption that the big-city revenue stream would continue ad infinitum. Voting to share the wealth could lessen the resale value of a franchise. Not surprisingly, large-market owners resist revenue-sharing to protect the return on their investments. Although cynics argue that the stock market carries no guarantees of a sure bet either, we should note that it is never the stockholders who cast the vote to buy high and sell low.

Ironically, revenue-sharing produces perverse incentives for the weaker franchises. Presumably, the league subsidies could be used by teams in weaker markets to hang onto (or sign) choice free agents. This, of course, would support the cartel's goal of promoting the product's legitimacy.

Professors Hadley and Gustafson, however, predicted that this will not be the case. An owner's decision to cast aside expensive talent for cheaper, lesser-quality players may lower the team's payroll, but it also hurts gate receipts. If the decline in attendance is too steep, management will think twice about dumping talent en masse.

Revenue-sharing insulates the owner from these harmful effects. Rather than to use the increased revenue stream to improve the roster, small-market owners can maintain inexpensive losing teams and rely on the larger, wealthier clubs to subsidize their existence. Professors Zimbalist and Shughart acknowledged this problem in labeling the Padres' infamous fire sale as "free riding." To the extent that weaker clubs willingly allow other clubs to swallow up the league's best talent, the cartel's desire to project an image of unrelenting competition on the field of play is tainted. In short, baseball's new revenue-sharing plan may represent good news to Pittsburgh Pirate management, but Pirate fans should not expect the income stream to translate into better talent on the field.

Salary Caps and Luxury Taxes. The belief that league rules constrain a club's profitability also explains the problems described by Professor Quirk as inherent in salary caps and luxury taxes. Free agent salaries escalate for one reason: because one owner voluntarily ups the bid to sign a free agent. Assuming that the owners have some semblance of business sense, the higher bid implies that the club expects to be more profitable by signing the player than by dropping out of the bidding.

Salary caps declare such rational behavior to be illegal. Teams nearing the cap must drop out of the bidding even though it would be more profitable for them to remain in the auction. Hence, clubs that feel handcuffed by the cap have powerful incentives to skirt the rules. Rather than outrightly break the rules, they seek loopholes that adhere to the cap while violating the rationale for creating it.[3]

Luxury taxes are not likely to be any different. If a tax system is instituted, individual clubs will seek out means of circumventing it. The same types of contract restructurings witnessed with salary caps should also become prevalent with luxury taxes.

Given that bending the rules of the salary cap/luxury tax could potentially drive partners out of business, why would a large-market owner conspire with an agent to circumvent the agreement? Again, the answer is the same: As long as other teams follow the cap/tax in the spirit in which it was intended, any individual franchise's attempt to avoid the cap/tax will result in increased profits. Breaking the rules is rational profit-maximizing behavior for the individual firm. Such behavior becomes self-destructive only when others follow suit. For this very reason, most economists view cartels as temporary phenomena: All cartel members have an incentive to bend the rules; when such rule-breaking becomes widespread, the cartel collapses.

Interestingly, disagreement among baseball owners is hardly a recent phenomenon. Economist Lance Davis (1974, 383) reviewed the 100-year history of professional baseball and drew the following conclusion in 1974: "The owners have proved easily seduced by the vision of short-term profits, and they have opted time and time again for policies that sacrifice long-term for immediate rewards. In practice, this tendency has led to continued cheating on cartel decisions, to the innovation of structures that permit members to circumvent cartel decisions when cheating is difficult, and to continued opposition to rule changes that would effect more equitable distribution of players and revenues."

The fact that Davis would draw such a conclusion over 20 years ago (and two years *prior* to the inception of free agency) is particularly notable. Baseball has experienced a near 100 percent turnover in ownerships since 1974. Yet the individual incentives for franchise owners to resist the league cartel that Davis observed 20 years ago still prevail today. With Jerry Jones suing the NFL for the right to break league revenue-sharing rules, with NBA and NFL owners inventing creative methods for eluding league salary caps, and with baseball owners with teams in large-market cities refusing to budge on revenue-sharing, the behavior described by Davis is likely to remain as much a part of baseball as popcorn and souvenirs.

The Players

One significant change has occurred, however, since Davis's observation. The lack of a union prior to the late 1960s eliminated the players' voice in any club or league decision. As a result, the players were mere chess pieces in the orchestration of the league. In the modern era, however, league policy must receive the approval of the Players' Association.

The inclusion of the players in league matters aggravates the problem considerably, because individual player incentives to resist cartel rules mimic those of clubs. To my knowledge, no NBA or NFL player has ever protested a contract designed to elude the salary cap. As long as the owner could make good on the payments, the player was only too happy to sign his name on the bottom line. Similarly, one doubts that Bobby Bonilla, Barry Bonds, and Doug Drabek lamented the plight of the weak-drawing Pittsburgh Pirates when the three jumped ship as free agents.

Baseball players have a long history of resisting any attempt by the league to develop safety-net rules that could protect weaker franchises. Proposals for player compensation led to a player strike in 1981, just as the push for a salary cap resulted in a walkout in 1994. More recently, the Players' Association insisted on having a say in any revenue-sharing plan adopted by the clubs. One can only suspect that the union leadership was aware that increased revenue-sharing could lower player salaries and preferred the scheme that places the greatest burden on someone else (Quirk and Fort 1992, 274). In the context of the analysis of Professors Hadley and Gustafson, we would expect the Players' Association to support the sharing of "fixed" revenues and resist increased sharing of variable revenue sources.

Of course, complicating matters is Professor Quirk's observation that the owners have been crying "Wolf!" for years. The analogy is, indeed, appropriate. The owners' forecasts of gloom and doom since the institution of free agency (and before) have been accompanied by skyrocketing franchise values and not a single bankruptcy or franchise relocation. For this reason, the players tend to view any safety-net proposal as a disguised attempt to turn the clock back to the days when management ruled the roost.

Nevertheless, both the players and owners should recognize that free agency has coincided with unparalleled growth in industry revenues (Zimbalist 1992, 48–59; Quirk and Fort 1992, 505). Local broadcast revenues were bursting at the seams throughout the 1980s and early 1990s, yet not all clubs were equal benefactors. What remains clear from the skirmishes that triggered the 1994/1995 strike is that MLB is totally unprepared to handle a stagnant or declining market. If individual franchises should approach bankruptcy, neither the owners nor the players will offer their assistance. Finger pointing will substitute for productive brainstorming, and with each principal staunchly insisting that some other party should bear the responsibility for salvaging the failing club (as any self-respecting cartel cheater should).

THE PLIGHT OF FRANCHISES IN SMALLER MARKETS

Despite the resolution among owners and the Players' Association regarding revenue-sharing and luxury taxes, fans in baseball's smallest markets may be whistling in the dark if they believe that any policy designed to stabilize franchise finances will keep their team close to home indefinitely. The fact that revenue-sharing, salary caps, and luxury taxes may keep Pittsburgh and Seattle in the black does not imply that maintaining franchises in these locations is in the best interests of the league.

Given the propensity for the reserve clause to transfer wealth from the players to the owners, one would be hard-pressed to believe that a franchise could have found itself in financial trouble prior to free agency, particularly in New York City: the biggest single market of all. Nonetheless, black ink did not keep the Brooklyn Dodgers from moving to Los Angeles or the New York Giants from going to San Francisco. In each case, the lure of even greater West Coast profits prompted the transfer.

Public relations fiascos aside, what motivation does the league have to block such moves? One would assume that the league prefers more revenue to less. With or without internal economic safeguards, MLB has a vested incentive to place its franchises in the most-lucrative locations.

The facts speak for themselves. In the 20 years of free agency, not one franchise has relocated. In contrast, eight franchise shifts occurred during the 20-year period leading up to the free agency era (Quirk and Fort 1992, 479–488).

Fortunately, small-market fans need not lose too much sleep worrying that their teams will skip town overnight. Despite the fact that MLB prefers the big money of New York to the pocket change of Pittsburgh, franchise mobility is significantly slowed by the long-term leases that inevitably accompany the construction of a new stadium.

Given the extraordinary cost of building a stadium, baseball has a powerful incentive to encourage taxpayers to pick up the tab. Of course, the local voters will not be willing to shell out $200 million for a new ballpark if there is a possibility that its primary tenant might leave after a couple of years. Only by promising to dig roots in the local community for an extended period of time can any owner reasonably expect a subsidy of that magnitude. Accordingly, most leases lock the team into the city for two or three decades.

The pros and cons of subsidizing local franchises were discussed by Professors Zimbalist and Fort. As both noted, the economic benefits generated by a major league franchise are invariably overstated. Local governments that attempt to lure a team for the sole purpose of generating income are likely to find that the taxpayers' expenditures exceed any economic benefits the team provides.

On the other hand, Professor Fort asserted that local beneficiaries from the existence of major league teams do exist, providing a logical foundation for at least some individualized subsidies. Further, professional sports teams represent a significant source of civic pride. A visit to the gift shop of any major airport will validate this contention. Although the existence of a ballclub can provide satisfaction to millions of local patrons, "value" of this sort is largely psychological and rarely winds up in anyone's cash register.

HOPE FOR THE FUTURE?

Economics is often referred to as the "dismal science" and the concluding analysis thus far does little to refute its unfortunate reputation. One might infer from this essay that baseball's necessary existence as a cartel dooms it to a future of work stoppages, name-calling, and other assorted goodies that alienate the fans.

There is, however, cause for optimism. Most economists share an undying faith in the ability of capitalism to benefit the consumer, and the free market may, indeed, be baseball's saving grace. In most industries, management and the union representatives calculate the pros and cons of allowing a strike or lockout to continue. The costs, of course, include the lost paychecks and revenues that accompany the work stoppage. When the costs of continuing the stoppage exceed the benefits, an agreement is reached.

In contrast, the notion that strikes and lockouts could actually damage the product is rather unusual (and definitely not taught in Collective Bargaining 101). Falling attendance and declining television ratings in 1995 sent a strong signal that repeated strikes and lockouts will not be tolerated by baseball fans. The message was not missed by players in other sports. Despite the efforts of Michael Jordan and company to decertify the NBA Players' Association and take management to court, the players overwhelmingly rejected the plan and voted for labor peace. Likewise, despite the fact that its collective bargaining agreement is burdensome and laden with inequities, the NFL players and owners had no problem agreeing to a contract extension that takes the league into the twenty-first century. Perhaps (and this is pure speculation), but perhaps there were even a few owners whose votes in favor of the new labor agreement were influenced ever so slightly by the decline in gate attendance that accompanied the last work stoppage.

Baseball proved the power of the free market: If you spend too much time arguing over how to share the wealth, the wealth may vanish. There is a lesson to be learned here by members on both sides of the bargaining table. Maybe they'll listen next time.

NOTES

1. For example, Daly (1992, 25) concludes that "interteam sales of first-line players are virtually nonexistent in major North American sports leagues." In sharp contrast, Quirk and Fort (1995, 1282) note "a long history of cash sales in all sports leagues."

2. Michael Canes (1974, 97) made an interesting observation regarding the importance of league standings. During World War II, when the calls to duty diluted baseball rosters, league attendance decreased. The greatest decreases occurred with teams whose winning percentages declined. More interesting was the fact that attendance actually rose for teams whose winning percentages increased. The implication is that fans tend to rely on relative quality measures such as win-loss percentages to infer the absolute quality of the individual teams.

3. For a fascinating insight into "cap evasion," see Barra (1995).

REFERENCES

Barra, Allen. 1995. How the 49ers Beat the Salary Cap. *New York Times Magazine* (January 5): 34–35.

Canes, Michael. 1974. The Social Benefits of Restrictions on Team Quality. In Roger Noll, ed. *Government and the Sports Busines,*. pp. 81–114. Washington D.C.: The Brookings Institution.

Daly, George D. 1992. The Baseball Player's Labor Market Revisited. In Paul M. Sommers, ed. *Diamonds Are Forever: The Business of Baseball*, pp. 11–28. Washington, D.C.: The Brookings Institution.

Davis, Lance E. 1974. Self-Regulation in Baseball, 1909–71. In Roger Noll, ed. *Government and the Sports Business*, pp. 349–386. Washington, D.C.: The Brookings Institution.

Forest, Stephanie Anderson, Jeff Hoffman, and Zachary Schiller. 1995. End Run in Cleveland, Straight Arm in Dallas. *Business Week* (November 20): 54.

Quirk, James, and Rodney D. Fort. *1992. Pay Dirt: The Business of Professional Team Sports.* Princeton, N.J.: Princeton University Press.

———. 1995. Cross-Subsidization, Incentives, and Outcomes in Professional Team Sports Leagues. *Journal of Economic Literature* 33 (September): 1265–1299.

Seymour, Harold. 1960. *Baseball: The Early Years.* New York: Oxford University Press.

Weisman, Larry. 1995. Jones Returns NFL Fire With Antitrust Suit. *USA Today* (November 7): C1.

Zimbalist, Andrew. 1992. *Baseball and Billions: A Probing Look inside the Big Business of Our National Pastime.* New York: Basic Books.

Appendix

As noted in the introduction, most of the essays in *Stee-rike Four!* were completed prior to the ratification of the labor agreement in November 1996. The settlement is timely both for baseball fans and this book. It allows us to summarize the terms of the new labor agreement and to predict their impact on the national pastime. We will confine our discussions to some of the more major issues covered in the deal.

LENGTH OF THE AGREEMENT

The new labor agreement begins with the 1997 season and lasts through at least the year 2000. At the players' option, the deal can be extended through the year 2001. However, should the players exercise this option, they will lose $24 million in postseason revenues and the minimum baseball salary will not be adjusted for increases in the cost of living in either the 2000 or 2001 seasons.

INTERLEAGUE PLAY AND EXPANSION

The agreement allows for interleague play to begin in 1997. The owners retain the option to expand the league by two teams which would begin play in the year 2002.

FREE AGENCY RULES

There will be no more repeater's rights restrictions governing free agency. A player with at least six years of experience becomes an unrestricted free agent at the expiration of his contract.

BASEBALL'S MINIMUM SALARY

The minimum baseball salary will be raised to $150,000 beginning with the 1997 season. This means that a rookie third-string catcher will earn nearly as much for the season as Albert Belle receives for every two games he plays. The minimum salary will continue to rise until it reaches a level of $200,000 (plus cost-of-living increases) in the final year of the labor agreement.

POSTSEASON PLAYER POOL

The players' share of gate receipts from postseason games will decrease from 80% to 60%.

SALARY ARBITRATION

Salary arbitration will continue to exist under the present rules. Unlike the past, however, each case will be heard by three arbitrators rather than one. In the context of the essays of Professors Dworkin and Kaempfer, the change from a one-person panel to a three-person panel is likely to benefit both players and clubs as it diminishes the likelihood of an aberrant arbitration decision.

LUXURY TAX

The new pact includes provisions for a luxury tax in its first three years. Clubs with payrolls exceeding $51 million in 1997 must pay a tax equal to 35% of the difference between the actual payroll and the threshold. The proceeds from the tax will be used in the revenue-sharing plan to be discussed later. The payroll threshold will rise to $55 million and $58.9 million in 1998 and 1999, respectively. Team payrolls will include the salaries of all players on the 40-man roster. The tax rate will remain at 35% for the 1998 season and fall to 34% in 1999.

Although only four clubs would have paid a tax had the rules been in effect in 1996, recent signings suggest that club payrolls are poised to rise over the life of the agreement. This would have little effect on the number of teams paying the tax because the agreement provides that no more than five teams will be liable for the tax in any given season. Rising payrolls, therefore, will affect the *amount* of money paid in taxes rather than the number of paying clubs.

There will be no luxury tax in the years 2000 and 2001 (assuming the players opt to extend the agreement). Reflecting on Professor Quirk's analysis, this provision is hardly a minor point. Salaries increase due to profit-seeking bidding wars waged by owners. Since rational profit-maximizers prefer not to pay a tax, the no-tax years would normally give big spenders like George Steinbrenner a convenient avenue for re-structuring contracts to elude the tax.

The owners have anticipated this possibility. The formula for team payrolls will rely on the *average annual value* of the player's contract rather than the stated salary for any given season. Further, the cost of player benefits will also be counted as part of the team payroll.

Having implemented controls designed to keep management from evading the tax, the task that lies ahead for the large-market owners is to exploit any remaining loopholes that exist. One possible loophole may lie in deferred compensation beyond the life of the player's contract. Such contracts were quite common in the days when federal income tax laws were highly punitive to individuals in the high tax brackets. During this era, fans may recall significant discrepancies in the reported annual salaries of George Brett, Willie Wilson, and Dan Quisenberry when the trio was signed to "lifetime contracts".

As noted in chapter 2, the absence of a tax in the final year of the agreement will work to the advantage of the players once negotiations on a new labor agreement begin. Should history repeat itself and the court enforce a "last best offer" injunction against the owners, the last best offer will not include a luxury tax. This has the effect of eliminating the luxury tax and forcing the owners to have to bargain with the union to get it back.

PLAYER SALARY TAX

In addition to the tax on team payrolls, the deal calls for a 2.5 % tax on player salaries for the 1996 and 1997 seasons. After this collective bargaining agreement runs its course, the owners will undoubtedly discover that the salary tax is a more effective means of re-directing income from players to clubs than the payroll tax. Unlike the payroll tax, the salary tax carries no perverse incentives for the owners.

REVENUE-SHARING

The new agreement will also phase in the owner's revenue-sharing plan. The plan becomes fully operational in the year 2000. At that time, the 13 wealthiest clubs will place roughly 22 % of their local revenues into a fund which will then be re-distributed to the other clubs.

Retroactive to 1996, this plan would re-distribute approximately $70 million in its first year. The Yankees will foot roughly $5.5 million of the bill. The largest subsidy will go to Pittsburgh ($4.7 million).

As of this writing, I have not seen the revenue-sharing formula in its entirety. The plan apparently targets all sources of a franchise's income, and is not limited to purely "fixed" or "variable" revenues as defined by Professors Gustafson and Hadley. In contrast to the sharing of fixed revenues, variable revenue-sharing has the added bonus (to management) of lowering player salaries. In fact, many economists view revenue-sharing as a more efficient means of reducing salary levels than caps or luxury taxes.

Although the plan promises to assist the finances of MLB's low-revenue clubs, Professors Gustafson and Hadley doubt that revenue-sharing will improve league balance. In fact, the combination of revenue-sharing and luxury tax subsidies could even *impair* competitive balance.

Consider the case of the Pittsburgh Pirates. By mid-December of 1996, Pittsburgh had disposed of every millionaire on its roster. All of these players were dealt away for cheap minor league talent.

In the absence of revenue-sharing, falling attendance and declining television/radio audiences would penalize Pirate owner Kevin McClatchy for replacing established players with inexperienced players. However, the Pirates were poised to receive MLB's most generous subsidy *prior* to these trades. One can only assume that the subsidy will rise as McClatchy's payroll falls in 1997. Does baseball's subsidy plan actually *reward* small-market teams for sporting low-quality, low-salaried rosters? If so, the new agreement will encourage free-riding and operate to the detriment of league balance.

LITIGATION AND SERVICE TIME

The Players' Association agrees to drop all litigation charges against management for its unfair labor practices during the strike. The agreement to drop litigation charges was apparently exchanged for the 75 service days that the players lost during the strike.

The restored service time affects far more than the 11 players who became free agents and the 50-plus players who became eligible for arbitration in 1997 because of the added service days. For most players, being docked one service day is the same as being docked 365 service days. Had the service days been lost, the vast majority of players would have become eligible for both arbitration and free agency one year later. The lost service time would have also impeded the retirement earnings of player because baseball's pension funding is tied to service days.

The lost service days may have also reduced the likelihood of a strike in the future. Most players have short careers and some could stand to lose more from lost service days than from holding out for a better settlement. My advice to the players is that they demand back pay in addition to service days next time they strike—they may get it.

THE ANTITRUST EXEMPTION

The players and owners will jointly ask Congress to eliminate baseball's antitrust exemption, but only as it applies to labor matters. There is much more here than meets the eye. At first glance, this appears to be an unconditional victory for players. Just as the NFL players obtained free agency by decertifying the union and suing the league, baseball players will have the power to use the court as a surrogate bargaining tool. In all likelihood, the owners conceded the partial exemption out of fear that Congress would act on its own volition to eliminate the entire exemption.

Much more telling is the apparent agreement by management and the Players' Association to retain the industry's exemption for non-labor issues. In fact, MLB's monopoly power benefits both management *and* the players. The recurring theme in many of the essays is that baseball uses its monopoly power to obtain taxpayer-financed stadiums and sweetheart leases. Such deals save a franchise owner roughly $200 million—money that the union will try to wrestle away at the bargaining table.

The bottom-line is quite simple—the only consensus among small-market owners is that the large-market owners should subsidize their businesses; the only consensus among small- and large-market owners is that the players should subsidize *their* businesses; the only agreement among players is that the clubs should subsidize their lifestyles; and the only agreement among player and clubs is that the taxpayers should subsidize *their* lifestyles. Perhaps it's time I started following women's softball—it's less frustrating.

REFERENCES

Dodd, Mike. 1996. "Four-year Struggle Ends," *USA Today*, (November 27): 3C.
Outside the Lines. Society for American Baseball Research Newsletter, Doug Pappas, ed. Fall 1996.
Pascarelli, Peter. "Critical Hour Fast Approaches," *USA Today Baseball Weekly*, (November 6-12): 4.

Selected Bibliography

Aaron, Henry et al. 1992. *Report of Independent Members of the Economic Study Committee on Baseball* (December 3).

Aaron, Henry. 1992. *Supplemental Statement: Report of Baseball Study Committee* (December 3).

Baade, Robert. 1994. Stadiums, Professional Sports, and Economic Development: Assessing the Reality. *A Heartland Policy Study* (April).

Baade, Robert, and R. F. Dye. 1990. The Impact of Stadiums and Professional Sports on Metropolitan Area Development. *Growth and Change* (Spring): 1–14.

Barra, Allen. 1995. How the 49ers Beat the Salary Cap. *New York Times Magazine* (January 5): 34–35.

Bernstein, Aaron. 1995. Let's See the Owners Pitch Their Way Out of This One. *Business Week* (April 3): 58.

Bernstein, Aaron, and David Greising. 1995. Owners: 1 Players: 0. *Business Week* (April 17): 32–33.

Bernstein, Aaron, and Kevin Kelly. 1995. A Three-Way Jump Ball in the NBA. *Business Week* (September 4): 58–60.

Besanko, David A., and Daniel Simon. 1985. Resource Allocation in the Baseball Players' Labor Market: An Empirical Investigation. *Review of Business and Economic Research* 21: 71–84.

Bodley, Hal. 1996. End of Labor Pains Gives Birth to Hope. *USA Today* (August 12): 7C.

———. 1996. Baseball Lifts "Dark Cloud". *USA Today* (November 27): 1C.

Chass, Murray. 1993. Owners Circle Bases Without Ever Scoring. *New York Times* (September 7): B11.

———. 1994. Owners Adopt Revenue Plan, But It's Tied to Salary Cap. *New York Times* (January 19): B11+.

Chipello, Christopher J. 1994. Stars' Bigger Salaries Threaten a Small Team. *Wall Street Journal* (November 21): B1.

Coase, Ronald. 1960. The Problem of Social Cost. *Journal of Law and Economics* 3 (October): 1-44.

Demmert, Henry G. 1973. *The Economics of Professional Team Sports.* Lexington, Mass. Lexington Books.

Dodd, Mike. 1996. Four-year Struggle Ends. *USA Today* (November 27): 3C

Drahozal, Christopher. 1986. The Impact of Free Agency on the Distribution of Playing Talents in Major League Baseball. *Journal of Economics and Business* 38: 113-121.

Dworkin, James B. 1981. *Owners versus Players: Baseball and Collective Bargaining.* Boston. Auburn House Publishing Company.

El-Hodiri, Mohamed, and James Quirk. 1971. An Economic Model of a Professional Sports League. *Journal of Political Economy* 79 (March/April): 1302-1319.

Fimrite, Ron. 1980. Yankee Stadium, Opening Day, 1980? *Sports Illustrated* 52 (March 3): 56-70.

Flanagan, Robert J., Lawrence M. Kahn, Robert S. Smith, and Ronald G. Ehrenberg. 1989. *Economics of the Employment Relationship.* Glenview, Ill. Scott, Foresman and Company.

Fleisher, Arthur A. III, William F. Shughart II, and Robert D. Tollison. 1989. Ownership Structure in Professional Sports. In Richard O. Zerbe, Jr., ed. *Research in Law and Economics.* Greenwich, Conn. JAI Press, 12: 71-75.

Fort, Rodney, and James Quirk. 1995. Cross Subsidization, Incentives, and Outcomes in Professional Sports Leagues. *Journal of Economic Literature* 33 (September): 1265-1299.

Greising, David, and Stephen Baker. 1995. The Bozos of October. *Business Week* (October 16): 50.

Helyar, John. 1994. *Lords of the Realm: The Real History of Baseball.* New York. Villard Books.

Impoco, Jim. 1994. Sliding toward a Strike. *U.S. News and World Report* 117 (August 8): 49.

Impoco, Jim, Sara Collins, and James Popkin. 1995. Down to the Last Out. *U.S. News and World Report* 118 (February 13): 66-68.

Jessell, Harry A. 1993. MLB's Local TV/Radio Take Tops $350 Million. *Broadcasting and Cable* (March 15): 39-42.

Kaplan, Jim. 1981. No Games Today. *Sports Illustrated* 54 (June 22): 17.

Kuhn, Bowie. 1987. *Hardball: The Education of a Baseball Commissioner.* New York. Times Books.

Kurkjian, Tim, and Tom Verducci. 1995. Time is Running Out. *Sports Illustrated* 82 (March 20): 38-40.

Major League Baseball. *Basic Agreement between The American League of Professional Baseball Clubs and The National League of Profess-*

ional Baseball Clubs and Major League Baseball Players Association, effective January 1, 1990.

McChesney, Fred S., and William F. Shughart II, eds. 1995. *The Causes and Consequences of Antitrust: The Public-Choice Perspective.* Chicago. University of Chicago Press.

McClellan, Steve. 1995. Broadcasters Balk at Admission Price. *Broadcasting and Cable.* (March 27): 34–37.

———. 1994. MLB Gets Its First Start. *Broadcasting and Cable* (March 14): 30–33.

———. 1995. The Baseball Network Stays in the Game. *Broadcasting and Cable* (March 27): 38.

———. 1996. The Foxification of Baseball. *Broadcasting and Cable* (March 25): 24–28.

McConville, Jim. 1996. Baseball Ad Sales Back in the Swing. *Broadcasting and Cable* (March 25): 28–32.

Miller, James E. 1990. *The Baseball Business: Pursuing Pennants and Profits in Baltimore.* Chapel Hill, N.C. The University of North Carolina Press.

Miller, Marvin. 1991. *A Whole Different Ball Game: The Sport and Business of Baseball.* New York. Birch Lane Press.

Neale, Walter. 1964. The Peculiar Economics of Professional Sports. *Quarterly Journal of Economics* 78: 1–14.

Noll, Roger G., ed. 1974. *Government and the Sports Business.* Washington, D.C. The Brookings Institution.

Outside the Lines. Society for American Baseball Research Newsletter, Doug Pappas, ed. Fall 1996.

Pascarelli, Peter. 1996. "Critical Hour Fast Approaches," *USA Today Baseball Weekly,* (November 6-12): 4.

Purdy, Matthew, and Richard Sandomir. 1994. Colleagues or Competitors? 28 Owners in the Spotlight. *New York Times* (August 22): A1+.

Quirk, James, and Rodney D. Fort. 1992. *Pay Dirt: The Business of Professional Team Sports.* Princeton, N.J. Princeton University Press.

Rosentraub, Mark. 1996. Does the Emperor Have New Clothes: Sports and Economic Development. *Journal of Urban Affairs.* 18 (April): 23–31.

Ross, Stephen F. 1991. Break Up the Sports League Monopolies. In Paul D. Staudohar and James A. Mangan, eds., *The Business of Professional Sports,* pp 152-174. Champaign, Ill. University of Illinois Press.

Rottenberg, Simon. 1956. The Baseball Players' Labor Market. *Journal of Political Economy* 64: 242–258.

Scully, Gerald W. 1989. *The Business of Major League Baseball.* Chicago.University of Chicago Press.

———. 1995. *The Market Structure of Sports.* Chicago. University of Chicago Press.

Seymour, Harold. 1960. *Baseball: The Early Years.* New York. Oxford University Press.

Shropshire, Kenneth L. 1995. *The Sports Franchise Game: Cities in Pursuit of Sports Franchises, Events, Stadiums, and Arenas.* Philadelphia. University of Pennsylvania Press.

Sommers, Paul M., ed. 1992. *Diamonds Are Forever: The Business of Baseball.* Washington, D.C. The Brookings Institution.

Stevens, Carl M. 1966. Is Compulsory Arbitration Compatible with Bargaining? *Industrial Relations* 5: 38–52.

Thomas, Evan. 1985. A Win for the Fans; the Owners Balk, the Players Walk, then Ueberroth Gets the Save. *Time* 126 (August 19): 44.

Voigt, David Quentin. 1983. *American Baseball: From the Gentleman's Sport to the Commissioner System.* University Park, Pa. Pennsylvania State University Press.

Will, George F. 1990. *Men At Work: The Craft Of Baseball.* New York. Macmillan Publishing Company.

Wulf, Steve. 1995. An Unwhole New Ball Game. *Time* 145 (April 17): 48.

Zimbalist, Andrew. 1992. *Baseball and Billions: A Probing Look inside the Big Business of Our National Pastime.* New York. Basic Books.

Index

About the Contributors

Daniel R. Marburger is Associate Professor of Economics at Arkansas State University. His research areas include labor economics, economic education, and the economics of sports. He has contributed chapters to the books *Diamonds Are Forever: The Business of Baseball* and *Baseball Economics: Current Research* and has published baseball-related articles in *Industrial and Labor Relations Review*, the *Journal of Labor Research*, *The Review of Black Political Economy*, *Contemporary Economic Policy*, *Managerial and Decision Economics*, and *The International Journal of Conflict Management*. He was also a presenter at the Baseball and the Sultan of Swat conference honoring the 100th birthday of Babe Ruth at Hofstra University in 1994. Marburger was retained as an expert in the baseball-related cases of *Renteria* v. *Professional Sports, Inc.* and *Keough* v. *City of Scottsdale*.

James Richard Hill is Associate Professor of Economics at Central Michigan University in Mount Pleasant, Michigan. His primary area of interest is in industrial and labor relations. Hill's published research on the business of major league baseball has appeared in *Industrial Relations* and *The Quarterly Review of Economics and Business*.

John L. Fizel is Associate Professor of Economics at Penn State University in Erie, Pennsylvania. His research interests include various applied microeconomic topics including the economics of sports. He coedited the book *Baseball Economics: Current Research*. He also has sports-related publications in *Journal of Sport Management*, *Applied Economics*, *American Journal of Economics and Sociology*, *Dispute Resolution Journal*, *Social Science Quarterly*, and the *Kentucky Journal of Economics and Business*.

James B. Dworkin is Professor of Organizational Behavior and Human Resources and Associate Dean of the Krannert Graduate School of Management at Purdue University. His areas of expertise include negotiations, labor-management relations, and dispute resolution. His fifty-plus publications include several articles on labor relations in sports. He also wrote the book *Owners Versus Players: Baseball and Collective Bargaining*. Dworkin has served as an arbitrator, mediator, and fact-finder in a variety of labor-management disputes in both the private and public sectors.

William H. Kaempfer is Professor and Chair of Economics at the University of Colorado at Boulder. In addition to his interest in the economics of sports, Kaempfer is an active researcher in the area of international political economy. Overall, he has published in excess of fifty articles. His sports-related work includes chapters in the books *Diamonds Are Forever: The Business of Baseball* and *Baseball Economics: Current Research* and an article in *Social Science Quarterly*.

James Quirk is currently retired after completing his distinguished academic career at Caltech. He has written extensively on general equilibrium theory, decision-making under uncertainty, qualitative economics and futures markets. He has published many papers on the economics of sports, and his theoretical models of professional sports are among the most significant contributions in this field. His published books include *Pay Dirt: The Business of Professional Team Sports* and *The Minneapolis Marines: Minnesota's First NFL Team*. He has also consulted extensively in the area of sports, including antitrust cases involving the World Hockey Association and the National Football League (*NFLPA* v. *NFL*), a Boston Celtics ownership dispute, and tax cases (*U.S. Department of Justice* v. *owners of the Atlanta Falcons* and *IRS* v. *owners of the Seattle Supersonics*).

Lawrence Hadley is Associate Professor of Economics at the University of Dayton. Prior to joining the University of Dayton faculty in 1977, he was a faculty member at Hartwick College and the American University in Cairo. For the past few years, his professional research has dealt with various economic issues in major league baseball. He coedited the book *Baseball Economics: Current Research*.

Elizabeth Gustafson has been Associate Professor of Economics at the University of Dayton since 1983. Previously, she held positions at Miami University and the University of Cincinnati. Gustafson's area of expertise is econometrics, and her research interests focus on applied econometric models with the most recent in the area of the economics of baseball. Along with John Fizel and Lawrence Hadley, she coedited the book *Baseball Economics: Current Research*.

James D. Whitney is Professor of Economics at Occidental College in Los Angeles. The economics of sports is among his research interests, and he has published two baseball-related articles in *Economic Inquiry*.

Bruce Johnson is the James Graham Brown Associate Professor of Economics at Centre College in Danville, Kentucky. His work on the economics of sports has appeared in academic publications such as *Diamonds Are Forever: The Business of Baseball*, and the popular press, including the *Boston Globe* and the *Atlanta Constitution*.

William F. Shughart II is Professor of Economics and holder of the P.M.B. Self, William King Self, and Henry C. Self Free Enterprise Chair at the University of Mississippi. He has published more than eighty scholarly articles and book chapters over his career, primarily in the areas of industrial organization, antitrust, and public choice. He has also written on transportation policy, education reform, and college sports. Shughart has contributed chapters to the books *Sportometrics* and *Advances in the Economics of Sport*. He has also published sports-related articles in *Atlantic Economic Journal*, *Journal of Institutional and Theoretical Economics*, *Kyklos*, *Economic Inquiry*, *Research in Law and Economics*, as well as in several newspapers. Shughart was retained as a consultant by the NBA in *National Basketball Association* v. *SDC Basketball Club*.

Rodney Fort is Associate Professor of Economics at Washington State University. His sports-related publications include *Pay Dirt: The Business of Professional Team Sports*, chapters in *Diamonds Are Forever: The Business of Baseball*, *Baseball Economics: Current Research*, *Advances in Sports Economics*, and an article in the *Journal of Economic Literature*. In addition to his scholarly work, Fort has served as a consultant on several sports-oriented projects.

Andrew Zimbalist is the Robert A. Woods Professor of Economics at Smith College. In addition to his work on the economics of sports, he has dedicated much of his academic career to the study of economic development in Latin America. His book *Baseball and Billions: A Probing Look Inside the Big Business of Our National Pastime* was listed by *Business Week* as one of the top eight business books in 1992. He also has sports-related publications in the *Seton Hall Journal of Sports Law*, a chapter in *Diamonds Are Forever: The Business of Baseball*, and articles in several newspapers and magazines. He is currently writing a book on the economics of college sports and coediting a book on the economic impact of sports teams on cities. Zimbalist has served as a consultant in numerous sports-oriented court cases, including the litigation of the NFL Players' Association's suit to obtain free agency. He has provided expertise to the Major League Baseball Players' Association and has testified before Congress on baseball antitrust issues on several occasions. He was also a consultant for the noted Ken Burns documentary "Baseball." Zimbalist has frequently appeared on radio and television and is an active participant on the lecture circuit.

ISBN 0-275-95706-3

90000>

EAN

9 780275 957063

HARDCOVER BAR CODE